Black Youth, Racism and the State

The Politics of Ideology and Policy

JOHN SOLOMOS

Lecturer in Politics
Birkbeck College
University of London

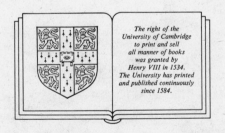

The right of the
University of Cambridge
to print and sell
all manner of books
was granted by
Henry VIII in 1534.
The University has printed
and published continuously
since 1584.

CAMBRIDGE UNIVERSITY PRESS

Cambridge

New York   New Rochelle   Melbourne   Sydney

Wingate College Library

Published by the Press Syndicate of the University of Cambridge
The Pitt Building, Trumpington Street, Cambridge CB2 1RP
32 East 57th Street, New York, NY 10022, USA
10 Stamford Road, Oakleigh, Melbourne 3166, Australia

First published 1988

Printed in Great Britain at the University Press, Cambridge

British Library cataloguing in publication data

Solomos, John
Black youth, racism and the state: the
politics of ideology and policy. –
(Comparative ethnic and race relations).
1. Great Britain. Young black persons.
Racial discrimination by society. Political aspects
I. Title. II. Series
323.1′1′96041

Library of Congress cataloguing in publication data

Solomos, John.
Black youth, racism and the state: the politics of ideology
and policy / John Solomos.
    p.   cm. – (Comparative ethnic and race relations)
Bibliography.
Includes index.
ISBN 0 521 36019 6
1. Blacks – Great Britain – Politics and government.
2. Youth, Black – Great Britain – Social conditions. 3. Youth, Black – Great
Britain – Economic conditions. 4. Racism – Great Britain. 5. Great
Britain – Race relations. I. Title. II. Series: Comparative ethnic
and race relations series.
DA125.N4S65 1988
305.8′96041 – dc19   88-3524 CIP

ISBN 0 521 36019 6

Comparative Ethnic and Race Relations

Black Youth, Racism and the State

Comparative Ethnic and Race Relations

Published for the Centre for Research in Ethnic Relations at the University of Warwick

Senior Editor
Professor John Rex *Associate Director & Research Professor of Ethnic Relations, University of Warick*

Editors
Professor Robin Cohen *Executive Director & Professor of Sociology, University of Warwick*
Mr Malcolm Cross *Principal Research Fellow, University of Warwick*
Dr Robin Ward *Head of Ethnic Business Research Unit, University of Aston*

This series has been formed to publish works of original theory, empirical research, and texts on the problems of racially mixed societies. It is based on the work of the Centre for Research in Ethnic Relations, a Designated Research Centre of the Economic and Social Research Council, and the main centre for the study of race relations in Britain.

The series will continue to draw on the work produced at the Centre, though the editors encourage manuscripts from scholars whose work has been associated with the Centre, or whose research lies in similar fields. Future titles will concentrate on anti-racist issues in education, on the organisation and political demands of ethnic minorities, on migration patterns, changes in immigration policies in relation to migrants and refugees, and on questions relating to employment, welfare and urban restructuring as these affect minority communities.

The books will appeal to an international readership of scholars, students and professionals concerned with racial issues, across a wide range of disciplines (such as sociology, anthropology, social policy, politics, economics, education and law), as well as among professional social administrators, teachers, government officials, health service workers and others.

Other books in this series:
Michael Banton: *Racial and ethnic competition*
Tomas Hammar (ed.): *European immigration policy*
Roger Hewitt: *White talk black talk: inter-racial friendships and communication amongst adolescents*
Richard Jenkins: *Racism and recruitment: managers, organisations and equal opportunity in the labour market*
Richard Jenkins and John Solomos (eds.): *Racism and equal opportunity policies in the 1980s*
Frank Reeves: *British racial discourse*
John Rex and David Mason (eds.): *Theories of race and ethnic relations*
Paul Rich: *Race and empire in British politics*
Robin Ward and Richard Jenkins (eds.): *Ethnic communities in business*

For Christine,
who has lived with this book for too long

Contents

Acknowledgements

In producing this book I have earned a number of intellectual and personal debts, which I would gratefully acknowledge. In particular I have been helped greatly by colleagues at the Research Unit in Ethnic Relations, University of Aston (1980–4) and the Centre for Research in Ethnic Relations, University of Warwick (1984–7). During the last stages of writing my present colleagues in the Department of Politics and Sociology, Birkbeck College, gave me the opportunity to work in a friendly environment. Among the numerous past and present colleagues who have provided valuable help I would like to mention Wendy Ball, Harris Beider, Parminder Bhachu, Robin Cohen, Malcolm Cross, Harry Goulbourne, Clive Harris, Richard Jenkins, Mark Johnson, Sasha Josephides, Heather Lynn and John Wrench. Outside my work environment I have been helped, at various points, by John Benyon, Paul Gilroy, Bob Miles, Andy Simpson, Paul Stubbs and Jenny Williams.

To complete a book one also needs friendship and support. In this regard I am particularly grateful to my family, whose support has always been there. Additionally, thanks to Claus Bredenbrock, Martin Chalmers, Mike Cowen, John Gaffney, Simon Jones and Bob Lumley for much intellectual and personal support. Finally, thanks to West Bromwich Albion, whose warm and friendly supporters kept my love of football alive during the writing of this book (and to George and Ian for minding me at various matches).

The labour that a number of secretaries put into the typing of this book is really too great to acknowledge fully. Many thanks to Rose Goodwin and Gurbakhsh Hundal for typing the final version, and for being such good friends. Charlotte Wellington and Lorraine Jones provided the administrative support on which my research depended. Finally thanks to Francis Brooke for being a helpful and encouraging publisher.

September 1987   Birkbeck College

Introduction

Background

The issue of the position of young blacks within British society, and particularly their role in the future of 'race relations', has been a hotly debated question for nearly two decades. Moreover, in the aftermath of the violent protests that have taken place since 1980, numerous state agencies, political organisations, voluntary bodies, academic researchers and media commentators have addressed themselves to the 'crisis of black youth' and its socio-political consequences from a wide variety of theoretical and empirical perspectives.[1] It came as no surprise when Lord Scarman's report on the Brixton riot of 10–12 April 1981 concluded that: 'The riots were essentially an outburst of anger and resentment by young black people against the police' (Scarman, 1981: 8.12).

While there seems to be a general consensus about the importance of the black youth question to any rounded analysis of the politics of racism in contemporary Britain, there is in practice much confusion about both what the category 'black youth' means, its structural location, and the nature of the crisis which young blacks face. This is exemplified by the terminological diversity in the academic race relations and policy literature; which quite interchangeably refers to young black people as 'the second generation', 'young West Indians and Asians', 'Afro-Caribbean youth', or more generally as 'black youth'.[2] There is, in addition some debate and confusion about whether the term 'black youth' can be used equally to refer to those young blacks descended from an Afro-Caribbean background or an Asian background.[3]

The terminological plurality evident in much of the academic literature and in public debate reflects both the complexity of the issues involved in analysing the situation of young black people and the increasing politicisation of debates around the future of young black people. The purpose of this book is therefore two-fold. First to provide a historically grounded political analysis of the genesis, formulation and use of ideological discourses about 'black youth', or more generally the black population that can no longer in any credible sense be considered as immigrant. The second objective is to provide a critical analysis of the policies which have singled out the 'problem' of black youth for special attention, whether in relation to social policy, law and order, unemployment policy, and more recently in the context of responses to urban disorder. The structure of the book is organised around these two objectives, with chapters 1 to 2 concentrating on the first, while chapters 3 to 7 look at various aspects of the response of the state and other institutions to young blacks. By exploring these processes it is hoped that this book will provide a basis for analysing the specific factors which have led to the social construction of black youth as a 'social problem', and perhaps to suggest ways in which this understanding can stimulate debate about what kind of policies can enhance the life chances of young blacks in British society.

Research on black youth

The initial stages of research on the social position of young blacks in British society, were governed by the twin concerns of the mid-1960s with the 'assimilation of immigrants into the host society' and the development of a more stable basis for 'good race relations' in the future. Thus during the period from the early sixties to the early seventies there were a number of studies which either focused specifically on the integration of 'second generation' blacks or analysed them as one aspect of a wider area of concern. These twin concerns were reflected in the ways in which the 'second generation' issue was treated in academic studies of the period (Patterson, 1969: chapter 5; Abbott, 1971; Deakin, 1970), in the report produced by the Survey of Race Relations in Britain on *Colour and Citizenship* (Rose *et al.*, 1969), and in the first report of the Select Committee on Race Relations and Immigration on *The Problems of Coloured School Leavers* (1969).

By the late sixties, however, a sizeable body of work began to emerge which distanced itself from the immediate policy preoccupations which dominated much of the early work and looked at specific institutional aspects of the experience of young blacks in relation to employment, education, and racism. Perhaps the most important studies to note are David Beetham's study of Birmingham school leavers (1967), Sheila Allen's research on the transition to work of black and white school leavers (1969; 1975), Gus John's study of Handsworth and his research on the youth service and young blacks (1970; 1981), Stuart Hall *et al.*'s study of the 'moral panic' about the involvement of young blacks in mugging (1978), Ken Pryce's study of Bristol (1979), Ernest Cashmore's study of Rastafarianism (1979) and Cashmore and Barry Troyna's edited volume on 'black youth in crisis' (1982). In addition, through the seventies the specific question of the socio-economic experience of young blacks began to receive some attention,[4] along with the related issues of policing, political alienation and homelessness.

Despite this relatively large body of work, however, there is still little guidance about how a framework can be developed which provides a coherent analysis of the politics of state policies in relation to black youth and the ideologies used to legitimate such policies. Most studies are concerned either with the general phenomenon of 'black youth' or with one specialised aspect of the history or the current situation. They provide little in the way of detailed accounts of the ideology, the institutional context or the outcome of state intervention dealing with the 'black youth question'.

Apart from a number of recent studies that have looked specifically at the question of the police and black youth, the dominant concern of researchers has been with the subcultural, identity and family aspects of being young and black in contemporary Britain. The dominance of this approach can be traced back to the early stages of both academic and policy debates over the future of the 'second generation of immigrants' or 'black British'. As Fisher and Joshua argue:

> In order that black youth might be sociologically, that is 'scientifically', explained, first a recognisable social group had to be identified and isolated. This isolating/explanatory process, however, rather than an exercise in even conventional academic rationale and method, demonstrated from its very beginnings a greater empathy with the social formulations, concerns and designs of the body politic. In short, that body of sociological literature purporting to deal with black youth was not primarily informed by any overwhelming desire to document and order the myriad of situations and strategies applicable to the black second generation. Instead, by far the more discernible were the influences of successive crises posed by young blacks and the corresponding social and moral panic of the state; both instructed by the problem orientated sociology associated with the first generation colonial immigrants.
>
> (1982: 131)

This is not to devalue individual contributions which are quoted elsewhere in this book, but it underlines the general lack of political perspective which still pervades the analysis of this and other race-related issues within British society.[5]

When the research work on which this book reports was first undertaken, in 1980–5, this absence of adequate work on the question of 'black youth' was perhaps more clear than it is now. The riots of 1980–1 and lately in 1985 have done much to stimulate interest in the subject matter of this book, both from academic researchers and policy practitioners. The Commission for Racial Equality (CRE), the Manpower Services Commission (MSC), other Central Government Departments (e.g. the Home Office) and numerous local authorities have devoted increasing attention to this issue, not least because of the popular concern that was voiced during 1980–1 about the drift of young blacks towards street violence and disorder. Lord Scarman's assessment, quoted above, acted as a further spur for such concerns by sensitising policy-makers and government agencies to the problems faced by young blacks in the fields of employment, housing and their relations with the police in inner city areas.[6]

More recent works from within the sociology of race relations and the political analysis of racism have touched on the question of the position of young blacks in contemporary British society. Examples of this growing interest are Cashmore and Troyna's introduction to the sociology of race relations (1983), Zig Layton-Henry's study of the politics of race (1984), Robert Miles and Annie Phizacklea's political economy of racism (1984), and Michael Banton's analysis of race relations policies (1985).

The increasing politicisation of the question of black youth has not, however, resulted in good research-based studies of the origins, development and political impact of this issue. It is precisely this gap which has concerned me and led to the writing of this book, which attempts to develop a specifically *political* analysis of the black youth question.

The political analysis of racism

During the early stages of my research on the inter-relationship between the state and black youth, it became clear that no adequate framework for the analysis of the *politics of racism* had been developed, despite the existence of numerous studies of the sociology and anthropology of 'race relations' in contemporary Britain. With a few notable exceptions (Rex, 1973; Katznelson, 1976; Hall *et al.*, 1978; Rex and Tomlinson, 1979), the majority of studies in this field contained little to guide any research project oriented specifically towards the study of the role of the state and political institutions in this field. As a discipline political science has done little to take account of the fact that a 'racialisation' of British politics has taken place during the post-war period (Solomos, 1986a).

This is not to say that no attempts have been made to analyse the politics of racism within the main body of sociological studies of racism. One of the central concerns of this literature, albeit implicitly and largely untheorised, has been the response to immigration and 'race' issues in a wide variety of political and policy settings, both in Britain and other societies (Ben-Tovim and Gabriel, 1978; Layton-Henry, 1984). The political expression of racism in the form of the immigration acts and the development of racist ideologies and ultra-right-wing racist groups has been a strong theme in those sociological studies of 'race' which have adopted a political sociology framework. Indeed, a number of writers have adopted as their starting point the need to understand the 'politics of race', and how racialised politics relates to other forms of political allegiance based on social class, gender, religion and nationalism.[7]

In addition to these contributions a small but growing body of work on race and racism has developed from within political science. In principle this body of research could be seen as the basis on which a more adequate framework for the analysis of the politics of racism could be developed. But as Ben-Tovim and Gabriel pointed out in their critical account of the political analysis of 'race' over the past three decades, the main issues which have dominated the field evince three broad areas of concern:

(a) the development and implementation of immigration controls and the political processes which led to such controls;

(b) the passage of legislation which has attempted to ameliorate the situation of black minorities and promote equality of opportunity;

(c) the policies of racist and anti-immigration groups, forms of black political organisation, and anti-racist politics. (Ben-Tovim and Gabriel, 1979)

Under these three broad headings there has been little room for the analysis of the role of political intervention on specific questions, such as the position of young blacks, the local politics of racism, the implementation of equal opportunity measures, and the genesis of specific racist ideologies and policies. The relative neglect of politics from within the mainstream of the sociology of race relations and the neglect of 'race' from within political science has meant that there are few areas under the heading of the *politics of racism* which have received adequate attention.

Elsewhere (Solomos, 1986a) I have suggested that the relative neglect of the politics of racism within political science and political sociology may be attributed to a number of factors, including the relative neglect of 'marginal' issues such as 'race' and gender from the agenda of the discipline, the identification of 'race relations' as a discrete discipline, the problems involved in researching an issue which is seen as a political minefield, and the relative neglect of 'race' even by the more radical neo-marxist approaches to British politics. I also argue:

> There is . . . much work to be done if the study of contemporary British politics is to reflect the fact that racism constitutes an important facet of political life in the 1980s. In particular, there are a number of issues which deserve much closer attention than they have been given so far. Apart from the questions of state policies and law and order . . . there is a need to know much more about the politics of racist organisations, the political identities of various racist groups, the relations between racism and sexism, the interface between nationalism and racism, the ideologies of the new right on race, and the political language of racism.
>
> (Solomos, 1986a: 324)

The main concerns of this book follow from this starting point and attempt to fill some of the gaps in the political analysis of racism, as well as question many commonplace assumptions about this area. Chapters 1 to 3 are interlinked by the twin concerns outlined above; namely how to develop an adequate analytic framework for a political analysis of racism and how such a framework can help us understand the massive politicisation of matters linked to black youth. These chapters are then followed by a number of case studies of how specific ideological and political responses to black youth have developed in relation to youth unemployment and street violence and disorder.

The politics of research on racism

I have referred in passing to some of the theoretical and methodological problems involved in doing research on 'race relations'. I have not, however, discussed the ethical and political aspects of doing such research, or what some scholars call the 'moral problems' of researching a powerless group's position in society from the outside (Blauner, 1972). This is an issue much debated during the Black Power period in the United States, when black militants and academics questioned the reasons why academic research was being done, the relations of such research to the controlling arms of the state, and the place of white social scientists in such research (Staples, 1976; Geschwender, 1977; Marable, 1983). In the British context this debate was refracted in the early seventies through the struggle at the Institute of Race Relations

(Jenkins, 1971; Sivanandan, 1974; Mullard, 1985) and by the development of fundamental criticisms of race relations research in radical black journals such as *Race Today*, *Race and Class*, the *Black Liberator* and many others.[8] More recently the focus of the criticisms has been on the objectives which research on 'race' should have, e.g. whether the main focus of research should be on minority communities and their cultural and family networks, or on the institutions of white racism.[9] In addition the politicisation of 'race' over the last two decades has raised a number of complex ethical and political dilemmas which confront any researcher working in this field, which are often somewhat simply put in the form of the question: 'whose side are you on?'

One important outcome of these developments is that it has become difficult even to think of doing research on this question from what is sometimes called a 'value-free' perspective. The core issues in this area have become so intensely politicised over the past two decades that the mere act of carrying out research on 'race relations' necessarily involves questions relevant to policy-makers and general political debates. Thus whatever the values and beliefs of the researcher, the research findings and beliefs about research findings, may gain currency outside the immediate academic environment. The combination of these pressures and the well-known methodological problems in doing 'value free' research, question the separation of the research function from practical political and policy dilemmas (Giddens, 1979; Keat, 1981; Touraine, 1981).

Although it is difficult to compare the American situation directly with the British, it may be useful to refer to some aspects of the American debates in order to clarify some issues. The experience of Lee Rainwater and David Pittman during their research on poverty and poor blacks in American cities is worth recalling in this context. Pointing to the inherently complex ethical and power issues involved in researching 'powerless' groups, they argue that the most important of these issues are the researcher's relationship to the communities that are being researched, problems of sponsorship and confidentiality, and potential use or misuse of research findings for questionable or unintended political and policy objectives. Speaking particularly about the last issue they argue:

> Concern for the effect of findings on public issues sensitised one to the question of how research results will be interpreted by others, and to his responsibility to anticipate probable misuses, and from this anticipation to counteract the possibility of misuse. That is, though we do not feel a researcher must avoid telling the

truth because it may hurt a group (problems of confidentiality aside) we do believe that he must take this possibility into account in presenting his findings and make every reasonable effort to deny weapons to potential misusers.

(Rainwater and Pittman, 1967: 361–2)

Giving specific examples of types of research which could be misused the authors refer to research on black family systems, subcultural lifestyles among young blacks, crime and delinquency in the ghettoes, and on mental health problems.

Perhaps a more familiar example, given the international notoriety which it achieved, is the controversy that has raged since the mid-1960s over the arguments of the Moynihan report on the black family in the USA, and its conception of the weaknesses of the black family structure as an explanation for the social problems faced by blacks in relation to poor housing, unemployment, bad schools, and poverty (Moynihan, 1965; Rainwater and Yancey, 1967; Billingsley, 1970; Berger and Simon, 1974; Anderson, 1976; MacDonald and MacDonald, 1978). What is particularly interesting about the controversy over the Moynihan report, apart from its immediate and subsequent academic and political fallout (Rainwater and Yancey, 1967), is the way in which it showed quite clearly that (a) whatever the academic arguments in favour of doing a specific piece of research it is politically naive and potentially dangerous to see research as autonomous from its contextual political environment, and (b) that governments and other interested groups necessarily take a strong role and have a stake in academic research about 'deviant' groups in society. In addition it highlighted the ways in which reform oriented strategies, which are ostensibly premised on the idea of 'helping' the poor and the powerless, can also become another strategy for extending government control and institutional power over such groups (Edelman, 1971). It is also an interesting example of how 'the media, policy makers and academics, when singling out black people for attention or special study, often concentrate on family structure rather than on other aspects of black life' (MacDonald and MacDonald, 1978: 2), particularly those that touch on the dominant power structures or economic institutions. This controversy is particularly relevant because of the way in which it connects with recent critiques of race research in Britain, which often see such research as reproducing a pathological image of black family life and as failing to prioritise racism. This is a point to which I shall return later.

More recent American studies refer to these and related issues, and emphasise the ways in which research on 'social problems' in black and other poor communities is liable to be used by government or other bodies in ways which do not necessarily 'help' the people with which it is concerned, and the ways in which research may help popularise myths about such communities and give them a 'scientific' gloss (Lowry, 1974; Ryan, 1976; Glasgow, 1981; Blau, 1981). One way in which this may happen is referred to by Kochman when he talks about the 'mythology of black pathology' (Kochman, 1972), while another is popularly referred to by the term 'blaming the victim' (Ryan, 1976). The pathological approach tends to see black and other poor communities as suffering from cultural and family handicaps which in turn help to create material conditions which help reproduce poverty and inequality. The 'blaming the victim' approach, on the other hand, sees such groups as victims of their circumstances and as suffering from a culture of poverty which unwittingly reproduces their own troubles.

Clearly not all these ethical and political issues can be said to have a direct purchase on the British situation. There is a remarkable similarity, however, between the terms of the debate that took place in the US in the aftermath of the civil rights movement and the 1960s riots, and the debate that has developed in Britain over the past decade or so. Although there have been many and diverse attempts to deal with the question 'what is race relations research for?' within the British context, it is possible to say that there have been three main sets of responses.

The first type of response is one which emphasises the need for research to be seen as autonomous from ideological and political commitments, or at best as having only a tangential link with existing political debates about racism. This school of thought is one with which a number of the early major race relations researchers have expressed some kind of sympathy (Patterson, 1969; Rose *et al.*, 1969; Deakin, 1970). Another version of this approach does not eschew the need to look at the political or policy aspects of race relations, but argues that the only way to influence legislative and administrative branches of government is not through political analysis but through the presentation of factual statistical information about discrimination in such areas as housing, employment, social services, etc. This approach is particularly associated with the work of the Policy Studies Institute (Daniel, 1968; Smith, 1977 and 1981; Brown, 1984). The end-result of this approach may be said to be an emphasis on race research as either a neutral academic discipline or uncommitted policy research which aims to present policy-makers with the facts on which they could base new policy initiatives.

The second response is more difficult to categorise. It has been most clearly articulated by John Rex in a number of his works since the early seventies (Rex, 1973a and 1981b; Rex and Tomlinson, 1979). The lineage of Rex's approach can be traced back to his engagement with the work of Gunnar Myrdal on racism in America (1969a, 1969b), and more broadly to the methodological problems which he addressed in carrying out research on the issue of racial discrimination in the Handsworth area of Birmingham (Rex and Tomlinson, 1979). Taking his starting point from Myrdal's important discussion of how American research on 'race relations' tended to be based on certain taken-for-granted assumptions and untestable hypotheses, Rex argues that similar biases can be found in much of the 'race relations' literature in Britain (Rex and Tomlinson, 1979: appendix 1). He notes, for example, the tendency in the literature to assume that various inadequacies in the culture or family life of West Indian and Asian immigrants are responsible for social problems brought about by racism, unemployment, low wages, menial occupations, poor housing and bad schools. While accepting, however, the reality of this tendency to 'blame the victims', he argues forcefully against the reduction of social science research on 'race' to the demands of special interests, whether it be those of the policy-makers or those of the black communities or political activists themselves. The burden of Rex's position is thus to question the terms of debate posed by the question 'whose side are you on?' and introduce what he sees as an intermediary position on which to base critical social science research. In the context of the debate at the Institute of Race Relations during the early seventies he provided an important statement of his position:

> I believe that we can do far more for the people of Notting Hill or Handsworth by setting their problem within a wider context of sociological theory than we can by *ad hoc* strategies which may involve mock heroics but which will be doomed to failure. For this reason there is a role for the community sponsored race relations research. There is also a need for people to man the barricades. And, in between no more or less important, there is a need for educators bringing to bear on experience the fruits of theoretical reflection and on theory the fruits of political experience.
>
> (1973a: 487)

This is a position which Rex has recently restated in a response to some criticisms of his work, which argued that there are inherent contradictions in trying to maintain a position for critical social science research that is distinct from policy oriented or community oriented research (1981b: 1–10). Arguing forcefully against both a neutral study of the 'facts' of racial disadvantage and a politically committed view of race relations, he maintains that, despite the increased politicisation of 'race' over the past decade or so, there is still room for independent research which aims to get beyond the everyday appearances to the factors which have produced and sustain forms of racial discrimination.

The third type of response cannot easily be pinned down to academic arguments as such, since its adherents argue for the impossibility of divorcing the research process from the political context of doing research on oppressed racial minorities. Reminiscent as it is of the arguments that raged through American sociology during the 1960s and 1970s (Ladner, 1973; Staples, 1976), the impact of this response on researchers in Britain has been minimal until the last few years. Although it gained a wide currency among sections of the black intelligentsia in the aftermath of the dispute at the Institute of Race Relations (Mullard, 1985) and the increasing involvement of government bodies in the funding and carrying out of research, the view that it was necessary to make research more politically oriented towards and linked to the black communities and their organisations, remained marginal in much of the race relations literature. It became identified either as a view held by black intellectuals or community leaders or simply as a view supported by politically committed Marxists or leftists. But despite its marginalisation within the context of academic debates it became a popular view in journals such as *Race and Class* and *Race Today*, and was reinforced by the relative paucity of community involvement in research and the relative absence of black research workers (Mullard, 1985; Solomos, 1986a).

Over the past few years, however, fundamental objections to the orientation of research on 'race' have been voiced within academic debates (CCCS Race and Politics Group, 1982; Miles, 1982) and by a number of radical writers and activists who have voiced strong objections to the ways in which research has been carried out on black communities (Bourne, 1980; Gilroy, 1980; Lawrence, 1981 and 1982; Parmar, 1981; Phillips, 1983). Error Lawrence's intervention has attracted much attention, partly because of the forcefulness with which he connects certain sociological studies of black communities with common sense ideologies of race which, he argues, see blacks as the cause of problems or as culturally deprived and inadequate. He links the popular images of black communities as suffering from communal helplessness and cultural handicap to the tendency of researchers to become preoccupied by the apparent social relations within black communal lifestyles at the expense of detailed studies of the personal and institutional mechanisms through which white racism operates. He argues that an exaggerated emphasis on factors of this sort only shifts attention from racism, and shifts the problems of 'race relations' onto the black communities as individuals or as collectivities. He gives as examples the tendency to compare the West Indian family structure negatively with the white family structure, the view of young Asians as 'caught between the two cultures', the preoccupation with the supposed 'identity crisis' which afflicts second generation black youth, and the view of black ghetto life as pathogenic. According to Lawrence this leads to marginalising the importance of racism in structuring the obstacles faced by blacks in British society, leading to 'blaming the victim' types of ideological images. In addition, Lawrence argues, the images presented of black communities tend to be ones which see them as passive, with little or no account taken of their capacities to respond positively and defensively to their historical experience of racism, either as individuals or collectively (Lawrence, 1982: 100–6 and 116).

A number of responses of Lawrence's argument have rejected specific aspects of his critique of the sociology of race as either over-generalised or misdirected, while others have accepted the relevance of some of his criticism while arguing that they need more clarification and verification. John Rex, for example, has responded by arguing that while it may be true that some research is based on assumptions which take for granted inadequacies on the part of West Indian and Asian communities, it is incorrect to label the mainstream of sociological research on race or his own works as 'blaming the victim' (Rex, 1981a). While accepting the dangers of ethnocentric and pseudo-psychological explanations of the attitudes of black communities or of their cultural values, he rejects the view that such research inevitably falls into the trap of seeing blacks as inadequate and as living in a 'culture of poverty' which reduces them to passivity (Rex, 1981a). Ernest Cashmore and Barry Troyna have also responded to Lawrence's critique, arguing that there are obvious dangers involved in studying black people rather than racism, but pointing out that their own work, along with other studies, is unfairly criticised as not looking at the ways in which racism structures the lives of black people (Cashmore and Troyna, 1981).

The complexities of this debate require a more detailed analysis, beyond the scope of this study. Nevertheless, the above summary of some of the central aspects of recent contributions should be enough to indicate that the question of what kind of research should be done on 'race', and by whom is far from being adequately resolved. The forcefulness with which it has been conducted may also be read, partly at least, as a reflection of increasing doubts over the usefulness or appropriateness of research on 'race' as a means of improving the social and economic inequalities experienced by black communities. But it can also be taken as indicating a degree of mistrust about the motives of largely white research teams doing research about 'race relations' in British society.

No doubt the heated nature of these exchanges has produced a very stunted and personalised debate, and one which has therefore had only a minor impact on the everyday conduct of research work. This is partly because there is a tendency to see criticisms of existing research as ideologically loaded and to treat them as having little value in guiding research on the ground. The problem with such a response is that while it is reasonable to see research as relatively autonomous from immediate political considerations, it is implausible to think that research on 'race' within the current political climate can be neutral in terms of its policy implications. Moreover the feeling that such research is too dominated by white institutions and values, and concentrates on issues which are policy-relevant rather than relevant to the interests of the minorities, is not *a priori* one which can be dismissed as value-laden. At a certain level it can be seen as a reaction against the 'colonial' image of race research, in the sense that such research inevitably gets caught up in the relationship between white institutional power and black communities (Blauner and Wellman, 1973). The fact that much of the recent research on race issues has been premised on the need to take action to overcome racism has not necessarily convinced those sections of the black communities that have been critical of research on their 'problems' that there is any more likelihood that public policy-makers will take the question of racism any more seriously.

While research cannot be seen simply as a guide to social action, neither can it be divorced from the social reality in which it is carried out, including its relations of power based on economic, class, racial and other social divisions (Fay, 1975). In this sense the challenge of doing critical research on the utilisation of 'race' in political debates and policy-making must be to draw out the public and hidden agenda on which policies are based, analyse their impact on minority communities, and make explicit the symbolic and real attainments of policy changes. Research which takes as given the value-free nature of policies on 'race' may in the long-term be seen as reproducing assumptions about 'race' which actually harm the interests of minority communities. Part of the agenda of doing research on the politics of racism must therefore be a continual process of self-critical awareness that research can have both intended and unintended political consequences.

One important issue to which I shall return in later chapters is the way in which 'social pathology' or 'blaming the victim' type arguments, which use the 'White Norms, Black Deviation' model (Murray, 1973: 66–8), are recurrent in the whole set of policies based on the principle of helping young blacks to cope better with the transition from school to work or unemployment. Although such images cannot be wholly blamed on the ways in which black youth have been researched, it seems implausible to say that research on 'race' played no role at all in producing and reproducing such stereotypes. Even if it is a question of social research findings being misused, such findings have played a certain rôle in shaping conceptions of 'problems', of the kind of 'help' needed, and legitimating certain explanations as opposed to others.

It is difficult not to reach the conclusion that most ethical and political problems, which have been a consistent feature of debates among those involved in doing 'race relations' research for the last twenty years, have defied resolution. At best they may have been clarified, yet their very persistence is indicative of a possible insolubility with the existing terms of reference. For example, the question of 'what is race relations research for?' cannot be answered simply, since it inevitably involves some consideration about research interests, funding, publication, political climate and political judgement. Until such questions become part of the theoretical and research agenda of those doing research on 'race' it is unlikely that the suspicion of research and the questioning of its relevance to the struggle against racism will end. For this reason alone, it is incumbent on researchers to make public the methods, values, and assumptions on which their work is based.

Finally, although I have argued that it is possible to combine a committed research view of the 'race' issue with a critical political perspective, it seems to me to be quite implausible to see research as speaking for or representing the view of communities which suffer from racism. Such a perspective would be tantamount to saying that the researcher can become a kind of representative of the oppressed, or 'speak' for them. My doubts about this do not exist because I am an outside researcher, or because I hold to some notion of value-free research, but result rather from my uncertainty about the utility of reducing all the voices of oppressed groups to the single voice of representatives who are supposed to speak for minorities. There is much value in Ben-Tovim *et al.*'s critique of the separation of race relations research from the politics of anti-racism (Ben-Tovim *et al.*, 1986), as there is in the call made by political activists for researchers to help change the current situation rather than just to study it. But it is a huge step to take from accepting the need for committed research to saying that researchers can actually 'speak' for minorities.

Such an assumption is problematic on a number of grounds, not least because there is no way in which a researcher can assume that all the black communities have one voice or interest, or that it is possible to speak for such communities as though they could not speak or struggle for themselves. This is not to say that research should not speak to current political and policy debates, or that it is indeed feasible to stay out of controversial issue areas. Indeed, a vital part of critical research on state policies must be addressed to those debates and processes which link policy outputs to actual political interests and pressures. What is at issue, however, is whether research evidence can be used to establish the 'interests' or 'needs' of social groups or classes. The plausibility of such claims does not, it seems to me, stand up, particularly when we bear in mind the complex social and political histories of the various black communities in Britain.

There are, no doubt, many more theoretical and political problems involved in doing research on 'race', which need to be discussed openly and across ideological paradigms but it is unlikely that all of these issues can be resolved easily. In the final analysis, however, it may be that the ethical and political problems involved in studying 'race' will only be resolved when critical research is shown to have made its contribution to understanding the origins and reproduction of racist structures and processes, and to have helped shape policies and political strategies which help undermine racist ideologies and racialist practices.

Politics, ideology and the state: some theoretical issues

This study of the politics of racism and black youth cannot pretend to have full pertinence at a broader theoretical or conceptual level. But it is worth emphasising that its broad analytical framework is derived partly from the growing number of neo-Marxist studies of the role of the state and its various institutional forms within the context of advanced capitalist societies. Leaving aside, for the purposes of this study, the wider theoretical conceptual intricacies of recent debates (but see Poulantzas, 1978; Jessop, 1982; and Carnoy, 1984), there are two central themes which seem to connect the various approaches to the state which can be seen as 'neo-Marxist'.

The first theme which has been addressed in this body of research is the massive expansion of the boundaries of state intervention, across a whole variety of public and private sector arenas. It has been shown that over a wide variety of policy arena the role of the state has not only expanded but has taken on new forms, adapting not only existing institutional structures but setting up new frameworks through which political decisions and programmes could be formulated and implemented. A good number of examples of this process can be given, including the contestation over the boundaries of economic policies, welfare policies, industrial relations policies and, more broadly, social policy. During the most recent period of capitalist development all these arenas have witnessed important struggles over both the extent and the form of state interventions (Offe, 1984 and 1985; Keane, 1984; Esping-Andersen, 1985). These struggles have resulted in complex and contradictory forms of state intervention which cannot be explained simply by reference to the laws of motion of capitalist accumulation. For example, the development of welfare and social insurance policies has been influenced not just by the economic conditions specific to each advanced capitalist country but by the political and ideological relations which have developed through class struggle and political party competition. In the Scandinavian countries Esping-Andersen's research has shown how the various stages of social and economic intervention by the state were structured by the balance of political and ideological struggles as well as by the material conditions of the accumulation strategies pursued by capital (Esping-Andersen, 1985: chapter 1). A similar point has been made by a number of studies which have analysed the role of state interventions in other advanced capitalist societies.

The above point links up to the emphasis which is evident in much of the recent literature on the state on the discontinuous and historically specific forms which 'the state' and 'state intervention' actually assume in each conjuncture of capitalist development. Rather than assuming that there is an 'essential nature' of the capitalist state which can be deciphered through an analysis of patterns of accumulation and economic change, much of the recent neo-Marxist and critical political science research has chosen to emphasise the historically contingent and contradictory processes through which ideologies of state intervention are formed and put into practice. Much of this book will be concerned with exactly these processes, and in this sense it has been influenced by the work of Nicos Poulantzas (1973; 1978), Claus Offe (1984; 1985), Bob Jessop (1982; 1985) and Adam Przeworski (1985). This does not imply that there is any necessary agreement between these authors, or that other influences are not evident in my general and specific interests in this book.[10] But in many ways the work of the above mentioned authors has acted as an inspiration and a constant influence for my own interest in the ideologies and practice of state intervention.

The second theme which has shaped much of the recent discussion on the state is the question of the relationship between the state and economic, class, non-class and international power relations. This has been encapsulated in the debate which started between Nicos Poulantzas and Ralph Milliband on the problem of the 'relative autonomy' of the capitalist state, particularly in advanced industrial societies.[11] The origins and current terms of this debate are complex and are related to a broader question about the applicability of the Marxist emphasis on the importance of production relations for the analysis of state and society to the historically specific 'processes of formation' which have shaped the national state forms of actual societies. When the question of the inter-relationship between the state and wider sets of social, economic and power relationships is posed as open rather than closed, a number of difficult questions arise, which both neo-Marxist and other social scientists have struggled to answer. For example, what is the relationship between 'states' and 'social classes', and how is it historically determined? What are the determinants of state autonomy and state capacities to implement official goals? What role do actual or potential oppositional forces from powerful social groups and recalcitrant socio-economic circumstances play in determining the capacities of the state? How are the capacities of the state to pursue specific kinds of social and economic policies determined in practice? (Evans *et al.*, 1985; Alford and Friedland, 1985).

The complex nature of these questions prevents any easy answers to the question of the inter-relationship of the state with other social relations and the limits and contradictions of the various policies which are pursued by states at any specific point in time. As will be clear from the following chapters the perspective adopted in this book is one which emphasises the need to see the state not as an abstracted monolith but as a set of institutions which have a direct and indirect impact on the content and workings of politics. To take the example of the responses to black youth unemployment, which are analysed in chapters 4 and 5, it seems necessary to contextualise these policy outcomes in relation to

(a)   the socio-economic and political environment within which the 'problem' of black youth unemployment took shape;

(b)   the processes which lead to the definition and implementation of policies to deal with this issue; and

(c)   the socio-economic and political pressures which determine in practice the capacity of the state to implement policy changes and reforms.

There are broad similarities here not only with the work of the authors cited above, but with the work of Theda Skocpol who has, in a number of provocative studies suggested a 'relational approach' for the analysis of the various historically and politically specific forms of state intervention and non-intervention. Skocpol argues against analyses of the state which maintain that the policies pursued by states are uniform and non-contradictory when in fact they grow out of the constant struggles, compromises, and transformations which state institutions undergo in particular historical periods.[12] It is with these issues of struggle, compromise and transformation that the bulk of this book will be concerned.

Political institutions and political practices

To concretise the argument developed above, the conception of the state on which this study relies is fundamentally anti-reductionist, in the sense that we see the capitalist state as a complex web of institutions which are partly structured by, but in turn structure the relations of civil society, i.e. the economic, class, political, ideological, gender and racial or ethnic relations which exist in specific societies.

Throughout this book an attempt will be made to give content to this conception by looking closely at the complex interactions and linkages between the institutions of the state and the wider sets of social relations within which they exist. The web of institutions forming the state structures of contemporary societies have necessarily developed interactions and linkages between them which often determine the mechanisms through which various agencies respond to specific issues and the resources available for specific interventions. To understand how immigration policies and 'race relations' policies have developed, for example, we would need to know the workings of the interests, institutions, organisational structures, personnel and resources which comprise the socio-political context within which they took shape. In addition, and no less importantly, we would need to know something about any linkages between these policies and broader transformations and crisis engendering situations in the society as a whole.

The British state has undergone complex processes of formation and reorganisation, and more recently has gone through what Tom Nairn has called a process of disintegration and crisis (Nairn, 1981). These questions are beyond the scope of this book, but one or two are worth probing further in order to arrive at some linkages between the theoretical arguments outlined above and the concrete form of political institutions and practices in contemporary Britain, particularly in relation to racism. This will be the central concern of chapter 1.

Perhaps the most important transformations, and the ones which have a direct bearing on the subject matter of this book, are (a) the structural changes in Britain's overall international position which have taken place during the past century; (b) the expansion of involvement by state agencies in such areas as welfare policy, economic policy and industrial relations; (c) the emergence of extra-parliamentary channels for the formulation of policy options and choices; (d) the expansion of the internal policing functions of state institutions; and (e) the articulation of an ideology of the British state which recognises the transition from an economically powerful colonial power to one where it was increasingly seen as an ex-colonial power which had entered a deep structural crisis.

These, and other, transformations have not taken place overnight and have matured over a long period. Andrew Gamble is surely right when he identifies the basic features of Britain's decline as involving in one way or another a search for a future in a post-imperial context where a number of other economies were developing much more rapidly and threatening the structures of British industry nationally and internationally (Gamble, 1981: chapter 1). Gamble dates this process to the beginning of the twentieth century, and this periodisation is supported by the study which Keith Middlemas has undertaken of the inter-relationship between the state and various interests groups, particularly industrialists and trade unions, over the last eighty years (Middlemas, 1979 and 1986).

This historical background should warn us against any notion that the genesis of 'Britain's decline' is related simply to post-war developments. But the depth and impact of the socio-economic and political crises on the policies pursued by successive governments since the 1960s seem to indicate that we can see the transformations in state policies over the past three decades as particularly important. Implicit in the 'crisis management' approach of successive administrations since the Wilson government of 1964–70 is the failure to come up with any kind of policies and initiatives that could reverse the decline of the manufacturing industries, the weakened international position, regional inequalities and declining technological competitiveness (Leys, 1983). In this view, although the British state may have been successful in managing the most immediate surface problems, it has not succeeded in overcoming the basic underlying contradictions.

During the 1970s and 1980s, as public concern has focused increasingly on the complex management of economic and social crisis tendencies, a fundamental reshaping of political institutions has also taken place. These processes have as their objective a wider area of policy concern than immigration and race-related issues, but as will be argued throughout this book, the forms of state management specific to 'race' cannot be understood fully if they are abstracted from the wider political economic context. It seems impossible, for example, to understand the increasing importance of unemployment in relation to black workers (particularly the young) if we do not link the growth of mass unemployment to the fundamental processes of economic restructuring which have taken place over the past three decades and the political and ideological responses to them. The struggle around the policies pursued by the

Heath government during 1970–4, the Labour administrations during 1974–9, and the three Conservative administrations since 1979, all represent aspects of the wider history of crisis management by the state. These will not be analysed in any detail in this book, but they will be referred to when they help to contextualise specific events or tendencies.

The emphasis throughout will be on the processes by which the policies by the state and its institutions are formed and re-formed, since it seems quite implausible to see the whole panoply of policy options which are part of the decision-making processes as unconnected to practices of ideological and political struggle. However, it must also be recognised that relations of power are by no means symmetrical, and that when we analyse the policies, programmes and discourses of political and state institutions we have to keep to the forefront their relationship to established inequalities in resources, status and power. A guiding theme of this volume is the importance of locating policies and political struggles as part of the wider structures of society, albeit in a contradictory and indeterminate fashion. Murray Edelman has made this point succinctly when he argues that

> The actions governments take to cope with social problems often contradict, as well as reflect, the beliefs used to rationalise such actions. While claiming to rehabilitate prisoners and the emotionally disturbed, authorities also constrain and punish them. While claiming to help the poor, public welfare agencies also control them and take pains to limit the help they offer. Governmental rhetoric and action, taken together, comprise an elaborate dialectical structure reflecting the beliefs, the tensions, and the ambivalences that flow from social inequality and conflicting interests.
>
> (Edelman, 1977: 19)

In other words, it is not just the meaning attached by policy-makers to state policies that has to be looked at, but the benefits and deprivations evolving from actions that follow from such policies for specific groups and classes of people. This points to the importance of analysing the institutional forms and political practices that are developed in each policy area.

Contextualising the research

The empirical information on which this study is based was gathered by using a variety of methods and a variety of sources. These included background statistical material, policy documents, parliamentary debates and media coverage. I have paid particular attention to the processes by which various policy initiatives were formulated, rationalised and implemented over the past three decades.

I have not assumed that the question which I have addressed in this study – why and how the social category of 'black youth' emerged as a politicised issue – can only be studied from the approach I have chosen in doing my research. In fact a number of useful studies of state intervention have been done using a wide variety of methods, ranging from action research, survey data collection, interviews, participant observation and a combination of all these methods. Other approaches have so far not made much impact on this field of study, e.g. we have few detailed ethnographic studies of the position of young blacks in either community or institutional contexts, when one would assume that they have much of value to tell us. Bearing this in mind, I would maintain that the approach adopted for this study, which has prioritised the detailed analysis of policy change, published and unpublished policy documents, newspapers, political debates inside and outside Parliament, official documents produced by race relations bodies, the police, and other important definers of political issues, has allowed me to cast some light on the questions with which I began this research from an angle which allows for the reconstruction of the political history of the black youth question. This is particularly true of parts two and three, which provide a detailed and critical analysis of how policies on the black youth question have been shaped, and how implicitly and explicitly they take on-board notions about black culture and social networks which emphasise their disorganised and pathogenic qualities. Chapters 5 and 6, in addition, reflect my concern to analyse the reasons why a gap has developed between the 'promise of reform' and the 'reality of continuing racial inequalities', which represents a critical dilemma for the legitimacy of policies premised on the notion of equality of opportunity.

In addition my focus is on the impact of institutionalised racialism on young blacks and so I have said little about their own alternative construction of reality or the cultural politics involved in responses to racism. This is a reflection (a) of my wish to move away from studies of the attitudes of young blacks as such to the study of how the institutions of white racism have a specified impact on the employment chances of young blacks, and (b) of the lack of research time in which to analyse their responses to discrimination and social marginalisation. Primarily, however, I would maintain that the focus of this study on how policymakers have come to perceive young blacks as a problem necessitates a concern with macro-level political and ideological processes.

The basic approach which I adopted in the early stages of the research, given the paucity of adequate background studies mentioned above, was one of searching thoroughly through the documentation on race produced by successive governments and race or race-related bodies ('the race industry') in order to trace out the history of how the categories of the 'second generation' and 'black youth' have been constructed and gained wide political and sociological currency. Because of the lack of much previous research this proved to be an arduous task, requiring not only detailed searches through documents dating from the 1960s and 1970s, but interviews with individuals involved in the debates about this issue within the 'race industry' and the 'youth industry', individuals involved either directly or indirectly in working with schemes catering for young blacks, local government officials and community activists.

In developing this broad historical overview of the processes which explain how the 'black youth question' came to occupy the position it does today, two basic problems emerged. First, it became clear that although one could develop a general overview of *how* the issue was socially constructed into a 'problem', it was more difficult to find out *why* specific changes in orientation actually took place. Second, although it was possible to define the central elements of an official ideology about the young black in British society it was impossible to argue plausibly that all these elements were shared by all the agencies involved or that they were fixed and unchangeable. Faced with these two problems, it seemed to me that the collection of detailed facts on each initiative could resolve only one dimension; namely that of why change occurs through immediate contingencies and sheer chance. But the empirical data on their own seemed to be unable to allow the researcher to explore non-contingent and structural determinants of change. Moreover, it is impossible to explain why a specific ideology of the 'black youth problem' came to dominate policy thinking through a reference to 'facts' alone, since there are clearly quite different interpretations of 'proof' and 'plausibility' available.

In attempting to explain how and why policies have changed over the past two decades, and particularly since the advent of relatively high levels of unemployment among young blacks and growing urban unrest, the basic concern of my research was not to develop a 'proof' of my explanation of events simply by reference to 'the facts'. Rather, since my concern was with the specific issue of political responses to the category of black youth, I oriented my research to the question of why certain responses had been adopted, how they were implemented and legitimised, how links and correspondences have developed between certain institutional arrangements of decision-making and the issues that can be processed by these same institutional arrangements. In other words, I attempted through a detailed analysis of political documents, debates and media coverage to develop a plausible, though not exhaustive, analysis of how a specific set of responses to black youth as a social category had come about.

It should be emphasised that throughout this analysis one point of departure was the empirical data produced by government agencies about the 'problems' faced by the young black in British society, and particularly in relation to unemployment and welfare issues. Indeed various documents and regular information papers produced by the Manpower Services Commission, the Commission for Racial Equality, and other official and quasi-official bodies proved to be an invaluable source of information on how young blacks have been affected by the collapse of the labour market in the current recession, as well as a useful tool in monitoring the impact of the various youth training measures on young blacks. This was supplemented by visits and conversations with project workers and participants in Youth Training Schemes, both in the Birmingham area and in London.

Other points of departure were a detailed analysis of media coverage on the black youth question, of parliamentary debates and papers, of documents produced by government departments, and by quasi-governmental bodies (most notably the Commission for Racial Equality and the Manpower Services Commission). After a series of interviews with key informants in the field I was able to pinpoint basic sources of information which provided me with full and detailed information about the various changes in official ideologies and policies, and some background information on how these changes were brought about.

The well-known restriction of official documents until thirty years after the event obviously provides the most important blockage to the analysis of contemporary policy developments, along with the related problems involved in analysing the complex real and symbolic meanings of political language (Edelman, 1977; Burton and Carlen, 1979). In addition the relatively recent (mostly post-1974) nature of interventionist strategies in the youth unemployment area and related fields makes detailed analysis of the origins of policies in these areas rather difficult, and the highly politicised nature of the issues makes for quite serious blockages in access to documents and minutes for debates. For example, it would clearly have been of some interest to know more about the detailed discussions that have taken place about the black youth question at both central and local government levels. Such discussions are more easily accessible at local government level, but there is no access available to the documents of central government policy formation within the past three decades. This represents an important limit on this study, as well as, of course, on all studies of contemporary policy changes.

Given these problems much of what follows in this study of policies concerning black youth makes no claim to being a definitive analysis of this question. This will have to await the availability of more detailed unpublished documentation. But what follows does, to my mind, provide a plausible case for the propositions which this study attempts to develop. Its originality lies in the way in which it traces the process by which the black youth question became a policy issue, in its detailed analysis of the form and content of policy developments since the emergence of black youth unemployment as a central problem, and in the analysis of the transformations in official thinking which were triggered by the 'riots' of 1980–1 and 1985. In addition, much of the source material relating to policy developments (e.g. government reports, parliamentary debates, quasi-official reports) has not previously been subjected to a critical analysis which aims to draw out the complex inferential structures and meanings on which they are based.

Order of presentation

The overall aim of this study is to analyse the political history which can help us understand the emergence, development and functioning of specific forms of state intervention which are aimed at managing the 'crisis of black youth'. The central task throughout is to combine the insights of a conceptual analysis of the form of state interventions with an analysis of actual types of policy action at both central and local levels.

Chapter 1 looks at the historical development of the politics of racism in post-war Britain, and locates the fundamental processes by which the central and local state have attempted to manage the 'race question'. The role of the political debates and state interventions is shown to have worked in the direction of seeing black communities, and specific groups within them, as social problems and sources of instability.

Chapter 2 explores the main sources of official, popular and policy images of black youth as a social problem. Tracing the shifts between ideologies based on notions of assimilation, integration and special needs, it shows that such changes were related to broader political questions about the future of settled black communities within British society.

This is then followed in Chapter 3 with a discussion of how the construction of linkages between race, crime and ghetto life made 'black youth' into a central component of the politics of racism, from the early seventies onwards. Taking the increasing concern of the police and social agencies with the involvement of black youth in crime it shows how images of 'race' and 'urban decay' were fused together to provide a common sense explanation of the social position of young blacks in inner city areas.

Chapters 4 and 5 examine the politics of black youth unemployment, an issue which became central in policy and political debates during the late seventies and eighties. Chapter 4 examines the processes by which youth unemployment among young blacks became a major issue in policy discussions about both race relations and unemployment. This is then followed in chapter 5 by a detailed analysis of the role of youth training programmes, particularly those run by the Manpower Services Commission, in relation to black youth and equal opportunity.

The focus on youth unemployment is expanded in chapter 6, which deals with the inter-relationship between the urban protests of 1980–1 and 1985 and debates about black youth, unemployment policy and social policy. This chapter deals in detail with both police and media responses to violent protest, particularly as they relate to the condition of young black people in inner city areas.

Chapter 7 examines the changing forms of racist ideologies and politics in the eighties, and looks at the various trajectories which may be followed over the next decade or so. This involves in particular a discussion of the changing role of the state and the impact of changes in political orientation on the future of 'race' politics and anti-racist strategies.

The book ends with a conclusion in which the theoretical arguments and empirical evidence reviewed in earlier chapters are drawn together in an attempt to clarify the nature of the crisis facing young blacks and the wider black communities, and the implications this has for political life in general.

PART ONE

Historical and political context

1

The politics of racism and state intervention

Introduction

The introduction outlined as the substantive concern of this book the question of why and how the 'black youth question' has become a major political issue over the past three decades, and the focus of specific forms of ideological discourse and state intervention. This chapter will discuss the overall political and policy context of 'race' and 'race-related' issues over this period, since it is within this broader context that we can understand the emergence of 'black youth' as a special category of concern for both central and local government. In addition some reference will be made to the general context of state intervention over this period, and the ways in which this has shaped the form of state regulation which has been developed to deal with 'race' and 'race-related' issues.

The specific questions asked in this chapter are: (a) What is the pattern of political and ideological response to 'immigration' and 'race' issues over the past few decades? (b) What accounts for this pattern? (c) What are the implications for the black communities in the United Kingdom? These questions direct us not only to the sources of the ideological and policy definition of the 'race' dimension in contemporary British politics but, more importantly, to the operation of particular types of policy and programmes aimed at managing or resolving aspects of the 'problem'. In addition, they allow us to trace the origins of the 'black youth question' historically through an account of the processes through which a distinct form of racialised politics has emerged during these decades.

The chapter shows first that the responses to black labour migration in the post-Second World War period were shaped by a complex articulation of political, ideological and economic developments, each with their own impact on the policy outputs in relation to immigration and 'race' issues. This reinforces the conclusion that the mediation of ideology and political intervention has been central to the process through which the 'race question' has been formulated as a problem. To elaborate this, the chapter focuses on the evolution of policy debates about 'race' and related questions, such as the issue of law and order and policing, and the riots of the 1980s. The ways in which successive governments have responded to these issues are analysed, and the emergence of the 'black youth question' is related to the important transformations in these and related issue networks.

Colonialism, migrant labour and the post-war conjuncture

In analysing the immediate post-war period scholars have traditionally made a distinction between the so-called '*laissez-faire*' period before the 1962 Commonwealth Immigrants Act and the subsequent phases of political and administrative intervention in the management of 'race' and 'race-related' issues.[1] A number of recent studies, however, have questioned the rigidity of this periodisation, and have suggested a more complex explanation for the origins and development of state intervention on such issues.[2] These studies have shown that during the immediate post-1945 period the attitude of the state was far from the popular image of *laissez-faire*, and that from a very early stage a preoccupation with the 'problem' of black immigration into the UK was evident in official thinking. Additionally, there is a wealth of evidence to show that although the period from 1945 to 1962 witnessed no restrictions on the entry of colonial labour both Labour and Conservative governments explored the possibility of such controls and the desirability of measures to discourage black workers from coming to the UK (Carter and Joshi, 1984; Carter, Harris and Joshi, 1987).

Some workers from the colonies, particularly the West Indies, had arrived in the UK during both the inter-war and the 1939–45 periods (Fryer, 1984; Ramdin, 1987). From 1948 onwards the flow of West Indian immigrants increased, but the actual numbers involved remained relatively small. The migration of workers from India and Pakistan increased towards the end of the 1950s, but once again it should be emphasised that the numbers involved remained relatively small. The numbers involved did not match the relatively high level of those who entered under the Polish war veterans and the European Voluntary Workers programme, but almost from the first stages of the arrival of black workers into the UK they were perceived, both within and outside government, as a 'problem' – particularly as regards the social and 'racial' conflicts which were officially perceived as connected with their arrival (Katznelson, 1976; Carter and Joshi, 1984: 63–70). In practice the publicity given to the arrival of 417 Jamaicans on the *Empire Windrush* in May 1948, and subsequent arrivals by groups of West Indian workers, helped to focus attention on the number of 'coloured' immigrants and obscure the fact that the majority of immigrants came from the Irish Republic, white Commonwealth countries, and other European countries (Patterson, 1969: chapter 1; Miles and Phizacklea, 1984: 45–8).

One consequence of these processes was that from a very early stage in the post-war period the notion that black immigrants represented a real or potential problem took root in both the official mind and in popular political debate. The emergence of the various elements of a racialised debate about immigration is a complex issue, which takes us beyond the boundaries of this volume.[3] But a number of features about this period are worth touching on, since they provide the backcloth against which 'black youth' emerged as a category of policy concern during the early 1960s.

First, from the earliest stages of the black migration process there emerged a debate about the implications of the growth of black settlement for the host society, and particularly in relation to issues such as housing, employment, white hostility to black migrants, cultural differences and the emergence of 'racial conflict' (see for example the early Cabinet Memoranda in CAB 129/28, 1948; CAB 129/40, 1950; CAB 129/144, 1951). This concern was made more acute by the fact that the vast majority of British subjects in the colonies and dominions retained a legal right to enter and settle in Britain. Notwithstanding the fact that at the end of the Second World War the British state had legislative powers in the form of the Aliens Legislation to control the entry of non-British subjects into Britain, the 1948 British Nationality Act confirmed the rights of colonial subjects to enter and seek employment (Deakin, 1972: part 1; Macdonald, 1983: 44–52). The 1948 Act made a formal distinction between British subjects who were citizens of the United Kingdom and Colonies and those who were Commonwealth citizens, but both categories had the right to enter, settle and work in Britain. The conflict between the pressures to regulate black migration and the absence of legislative mechanisms which allowed for such control is encapsulated in the debates within the Cabinet and a number of government departments during the period from 1948 onwards,[4] and at a public level in the emergence of a political and ideological debate about the issue of 'colonial immigration'.[5] The ambivalence of the official response is captured in a recent study of the official records of the early 1950s, which concludes by questioning the whole idea of an 'age of innocence':

The period between the 1948 Nationality Act and the 1962 Commonwealth Immigrants Act is frequently characterised as one in which the principle of free entry of British subjects to the UK was only relinquished with great reluctance and after considerable official debate. This was not the case. On the contrary, the debate was never about principle. Labour and Conservative Governments had by 1952 instituted a number of covert, and sometimes illegal, administrative measures to discourage black immigration.

(Carter, Harris and Joshi, 1987)

It was a short step from the articulation within governmental institutions of measures to discourage black immigration to the attribution to black migrants of negative stereotypes, and the emergence of ideologies which see blacks as a problem can be traced back to this immediate post-war conjuncture.

This leads to the second feature of this period which needs to be mentioned: namely, the construction of 'race' and 'immigration' as synonymous, or what is sometimes called the 'immigrant–colonial nexus' (Freeman, 1979: 28–9). The evolution of political and public debate on immigration during the immediate post-war period became closely tied to the 'race' dimension in an almost seamless manner, with the focus of concern not being the arrival of immigrants *per se* but the threats posed to British society and culture by 'undesirable immigrants'. The terms of this debate were by no means fixed purely by party political ideologies, and there was a widespread discussion both within the Conservative and Labour parties about the impact of coloured immigration on housing, employment, welfare, and related social and economic issues.[6] This debate focused on both local and national issues, and successfully defined subsequent debates about 'coloured' immigration along problem-oriented criteria.

Within the terms of this overarching view of the 'problem' successive internal government documents and public pronouncements through the early 1950s reveal an ideology which exemplified a perception of the consequences of allowing 'undesirable immigrants' along the following four lines of argument: (a) economic and employment issues; (b) housing and environment; (c) long-term social consequences; and (d) responses to black immigration by whites. During the period leading up to the passage of the 1962 Commonwealth Immigrants Act the terms of the debate around all four issues were constantly in flux, as can be exemplified by reference to confidential government documents which have only recently been made available.[7] But even the most casual scrutiny of the period of the early 1950s to 1962 shows that the question of controls on 'coloured immigration' had already been placed on the margins of the political agenda, and was gradually moving to centre stage. Controls on immigration from the colonies had been discussed as early as 1948, and the need for legislation had been assessed and rejected during 1950–1 (CAB 128/17, 1950; CAB 128/19, 1951; Carter and Joshi, 1984: 63–70). During 1955 and 1956 a draft Bill was circulated by the Home Secretary and a Committee of Ministers was constituted with the following terms of reference:

> To consider what form legislation should take, if it were decided that legislation to control the entry into the United Kingdom of British subjects from overseas should be introduced; to consider also the intended affect of such legislation upon actual immigration, how any such control would be justified to Parliament and the public, and to the Commonwealth countries concerned; and report to the Cabinet.
>
> (CAB 129/81, 1956: CP(56) 45)

The concern with how a policy of control and exclusion could be justified was displayed in official government documents throughout this period (Carter, Harris and Joshi, 1987; Harris, 1987) and explains the reticence to follow the advice of some MPs and others who called for immigration controls to be introduced to change the rights enjoyed by colonial citizens under the 1948 British Nationality Act (Deakin, 1972: part 2; Miles and Phizacklea, 1984: 20–44). But by the early 1950s the ideology that 'too many' black immigrants were a potential 'problem' had already become institutionalised. This, in turn, laid the ground for the move towards the implementation of legislative controls on immigration, since it situated the question within the broader context of the social and political problems which were perceived as linked to the arrival of black immigrants.

Processes of racialisation and political ideologies

To summarise the argument so far: With the growing emphasis on the control of 'coloured' immigration the terms of ideological and policy debates about the future of black workers in the UK turned on two themes which were to prove influential later. First, a vigorous debate took place in and out of parliament about the possibility of revising the 1948 British Nationality Act so as to limit the number of black immigrants who could come and settle in the UK. The terms of this debate were by no means fixed purely by party political ideologies, and there was much opposition to the call for controls on black immigration from Conservative and Labour politicians, as well as from immigrant groups, pressure groups and individuals (Fryer, 1984: 367–86; Ramdin, 1987: 210–31). Second, a parallel debate developed about the problems caused by 'too many coloured immigrants' in relation to housing, employment, crime and social welfare (see for example CAB 129/78, 1955; CAB 129/81, 1956).

This debate linked up with the construction of a political argument in favour of controls; a link which was made apparent during the public debate about the 1958 riots in Notting Hill and Nottingham (Wickenden, 1958; Ramdin, 1987: 204–10). These events, and the period from 1958 to the announcement of the Commonwealth Immigrants Bill in October 1961, are traditionally conceived as a watershed in the politics of racism in contemporary Britain. A number of writers have argued that the outbreak of 'racial violence' on the streets of two major cities, Nottingham and London, symbolised a move from a 'pre-political' to a 'political' stage in the history of post-war racism (Deakin, 1970: 96–100; Foot, 1965: 130–2). Yet others have seen the events as a symbol of the emergence of racist ideologies within British political life in response to the growing presence of settled black communities in many urban localities (Hall, 1980: 27–8; CCCS Race and Politics Group, 1982: 15–17). Katznelson's account of the 1958 riots is a case in point. He locates the riots as part of a longer term process involving the politicisation of 'race' both at a national and local level (1976: 129–32). Thus he argues that 'Largely as a result of the violent racial clashes that erupted in London and Nottingham in the summer of 1958, the issue of race moved from the periphery to the centre of political debate' (1976: 129). According to this model the 1958 events played an important role in opening up the road towards the institutionalisation of legislative controls on black immigration. From this perspective the riots helped to speed up the process of racialisation, and structured official ideologies about the consequences of black migration and settlement.[8]

While Katznelson and others have failed to contextualise the 1958 riots in their proper historical context, and may have exaggerated the impact of the riots at the political level, it is nevertheless true that by the 1958–62 period the mobilisation of opinion inside and outside Parliament against black immigration had reached a peak.[9] Thus although the 'riots' themselves consisted largely of attacks by whites on blacks, the political climate was such that they were interpreted largely through a racial model or as an outcome of 'unrestricted immigration' (Harris and Solomos, forthcoming). Thus a number of Conservative MPs used the riots as yet another plank on which to construct their case in favour of immigration controls. The years between 1958 and 1961 witnessed a series of debates in Parliament, within the major political parties, in the media and other public forums about the desirability or otherwise of immigration controls.[10]

The outcome of these debates became evident in October 1961, when the Conservative government announced its intention to legislate for the control of black immigration. The Commonwealth Immigrants Bill was legitimised in Parliament by arguments about the need to control the rate of immigration because of the limited ability of the host society to assimilate immigrants (*Hansard*, vol. 649, 1961: cols. 687–824; vol. 650, 1961: 1159–500). But perhaps Hugh Gaitskell, the Labour party leader, was closer to the mark when he said the Bill represented a crude attempt to amalgamate the question of 'immigration' with 'race'. According to Gaitskell, Labour's opposition to the Bill was based on a fundamental difference in approach to that of the Conservative government:

> It is no part of our case to pretend that any amount of immigration of people of different colour and social customs and language does not present problems, though I urge that we should beware of exaggerations here. Does the Government deal with it by seeking to combat social evils, by building more houses and enforcing laws against overcrowding, by using every educational means at their disposal to create tolerance and mutual understanding, and by emphasising to our own people the value of these immigrants and setting their face firmly against all forms of racial intolerance and discrimination? That is what we believe, and that is what I hope the Government believe, but it is not what is implied in the Bill. Indeed, there is no shred of evidence that the Government have even seriously tried to go along this course and make a proper inquiry into the nature of this problem. They have yielded to the crudest clamour, 'Keep them out'.
>
> (*Hansard*, vol. 649: col. 801)

Gaitskell's opposition to the Bill was not shared by all Labour politicians, who often took a more ambiguous stance on the question of control (*IRR Newsletter*, December 1961 and May 1962). But the contrast between the position taken by the Labour and Conservative parties was partly the outcome of the debates about immigration which developed during the 1950s. The debates about the Bill in Parliament, and the public discussion of the 1962 Commonwealth Immigrants Act, were an outcome of the long process of politicisation which I have outlined above.

The 1962 Act introduced a distinction between citizens of the UK and colonies and citizens of independent Commonwealth countries. All holders of Commonwealth passports were subject to immigration control except those who were (a) born in the UK, (b) held UK passports issued by the UK government, or (c) persons included in the passport of one of the persons excluded from immigration control under (a) or (b) (Macdonald, 1983: 10–12). Other Commonwealth citizens had to obtain a Ministry of Labour employment voucher in order to be able to enter the UK. During the period from 1963 to 1972, when the voucher system was abolished, there was pressure to cut back the number of vouchers allocated, and this was reflected in a steady fall in the number of vouchers issued and the number of voucher holders admitted. This reduction in the pattern of primary migration did not depoliticise the issue of immigration as a whole, however, since even after the 1962 Act the wives and children of immigrants already settled continued to arrive. The continuing influx of the dependents of black immigrants therefore helped to keep alive the political debate about the impact of Commonwealth immigration on British society.

Immigration controls and race relations legislation

The racialisation of the immigration issue during the 1950s laid the foundations for the move towards the control of black immigration, an objective which was first implemented through the 1962 Commonwealth Immigrants Act. This Act prepared the ground for further pieces of legislation to control black immigration: most notably the 1968 Commonwealth Immigrants Act, and 1969 Immigration Appeals Act, and, most importantly, the 1971 Immigration Act (Macdonald, 1983: 1–20; Miles and Solomos, 1987). But the 1962 Act is important from both a practical and a symbolic political perspective. It marks a definite break with the rights which were enjoyed by colonial immigrants under the 1948 British Nationality Act. While successive Labour and Conservative governments had been reluctant to implement such a fundamental shift in policy, by 1961 the main dilemma which seemed to be faced by the government was exactly how to legitimise a policy which aimed to control black immigration and how to present it as a more universal measure. William Deedes, who was then a Minister without Portfolio, recalls that

> The Bill's real purpose was to restrict the influx of coloured immigrants. We were reluctant to say as much openly. So the restrictions were applied to coloured and white citizens in all Commonwealth countries – though everybody recognised that

immigration from Canada, Australia and New Zealand formed
no part of the problem.

(Deedes, 1968: 10)

This quotation serves as a measure of the extent to which the 'problem of
immigration' had been codified along racial lines in the period leading up
to the 1962 Act – 'commonwealth immigrants' were not a 'problem' as
such; they were perceived as a 'problem' if they also happened to be
black (Freeman, 1979: 45–52). More generally, black immigrants were
seen as linked to other 'problems', such as pressure on housing,
unemployment, racial conflict and urban decay. The objective of state
policy was therefore to prevent these 'problems' from becoming a source
of conflict in the future. This was to be achieved by placing restrictions on
the arrival of black migrants and introducing measures to help their
integration into the majority society.

Two competing models have been used to explain the move towards
immigration controls. Some scholars have seen the 1962 Act and
subsequent legislative measures as a response by the state to the pressure
of popular opinion against black immigration, and therefore as an
abandonment of earlier principles (Foot, 1965: chapter 7; Rose *et al.*,
1969: chapter 16). According to this model the main rationale behind
immigration control legislation was the need to placate anti-immigrant
lobby groups and racialist popular opinion. Successive Conservative and
Labour governments during the 1960s and 1970s are seen as acting not on
the basis of principle or rational policy-making, but largely on the
defensive premise of placating opposition to black immigration.

Yet other scholars have argued that the state was not merely responding to popular political pressures, but was also acting to protect the
economic interests of the capitalist class, which required that the rights of
colonial workers to migrate and settle freely in the UK be undermined
(Freeman and Spencer, 1979: 63–8; Sivanandan, 1982: 101–26). According to this analysis the role of the state is determined by the interests of
the capitalist class in the super-exploitation of black labour. Thus the
passage of immigration legislation can be seen as one aspect of this
broader political strategy, since it is argued that the net effect of the
controls imposed by the 1962 Commonwealth Immigrants Act and
subsequent measures has been the imposition of a quasi-migrant labour
system in Britain. Such a system approximates the experience of other
European countries, most notably West Germany, where migrant
workers are effectively denied citizenship rights enjoyed by other
workers (Castles and Kosack, 1973; Castles *et al.*, 1984). Both explanations have been widely used in the literature on the politics of

immigration.[11] They do, however, raise a number of problems when used as explanatory models for analysing the development and implementation of particular policy initiatives. It seems inadequate, for example, to view the actions taken by the state as purely responsive, whether to the demands of popular opinion or to economic interests. Throughout the period from 1948 to 1962, and subsequently, a substantial amount of recent research evidence has shown that state institutions were actively involved in monitoring and regulating the arrival of black workers. Government departments, quasi-governmental agencies and political parties were all actively involved in the complex processes which helped to articulate a definition of the immigration question which was suffused with racialised categories.[12]

But the state has by no means been preoccupied simply by the issue of immigration controls. Throughout the period since 1962, successive governments have also been faced with the question of how to deal with the position of those black communities which were already settled in Britain, and which could not simply be excluded from the citizenship rights enjoyed by white citizens (Brier and Axford, 1975: 2–21; Freeman, 1979: 120–3). They have also been faced with the need to respond to the political pressure which such minority groups have sought to extend through the political system, and the need to legitimise immigration control which seemed to be aimed at a specific group defined by colour and ethnic origins (Heineman, 1972: 16–52; Ramdin, 1987: 370–456).

This aspect of the state's response has led to the emergence of a dual strategy which has aimed at both the control of primary immigration and the 'social integration' of those who had already entered and settled in the UK, or who were likely to settle in the future. The first clear statement of this strategy was made by the Labour government in 1965, in the form of the White Paper on *Immigration from the Commonwealth*.[13] Between 1962 and 1965 the Labour party moved away from its opposition to immigration controls and began to articulate a dual strategy of maintaining and strengthening controls while at the same time promoting the 'integration' of immigrants already settled (Foot, 1965: 161–94; Dummett and Dummett, 1982: 97–126). The 1965 White Paper rationalised this shift by linking the maintenance of immigration controls to measures to deal with the 'social problems' and 'conflicts' arising from immigration. Harold Wilson introduced the White Paper along these lines when he argued that controls needed to be supported by measures 'to promote integration in the widest sense of the word, in terms of housing, health, education and everything that needs to be done to minimise the possible social disturbance arising from this social problem' (quoted in Deakin, 1969: 5).

According to Roy Hattersley's famous statement, 'Integration without limitation is impossible; limitation without integration is indefensible' (*Hansard*, vol. 721, 1965: col. 359). Broadly speaking common sense notions such as this exercised a heavy influence on official policy, and created a political climate which allowed the 'balancing' of immigration control legislation with integration measures. Thus in 1965 the Labour government passed the first Race Relations Act. This Act was fairly limited in scope, but its genesis and implementation can be traced to the dual strategy which became part of the dominant political consensus during the mid-1960s (Kushnick, 1971: 233–68; Katznelson, 1976: 139–51). During the tenure of Roy Jenkins as Home Secretary in the Labour government, this dual strategy was implemented enthusiastically because of the fear that the social exclusion of racial minorities in Britain could lay the basis for violence and disorder on the American model (*IRR Newsletter*, June/July 1967). Given these assumptions the Race Relations Acts of 1965 and 1968 were based on the twin objectives of

(a) setting up special bodies to deal with the 'problems' faced by immigrants in dealing with racism discrimination, social adjustment and welfare; and

(b) helping to educate the population as a whole about 'race relations', and hence minimising the risk of racialised conflicts developing in Britain as it had done in the United States.

These twin objectives dominated the thinking of successive Labour and Conservative governments during the 1960s and 1970s.[14] Significantly, however, the state did not seek to use mainstream government departments and spending programmes to tackle this issue. While the Home Office was directly responsible after 1962 for the enforcement of strict immigration controls, the responsibility for enforcing the 1965 and 1968 Acts was given to weak quasi-governmental bodies. The objectives of such bodies were to tackle racial discrimination, but their ability to implement them was severely limited throughout (Jenkins and Solomos, 1987; Solomos, forthcoming: chapter 5).

At the same time the Commonwealth Immigrants Act of 1968 and the Immigration Act of 1971 further institutionalised controls on black immigration. The 1968 Act was passed specifically to bring the East African Asians under immigration control, and signalled the institutionalisation of the radical break with Gaitskell's position on the 1962 Act which had emerged during the mid-1960s. The 1971 Act distinguished between citizens of the United Kingdom and colonies who were 'patrial' and therefore had the right to settle in Britain, and 'non-patrials' who did not. The most important categories of patrials were:

(a) citizens of the United Kingdom and colonies who had that

citizenship by birth, adoption, naturalisation or registration in
the United Kingdom, or who were born of parents, one of whom
had United Kingdom citizenship by birth, or one of whose
grandparents had such citizenship; and

(b)   citizens of the United Kingdom and colonies who had at any time
settled in the United Kingdom and who had been ordinarily
resident in the United Kingdom for five years or more (Macdonald, 1983: 52–6).

Under the 1971 Act, therefore, all aliens and Commonwealth citizens
who were not 'patrials' needed permission to enter Britain. While before
this Commonwealth citizens entering under the voucher system could
settle in Britain, after the 1971 Act came into force they entered on the
basis of work-permits. Thus Commonwealth migrants who were not
patrial were reduced to the effective status of short-term contract
workers rather than settlers (Sivanandan, 1982: 108–12; Castles *et al.*,
1984: 11–29).

The 1971 Immigration Act completed the course of action signalled by
the 1962 Commonwealth Immigrants Act: it took away the right of black
Commonwealth migrants to settle in Britain. It represented the culmi-
nation of what was popularly seen as a 'White Britain Policy'. This
strategy left little room for effective measures to tackle racial discrimination within Britain. A strong lobby by liberal pressure groups, black
organisations and sections of political opinion in favour of more effective
policies to tackle racism and racial inequality was resisted by the
Conservative government from 1970 to 1974 (Layton-Henry, 1984:
75–86; Solomos, forthcoming: chapter 5). But when the Labour party
came back to power in 1974 it proved to be more responsive to this
pressure. In September 1975 it published a White Paper on *Racial
Discrimination*, which called for recognition of the fact that black
communities were 'here to stay' and for the need to introduce more
effective measures to tackle racial discrimination. Interestingly enough,
the White Paper saw the younger generation as becoming increasingly
frustrated by racial discrimination and a lack of equal opportunity, and
warned that the government and the race relations institutions needed to
take positive measures to overcome the specific problems faced by the
second generation of young blacks who were no longer 'immigrants', but
who shared the economic, social and cultural injustices suffered by their
parents (Home Office, 1975: 4–6). The 1976 Race Relations Act followed the White Paper and came into force in 1977. Although based
essentially on the model of the 1965 and 1968 Acts, the 1976 Act
extended the law against discrimination in three ways. First, it extended
the law to cover not only intentional discrimination but indirect discrimi-

nation. Second, it set up a joint agency to replace the Race Relations Board and the Community Relations Commission. The Commission for Racial Equality was seen as a stronger agency for tackling racial discrimination. Third, cases of discrimination in employment were to be handled by the industrial tribunal system (Lustgarten, 1980: 3–37). Despite these changes, however, the impact of the 1976 Act in tackling the root causes of racial discrimination seems to have been quite minimal (Feuchtwang, 1981: 107–15; McCrudden, 1982: 336–67).

The lack of 'balance' between the strict immigration controls institutionalised between 1962 and 1971 and the Race Relations Acts of 1965, 1968 and 1976 highlights the dominance of the 'immigration–race' amalgam in official ideologies and policies. While successive governments have been able to impose controls on black immigration very effectively, they have shown little inclination to tackle the roots of racism in British society. They have thus created a situation where the legitimacy of state actions in this field has been questioned from a number of perspectives.[15]

Racism, economic decline and crisis management

If the main rationalisation of the immigration controls and the race relations legislation was the objective of producing an atmosphere for the development of 'good race relations' and integration, it needs to be said that they failed to depoliticise the question of 'race' as such. The restrictions imposed by the 1971 Immigration Act and successive Immigration Rules have seemingly fulfilled the ostensible objective of government policies since 1962, which has been to control primary immigration and restrict secondary immigration, but the politicisation of 'race' has proceeded apace during this time. In 1986, for example, the Conservative government produced a statement for an international conference on immigration policy which stated the broad objectives of governmental policies over the past few decades in the following terms:

> In recent decades, the basis of policy in the United Kingdom has been the need to control primary immigration – that is, new heads of households who are most likely to enter the job market. The United Kingdom is one of the most densely populated countries in Europe. In terms of housing, education, social services and of course, jobs, the country could not support all those who would like to come here. Firm immigration control is therefore essential, in order to provide the conditions necessary for developing and maintaining good community relations.
>
> (OECD, 1986: 1)

Yet, what is also clear is that although the various Acts and regulations which restrict and control black immigration have been legitimised along these lines there has been no noticeable change in the racialisation of political ideologies and practices. Indeed if one looks at the past decade as a case in point there has been a noticeable racialisation of policy debates in relation to a growing number of national and local political issues (CCCS Race and Politics Group, 1982: 15–36). Perhaps the most important issues in which this process is clear are education, employment, policing and urban policy (for some perspectives on these issues, see Troyna and Williams, 1986; Gilroy, 1987).

It should be no surprise that the management of 'good race relations' has assumed a central and expressive role in the context of this deep-seated crisis. There is no one-to-one correspondence between the 'crisis of race' and the wider crisis tendencies within British society. Yet 'race' is always present, whether the issue under discussion is the growth of unemployment, the role of the police, educational problems or urban disorder. The morphology of racism during the past four decades needs to be contextualised against the wider set of social transformations which have taken place, and which influenced the perception and response of the 'race problem'. As Stuart Hall argues:

> At the economic level, it is clear that race must be given its distinctive and 'relatively autonomous' effectivity, as a distinctive feature. This does not mean that the economic is sufficient to found an explanation of how these relations concretely function. One needs to know how different racial and ethnic groups are inserted historically, and the relations which have tended to erode and transform, or to preserve these distinctions through time – not simply as residues and traces of previous modes, but as active structuring principles of the present society. Racial categories alone will not provide or explain these.
>
> (Hall, 1980: 339)

The new morphology of racism in the eighties needs to be located against the background of these social relations, and the fundamental transformations which are being experienced at all levels of economic, social and political life in contemporary Britain.

This may sound like an obvious point to make, but there is still a strong tendency to analyse questions of 'race' apart from the wider social context. The question of racial discrimination in employment is a case in point. There is still a tendency to conceive of the issue of racism in employment as a problem linked only to 'race', when in fact it is also determined by processes external to the 'race' issue as such. These include the restructuring of employment in the British economy, changes in the structure of the labour market, regional and local de-industriali- sation and international economic relations. Any analysis of the question of racism in employment therefore cannot ignore the wider context, and it certainly cannot ignore the dynamics of change in relation to the 'social fabric' of British society.

The contradictory nature of this interplay between 'race' and the wider social totality can be grasped more concretely if we look at the changing forms of state intervention and ideologies which legitimise policy in this field.

Law and order, racism and the 'enemy within'

Perhaps the most important development in this field during the 1970s was the move away from a preoccupation with immigration *per se*, and a shift towards a concern with the development of the black communities already settled in the UK.

The political language used still referred to 'immigrants', but by the mid-1970s the reference point was not only new arrivals but the black communities already settled in Britain. Particular sections, or indeed whole black communities, were perceived as a kind of 'enemy within', growing in size and changing in composition within the confines of Britain's inner city areas (CCCS Race and Politics Group, 1982: 27–35). The image of inner city areas becoming 'black enclaves' where 'British' law and order could not be easily enforced became a theme in a number of official reports and studies during this period. The very presence of black communities was seen as a potential or real threat to the 'way of life' and culture of white citizens (see Solomos, forthcoming, for an extensive discussion of these issues).

Sections of the extreme right, and even sections of the Conservative party, agitated around such symbols and images throughout the 1970s. But by the mid-1970s it became clear that such agitation focused as much on the supposed dangers of an 'alien wedge' as on the question of the arrival of new immigrants. The dangers of immigration were equated not just with the 'hordes waiting at the gate' but with the 'enemy within'; who was in many cases born and bred in Brixton, Hackney, Tottenham, Handsworth, Moss Side, Toxteth and other urban localities. During the debate on the 1981 Nationality Bill, Ivor Stanbrook, one of the most outspoken of Conservative MPs on 'race' issues, made this point succinc- tly when he argued:

> On the issues dealt with by the Bill we are in the grip of forces which, because of the large influx of immigrants into Britain, we

seem unable to control. Racial violence is occurring with increasing frequency. The British people are sick at heart about it all. We badly need honest and forthright politicians to express their feelings without fear of being condemned on moral grounds. It is, therefore deplorable that Church leaders should have condemned the Bill as being racially discriminatory. Any nationality law that is based upon place of birth or descent from one's parents is bound to favour those who are born or who are the children of those born in the country concerned ... Most people in Britain happen to be white-skinned. Most of those who would like to become British citizens happen to be black-skinned.   (*Hansard*, vol. 5, 1981: col. 1180)

Arguments such as these focused as much on the 'influx of immigrants' as on the domestic consequences – 'forces we seem unable to control'. The image used is one of a society under threat from outside and from within.

What explains this transformation during the past two decades? A number of issues are involved, and not all of these can be analysed in this chapter but at least two are worth noting. The first concerns the transformations of the broader social and economic, as well as political, structures of British society during this period. 'Immigration' and 'race' questions have not existed in isolation and, as I have argued above, the complex interaction between social, political and economic change since the 1970s is an important background factor in explaining changing ideologies about 'race' and related issues. For example, the rapid transformation of many inner city localities has provided a fertile ground for the racialisation of issues such as employment, housing, education, urban policy and law and order. But this racialisation process has moved public and political debate beyond immigration *per se*, with the focus moving towards the identification and resolution of specific 'social problems' linked to 'race'. The link with the immigration question is maintained at another level, because it is the size of the black population, whether in the schools or the unemployment queue which is identified as the source of the problem (Miles and Phizacklea, 1984: 79–117).

The second issue which needs to be looked at, and which will be emphasised throughout this book, is the role of ideological symbols in reproducing common sense notions about the question of 'race'. Political language is both a way of emphasising what one wants to believe and of avoiding issues that one does not wish to face (Edelman, 1977; 1–21; Katznelson, 1986: 307–10). A good example of this dual usage of political symbols are the calls for more controls on immigration, which continue to be made even in the context of strict racially specific controls. Such calls have been made continuously in the period since the 1971 Immigration Act (*Hansard*, vol. 865, 1973: cols. 1469–582; vol. 914, 1976: cols. 964–1094; vol. 973, 1979: cols. 253–382), and are often laced with references to the 'number' of actual immigrants or to the 'large numbers' who potentially could arrive and 'swamp' British culture with 'alien values' (Barker, 1982; Miles and Phizacklea, 1984: 159–76). Such statements are not based on 'the facts' in any recognisable sense, nor do they need to be in order to be effective. Rather references to statistics and trends in immigration are often highly selective, and emphasise symbolic fears about the present and the future. Good examples of this process are the debates which occurred during the mid-1970s about the Hawley Report on immigration from the Indian sub-continent (*Hansard*, vol. 914, 1976: cols. 964–1004), and the Select Committee's Report on Immigration (Select Committee, 1978: Report, vol. I; *Hansard*, vol. 975, 1979: cols. 253–372), as well as a number of more recent debates in and out of Parliament.[16] A more recent case is the introduction in 1986 of visa controls for visitors from India, Pakistan, Bangladesh, Nigeria and Ghana. These controls were legitimised as necessary in order to control the number of illegal immigrants from these countries (*Hansard*, vol. 103, 1986: cols. 77–138). The fact that only 222 out of 452,000 visitors from the five countries absconded as illegal immigrants in 1985, did not prevent the symbolic use of visa controls as yet another means of 'holding the tide' of immigration (*The Guardian*, 2 September 1986).

The combination of images of 'large numbers' of immigrants, urban decline and the growth of concentrated black communities has been a theme in much of the recent neo-Conservative writings on 'immigration' and 'race'. During the 1978–9 period, leading up to her 1979 election triumph, Margaret Thatcher made a number of astute interventions on the subject, including her statement about the 'swamping' of white communities by immigrants (*The Guardian*, 1 February 1978; *Daily Mail*, 13 February 1978). Since 1979 this theme has been returned to a number of times by some sections of Conservative opinion, and has been articulated around substantive issues such as policing, urban decline and violent urban disorders.[17]

Responses to the 1980–1 and 1985 riots are a case in point. One of the central themes in both public and parliamentary debates about the riots was the question of 'race', 'young blacks' and 'black inner city enclaves' (Solomos, 1986: 14–22; Benyon and Solomos, 1987: introduction). A number of the popular papers and a section of the Conservative party focused on the role of young blacks during the riots, and the linkage between the emergence of violent protest on the streets of British cities and the growth of 'immigrant communities' and 'black ghettoes'.

Through this process of identification of the riots with a specific section of society common sense images of 'black youth' as a danger to social stability and order, as an 'enemy within', were given further credence and political legitimacy.

During both the 1981 and 1985 riots Enoch Powell, and a number of other MPs constructed an interpretation of the riots which saw them as intimately linked to the size and concentration of the black population in certain localities. Thus, in 1981 Powell proclaimed that the riots were a vindication of his warnings about immigration since 1968, and he linked this assessment to a renewed call for repatriation as the only solution (*Hansard*, vol. 8, 1981: cols. 1312–13; vol. 84, 1985: cols. 375–7). Such an assessment was by no means widely accepted, and indeed it was widely criticised by politicians and commentators from all shades of political opinion.[18] But his analysis of the events in 1985 stands out as an example of the political implications of the extreme racialisation of the riots. He argues that

> In the foreseeable future not less than one third of the population of inner London will be New Commonwealth and Pakistan ethnic, and . . . this will apply to major cities throughout the length and breadth of England ... The Hon. Member for Birmingham Selly Oak (Mr Beaumont-Dark) drew attention to the profound change that has taken place in the composition of the population in inner London, in his city and mine, and in other cities. He did not draw attention to the fact that this phenomenon is not static, but dynamic. It marches on. What we have seen so far in terms of the transformation of the population, like what we have seen so far in terms of urban violence, is nothing to what we know is to come. This knowledge, which is not hidden from ordinary people who live in those places, overshadows those cities and inner London.
>
> (*Hansard*, vol. 84, 1985: cols. 375–6)

There is still, of course, an important difference between Powell's repatriation scenario and the policies of the state. Yet within the popular consciousness, and not just the media, Powell's analysis exemplifies the way in which the issue of 'race' came to occupy the central role in accounts of why the riots have taken place in specific areas.

Within the context of growing urban unrest and structural change in the economic and cultural relations of inner city areas it becomes all too easy to portray black communities as a whole, or sections of them, as a kind of 'social time-bomb' which could help undermine the social fabric of the localities in which they live or even of British society as a whole.

Growing urban unrest and violence create a space for the Powellite imagery of a 'racial' civil war to take root in popular common sense, for the 'real fears' of the majority white population to be deflected onto the 'enemy within'. The policies pursued by the Conservative government since 1979 have helped to give further credence to such 'real fears'. While emphasising the need to maintain and strengthen controls on immigration because 'of the strain that the admission of a substantial number of immigrants can place on existing resources and services' (Leon Brittan, *Hansard*, vol. 83, 1985: col. 893), it has steadfastly refused to strengthen legislation on racial discrimination.

'Race' and crisis management in the 1980s

The above analysis leads directly to the question which will occupy the rest of this book: namely the construction and amplification of a racialised discourse about 'black youth'. It will be argued in this volume that the identification of young blacks as a 'problem group' has resulted from the overall categorisation of black communities as a 'problem'. Just as in the 1950s and 1960s the 'numbers game' mobilised a conception of the 'problem' which focused on the need to keep black immigrants out, the language of political debate during the 1970s seemed to shift towards the view that 'black youth' were a kind of social time-bomb which could help undermine the social fabric of the 'immigration–race relations' amalgam and possibly society as a whole.

The processes which helped to construct a racialised discourse about 'black youth' are themselves complex, and will be discussed in detail in the following chapters. But the whole question of the relationship of the state and its institutions to young blacks cannot be analysed apart from the wider processes which have been briefly outlined in this volume. As will be argued in chapter 3, for example, the generation and amplification of the 'mugging' issue in the early seventies, has to be contextualised against both the wider racialisation of British politics and the social and economic changes which were taking place in inner city localities. Similarly, the arguments in chapters 6 and 7 about the relationship of urban unrest to the black youth question cannot be understood without some reference to the policies pursued by the Conservative government since 1979 in relation to employment, policing, inner city areas and 'race'.

Additionally, it is important to note that the current situation which we confront in the 1980s did not come about by accident. It resulted from the actions and non-actions of successive governments and political actors. Throughout this volume, therefore, I shall be attempting to analyse the

impact of particular actions on the political environment of 'race relations' and wider political relations. Two central questions will be asked
throughout: First, what are the factors which can explain the construction of 'black youth' as a political issue? Second, what impact has this
construction had on the politics of 'race' within British society? Such
questions are difficult to answer, but the account of the origins, development and articulation of state policies towards the black youth question
may at least provide some tentative answers. In so doing I hope to
challenge some of the fundamental assumptions of past and present
policies, and suggest how a more positive approach can be developed.

This case study will therefore allow us to reflect on some of the more
general aspects of the inter-relationship between 'race' and wider social
transformations. This will provide the focus for chapter 7, which will be
the question of how the issue of 'black youth' has been re-interpreted in
the mid- to late eighties around the themes of urban protest, youth
unemployment and social policy. This will provide us with an opportunity to return to the question of how the re-working of racial ideologies
in the eighties has hinged around notions of blacks as 'enemies within'
the very heart of British society.

Conclusions

This chapter has attempted to present a general introduction to the
racialisation of British politics, and in particular to outline the assumptions, arguments and beliefs that guided policy on both 'immigration' and
'race relations' issues. In this sense the account provided above will be
treated as a base line for the analysis and evaluation of policies in relation
to the question of 'black youth', a theme that will occupy the rest of this
book. The main arguments developed in this chapter can be summarised
through the following four propositions:

(1)   State intervention in relation to 'race' questions since the 1940s
      has been dominated by perceptions of black immigrants as a
      'problem group'. In a very real sense black people have been
      constructed into the bearers of ascribed characteristics.
(2)   During the past four decades, however, there has been a
      noticeable shift in official concerns away from black immigration
      per se; with a consequent preoccupation with the management of
      the black communities that are already domiciled in Britain.
(3)   The logical consequence of this shift is to displace conflicts and
      strains in 'race relations' onto the black communities as a whole,
      or to specific sections of them.
(4)   In so far as a displacement of conflicts onto the black communi-

ties becomes a part of political debates, common sense ideas of blacks as an 'enemy within' or 'alien' are able to take further root.

One last point needs to be made. In pointing to the general tendencies which have characterised political interventions and debates, we should be wary of drawing the all too easy conclusion that there are no tensions and contradictions which influence the inter-relationship between 'race' and politics in contemporary Britain. It is precisely such contradictions which will be explored in the rest of this book. The interplay of ideology and policy in relation to the 'black youth' question will be used to pin down the sources of state policies and to examine their consequences for the politicisation of 'race'.

PART TWO

Dimensions of the black youth question

2

From assimilation to special needs: ideologies and policies

Introduction

When the Select Committee on Race Relations and Immigration was set up in 1968 it chose the issue of *The Problems of Coloured School Leavers* for its first inquiry. It justified this choice on the basis of the following three reasons:

(a) The issue of 'coloured' school leavers was likely to be a continuing problem. Even if immigration were to stop immediately, children from minority ethnic groups would continue to leave British schools and seek employment and acceptance in British society.

(b) The treatment of these school leavers was in a sense a 'test case' in race relations, because if the country failed to give them full, fair and equal opportunities on entering adult life it was unlikely to succeed in any other sector of race relations.

(c) The proper treatment of these young people was in the direct interests of the British people because discrimination against them in employment was not only a waste of the resources of the schools, but also damaging to the national economy (Select Committee, 1969, Report: 5–7).

The Committee's choice of topic and the reasons it gave for its decision represent an interesting case study in the development of an official response to the 'second generation' of the black community, and one to which I shall return later on in the chapter. But what is important to emphasise at this juncture is the fact that during the period of the mid-1960s the shift in the political language of 'race relations' which I have analysed in the previous chapter began to have an important impact on the position of young black people growing up in British society. Not only were this group perceived as a 'continuing problem', but the main institutions of the emerging race relations industry became intimately concerned with the question of the 'second generation' of black British and their future.[1]

It is to this issue that I now turn my attention in this chapter. In particular I shall be exploring the complex reasons why young blacks were constructed politically and socially into a 'problem group'. Given the wider context of the racialisation of British politics described in chapter 1, the questions I shall be asking in this chapter are: Why were young blacks seen from an early stage as a danger to the social fabric of British society? How did various agencies attempt to respond to the 'threat', and what were the practical policy consequences of the perception of young blacks as a 'social problem'? Finally, what explains the ideological shift, from the late sixties onwards, towards the ideology of 'special needs' in contrast to earlier notions of assimilation? Throughout this chapter detailed use will be made of contemporary official reports, policy documents and newspaper coverage in order to show the dynamics of political and policy debates about this question. Additionally, reference will be made to the changing parliamentary discourses on this subject.

From black immigrants to black British

Within the context of the changing role of state intervention on 'race' and immigration issues, the question of the 'second generation' of 'coloured teenagers' emerged as a focus of concern during the earliest stages of black migration and settlement. Indeed some scholars have argued that an important theme in official political language during the inter-war period was the question of youth, particularly the position of 'half-caste' children produced as a result of mixed marriages (Rich, 1986: 120–44; Harris, 1987; Ramdin, 1987: 60–99). Certainly, there is much evidence to support this argument when one looks at some of the contemporary debates about black communities in the port towns, including Liverpool, Cardiff and London. A number of investigations into the 'social conditions' of such areas contained accounts of the employment and social position of the children of the black communities (Fletcher, 1930; HO, 213/352).

St Clair Drake's study of Cardiff's black community is a good example of the focus of such early studies (Drake, 1954; 1955: 197–217). According to Drake various facets of the contact between black and white people in twentieth-century Britain were socially constructed into 'social problems', ranging from employment, housing, welfare to youth questions. Such definitions of the 'social problems' associated with the presence of 'coloured people' were not, according to Drake, the consequence of a natural process of development but resulted rather from a complex series of attempts to mobilise public opinion, produce reports that defined the nature of the 'problem', and develop agencies to 'seek solutions' (Drake, 1955: 210–12).

Other studies of long-established black communities have pointed to the same phenomenon. They have shown how the 'youth question' was not only a major theme in media coverage of those settlements,[2] but a major focus of concern for the voluntary agencies which were most intimately involved in managing the 'problems' faced by them. A number of reports were produced on the question of 'half-caste' children, the problems they faced in schools and in the labour market, and their social integration into the majority society (Little, 1947; Banton, 1955 and 1959; Collins, 1957; Fryer, 1984; Ramdin, 1987). Much of the language used to discuss their situation is similar to that used to describe that of young blacks during the 1970s and 1980s.[3] A report on the 'growing number of half-caste children' in Liverpool painted a grim picture of the employment situation of this group:

> It is difficult to obtain employment for these children for the following reasons: The juvenile employment situation in Liverpool on the whole is bad. There is evidence of conscious discrimination against half-castes which one can expect, and there is reason to believe that unconscious discrimination goes further.
>
> (HO, 213/350, 1936)

Such children were perceived by employers as being unpunctual, lacking discipline and untrainable for certain kinds of jobs. More generally, these children were seen as suffering from a combination of 'racial traits' and social disadvantages which could produce a permanently disadvantaged and alienated group within cities such as Liverpool and Cardiff (Harris, 1987).

During the Second World War the 'problem' in terms of governmental concern was expanded even further by the arrival of black workers from the colonies to help with the war effort and the arrival of black American soldiers (Rich, 1986: 145–68; Ramdin, 1987: 86–99 and 187–96). While both groups were important in the general politicisation of the black immigration issue, it is also relevant to note that their arrival helped to bring about a new stage in the discussion about the 'problem of youth' in relation to black communities.[4] The inter-war preoccupation with 'half-caste' or 'brown' children persisted but to it were added other concerns. Thus a Colonial Office report on the social situation in Cardiff and

Liverpool argued that black migrants were facing problems of (a) finding employment, (b) getting access to adequate accommodation, and (c) achieving equality of opportunity for their children. It described the situation in the following graphic terms:

> During the past 30 years groups of colonials have been domiciled in Great Britain. Originally they came here as seamen in the 1914–18 war. After the war, many settled down, married and have lived here ever since. They have produced a group of citizens of mixed birth. During the depression periods, the original settlers endured, in common with other workers, years and years of unemployment and for the most part their familes were reared during these periods. Upon reaching working age their off-springs had little opportunity for employment, partly because of the economic depression, but more so on account of racial prejudice. These family units therefore became social problems.
>
> (CO, 1006/2, 1948)

During the period from 1941 to 1948 a number of reports repeated this kind of analysis, and added the additional dimension of the impact of newly arrived black migrants and black American soldiers on these black communities and on the 'race problem' more generally.[5] But the broad focus of concern remained constant throughout: namely, how to take action to prevent this 'social problem' from becoming more serious? After all, if 'the future prospects of these children are not good' (CO, 876/39, 1944–5) what was the likelihood of harmonious 'race relations' developing in areas of black settlement? What was the likelihood of such areas becoming centres of social deprivation, crime and lawlessness?

The concerns which were evident during the inter-war period were continued into the immediate post-war conjuncture. But within the context of this period the issue began to shift away from a concern about the position of 'half-caste' children as such and towards a broader category: namely, the younger generation of blacks who were going to become adults and enter the world of work over the next decade or so (McCowan, 1952; Mackenzie, 1956; Little, 1958). The growth of black migration and settlement outside of the port towns broadened the debate about the younger generation of blacks away from the 'half-caste' issue as such. Additionally, concern within official circles began to shift from the port communities to the newly arrived migrants and their children.[6]

This shift can be traced through the 1950s by looking at some of the debates that took place about the migration of black workers into Britain and their settlement. These debates were taking place at a number of levels. First, within the Cabinet, government departments, voluntary bodies, and in informal inquiries by various agencies of the state; second, in Parliament and within political institutions more generally; third, in the national local press, which from the earliest stages of black migration had run a number of stories on the new arrivals and their reception.

A good example of official debates during the early 1950s can be found in the parliamentary debates and questions on the subject (*Hansard*, vol. 491, 1951: cols. 805–14; vol. 540, 1954: cols. 1887–8) and in the confidential discussions within government policy-making institutions about immigration. In a parliamentary question in October 1950 the Conservative MP Cyril Osborne asked the Home Secretary to provide him with figures for the number of immigrants from 1945 onwards, with 'separate figures for white and coloured peoples' (*Hansard*, vol. 478, 1950: col. 259). The Home Secretary reponded that such figures were not available, but questions such as this were the early signs of the politicisation of the issue of 'coloured immigration'. Both Conservative and Labour MPs were to ask questions in Parliament about this issue, and later were involved in the public debate about the control of immigration from the colonies.[7] An important early debate on immigration took place in Parliament on 5 November 1955, when Labour MP John Hynd initiated the discussion by asking how the regulation of colonial immigrants could be brought about despite the fact that they were British citizens (*Hansard*, vol. 532, 1954: cols. 822–3). Among the problems he related to the newly arrived immigrants, the important ones were housing, employment, sexual relations and possible conflicts in dance halls and places of entertainment (*ibid.* cols. 825–6).

Although the arguments of MPs such as Osborne and Hynd remained a minority view in Parliament, and received only limited support within the Cabinet, their interventions did help to keep the immigration issue alive and to draw the attention of sections of the media to it as well. Throughout the period of the early 1950s reportage on the immigration issue in the press ran along two general lines. First, there were articles reporting on the arrival of groups of immigrants, on specific localities, and on confrontations between blacks and whites. Second, feature articles were written which considered the prospects for 'race relations' and conflicts more generally within British society. Examples of the latter kind of coverage include the following:

- 'The West Indian settlers: first signs of a British colour problem' (*The Times*, 8 November 1954)
- 'Journey to heart-break: and now for the dole' (*Daily Sketch*, 5 January 1955)

- 'More firms refuse to take coloured staff' (*Daily Telegraph*, 7 February 1955)

Stories such as these did not necessarily state a case for the control of black immigration, but they helped to politicise the public debate about the 'problems' which were perceived to emanate from 'too much' migration of black workers.

A particularly forceful statement of the case for control of immigration was made in a question by Thomas Reid, Labour MP for Swindon, when he asked the Home Secretary whether:

> He will speedily introduce legislation giving our government control over the immigration to this overcrowded island of aliens, and citizens of British Dominions and Dependencies, of whom the latter can now enter regardless of their health record, means of subsistence, character record, culture, education, need for them economically or otherwise, or of the wishes of the British people.   *Hansard*, vol. 535, 1954: col. 190)

The 'case for control' was thus legitimised by MPs such as Reid on a number of grounds: but the thread running through all of them was the notion of 'immigrants' as carriers of specific social characteristics or personal attributes which made them into 'undesirable immigrants'. These issues were seen as having both a short-term and a long-term context, particularly in relation to the questions of employment and housing.

In 1956 a Cabinet Committee on Colonial Immigrants considered not only the immediate social, housing, political and economic issues but long-term questions about the future of 'race relations'. The chair of the Committee was the Lord Chancellor, Viscount Kilmuir, and he asked the following questions:

> Are the following risks serious –
> (i) Miscegenation on any significant scale, with its gradual effect on the national way of life?
> (ii) The creation, on any significant scale, of a plural way of society, with the prospect of race riots, colour-bar incidents, and the emergence of a set pattern of politics cutting across ordinary political issues?
>
> (CAB 134/1210, 10 February 1956)

Like previous investigations during the 1950s the Committee's final report did not support the introduction of controls on immigration immediately, though it did say that 'some form of control over coloured immigration will eventually be inescapable' (CAB 129/81, 1956: CP (56) 145).

Thus in the period of the early 1950s the debate on immigration in and out of Parliament was crucial in focusing attention on the 'social problems' associated with newly arrived black workers, and the 'incalculable' consequences of migration in the longer term. It was a period when the terms of political debate about this issue were fixed firmly on the question of control, but the government held back from carrying out the legislative measures proposed by the anti-immigration lobby. The questions, however, remained: How long would the 'need for control' be kept off the political agenda? What actions could be taken to regulate the position of black migrants already settled?

These were the questions that came to dominate debate about black immigration during the late 1950s. And it was within this context that the issue of the younger generation of immigrants, and the children of immigrants, began to assume an important role in these debates. During these early stages of debate about this issue the overall question of immigration continued to dominate, but the period from the late fifties to the early sixties remains central to any historical analysis of the genesis of the present preoccupations about the young blacks. It was during this period that public debate about the role of 'race' in relation to housing, employment, social welfare and urban violence reached its high point. A number of debates took place in Parliament about the 'problems' of 'coloured immigration' and the consequences for British society nationally and for specific localities. Marcus Lipton, MP for Brixton, had raised the question of the arrival of black immigrants in Lambeth and their impact in increasing pressures on housing (*Hansard*, vol. 535, 1954: col. 168; vol. 578, 1957: cols. 767–8). Similar experiences were reported in other cities across the country during this period. The *Birmingham Evening Despatch* reported that areas of the city such as Balsall Heath were seen locally as 'problem areas' because they housed a large number of immigrants (8 July 1958). *The Times* reported that there was local pressure in the Birmingham area for a 'Ban on coloured people's dances' because it was claimed that 'toilet facilities were ignored, alcohol was consumed and a good deal of noise created when the dances broke up' (29 April 1958).

The period of 1958–62, which has been shown in chapter 1 to have been a turning point in the racialisation of British politics, was also central to the transformation of political and welfare debates about the 'second generation' of young blacks.[8] The lead up to the 1962 Commonwealth Immigrants Act represented a new stage in the genesis of an official ideology about future generations of black citizens and their social position within British society. The 1958 riots in Nottingham and Notting Hill further politicised debates about black immigration, and in the aftermath a furious debate took place in both the Conservative and Labour parties about the various policy options which confronted both central and local government (Griffith *et al.*, 1960: 125–48; Miles, 1984; Harris and Solomos, 1987; Ramdin, 1987). The riots in a sense forced the governments to rethink the issue of immigration, and most importantly to look at two issues:

(a) the long-term consequences of the settlement of racial minorities, and their integration or non-integration into British society; and

(b) the possibility that conflicts around immigration could produce a racialisation of British politics.

By forcing issues such as these onto the political agenda the riots helped to shift both common sense and official thinking on this issue onto new and contentious policy questions, requiring more than the piecemeal responses evident throughout the 1950s.

In the aftermath of the 1958 riots a series of press stories discussed the consequences of the disturbances for the future of 'race relations'. *The Daily Telegraph* talked of the disturbances in these terms:

> Events at Nottingham on Saturday night have come as a considerable shock to the tranquil, tolerant British public. Here was a racial riot; of a kind to which we are totally unaccustomed, involving hundreds of men and women in a pitched battle. The cry of 'lynch the blacks!' has been heard in the streets of Nottingham. All this has an ugly ring which should shake our complacency to its foundations. Why do these things happen? And why are they now happening here?
>
> (26 August 1958)

These were the kind of questions that resonated through the press coverage of 'immigration' and 'race' issues throughout 1958 and 1959, and which helped to bring the question of racism and ethnic divisions onto the political agenda.[9] This, in turn, focused attention on specific aspects of the 'problem', and on the possible resolutions which could be implemented through state intervention. These policy solutions ranged from proposals for controls on immigration and repatriation of 'undesirables' to measures aimed at ameliorating pressures on housing, employment and on local authorites.[10] But the posing of such questions as 'why are race riots happening in Britain' helped to focus attention not only on the black migrants themselves, but on the wider context of social, economic and political relations within which they were being incorporated. The riots and political responses to them helped to increase awareness of the reality that a category of 'black British' citizens was becoming an established feature of many cities, factories and places of entertainment.

A report by the Family Welfare Association entitled *The West Indian Comes to England* (Manley et al., 1960) provides us with an important indication of the shifting grounds of ideologies about black immigrants. It focused on such issues as the cultural background of immigrants, their family structures, community associations and their social integration into the wider British society. It argued that few of the migrants were likely to return to their countries of origin and that it was necessary therefore to stop thinking of West Indians and other black settlers as a transient phenomenon, and to see them as an integral element of the present and future population of Britain. Similar sentiments were expressed by the authors of a survey carried out after the 1958 riots by the Institute of Race Relations, which argued that the future of 'race relations' was one of the main issues that should concern politicians and decision makers (Griffith *et al.*, 1960). Significantly this report warned that although it was difficult to judge the question of how much discrimination was directed at black children, largely because most of them were still in school, there were danger signs. It pointed out that:

> When coloured children leave school . . . they leave a cosy world where they are judged by their skill at games or the colour of their blazer and enter the adult world where the colour of their skin may be more important. The placing of coloured teenagers in unskilled jobs seems to have presented few problems to Youth Employment Officers, but they have found it difficult to find apprenticeships for coloured youths.
>
> (*Ibid.* 20)

The investigators reported finding evidence of this trend in Birmingham, Coventry, London, Manchester and Newcastle. They report the reasons for this as (a) the preference by employers for the white boys whose background they know, and (b) the belief by employers 'that coloured boys will not stick at their training or, if they do, that they will go back to their own country at the end of their courses'. They go on 'It is difficult also to place coloured boys and girls in clerical jobs even if they hold the General Certificate of Education. Some girls have had to take up factory work after looking fruitlessly for office appointments' (*ibid.* 20). Though the report concluded that the employment situation 'does not yet seem to be a worrying problem in these towns', it did argue that this issue represented a dimension of the issue that was likely to grow in importance when the young black children in primary and secondary schools started to leave school and search for work. Similar expressions of concern can be found in both press coverage of the time and in other studies carried out in London and elsewhere.[11]

The immediate post-war period thus saw a shift in concern away from the migration process *per se* and towards a new area of policy debate: namely, what to do with the future generations of 'black British' once they had settled and established themselves (Drake, 1955: 197–214; Deakin, 1972: part 2). There appear to have been three reasons for this shift. First, although the pressures for the control of black immigration had placed the need for legislative measures to regulate the migration process onto the main political agenda, there was also widespread recognition that control itself would not resolve the question of the future of those migrants who had already settled. Second, there was a fear that future generations of blacks could grow up in conditions of social isolation and economic inequality which fostered resentment and feelings of isolation among them. Third, the educational position of black children in schools was beginning to emerge as an issue of concern, particularly in some local contexts. These were the issues that were to emerge as the main areas of concern about the 'second generation' in the early 1960s.

Defining the 'second generation'

The emergence of an official ideology about the 'problems' faced by the growing number of second generation of 'black British' did not take place in a political or ideological vacuum. Throughout the period of the early to late sixties official reports, conferences and inquiries attempted to provide a rationale and an ideological basis of understanding the 'problems' faced by this social grouping and the forms of intervention necessary for overcoming them. For example, in 1964 the Commonwealth Immigrants Advisory Council produced a report on 'what happens to young immigrants when they leave school and first seek employment' (CIAC, 1964b: 3). During the period from 1962 to 1970 a number of reports on this issue and related themes were commissioned and produced, both by government bodies and by voluntary agencies.[12] A number of conferences and seminars were held to discuss various themes, such as education, employment, the police and homelessness in relation to young blacks.[13] During this same time a number of stories in the press focused attention on the social conditions faced by the second generation, their special position 'between two cultures' and the signs of their emerging 'alienation' from the mainstream values of British society.

What explains the priority given to the issue of young blacks during this period? The causes of this process are complex. The politicisation of the question of the 'second generation' during the 1950s provides the backdrop against which the events of the 1960s took place. But we also need to know why this change occurred at the time it did, and what were its basic consequences.

There were in fact three central factors in the early 1960s which governed the developments of an official ideology about the 'second generation' of young blacks: (a) the institutionalisation of a dualistic consensus around the principles of immigration controls and integration; (b) the fear that deprivation and unemployment among young blacks could push them in to a 'cycle of deprivation' along the American model; and (c) a perception that the 'second generation' were caught between the (sometimes) conflicting cultures and were in need of 'special help' to help them adjust to the realities of their life in contemporary Britain. During the early sixties the genesis of a specific ideology about young blacks relied on all three factors, and it is therefore necessary to say something about each of them in turn.[14]

(a) Integrating the 'second generation'

The impact of the dualistic consensus which legitimised the need both for immigration controls and integrative measures at the level of 'race' policies generally has been analysed in chapter 1. This does not itself tell us much about how the position of the second generation was seen within this consensus, although it does locate the general parameters of race relations policies from the 1962 Commonwealth Immigrants Act onwards.

The concern of state institutions was no longer with the question of immigration as such, but with the growing number of black settlers and their families who were permanent residents. This grouping had been growing through the 1950s, and although much of the political agenda was dominated by the question of control there was also a growing awareness within and outside the state that the question of 'integration' of the settled black population was perhaps the main long-term issue.[15]

The 1964 report by the Commonwealth Immigrants Advisory Council is a case in point, though it is by no means the only primary evidence that could be cited from this period. The report is important, nevertheless, since it represents the first consistent attempt to define the various dimensions of the phenomenon of the growth of a permanent black population in Britain, many of whose children would grow to maturity in the 1970s and 1980s. The report warned against complacency by arguing:

It is sometimes tacitly assumed that the problem is temporary and that this influx of immigrants, like various others in the past, will be so completely absorbed as not to constitute a distinguishable group. This is highly desirable, but the assumption ignores the fact of physical differences which are visible and which will be handed on to the children. We shall for several generations at least have school-leavers seeking work who in appearance are different from the rest of the community; the object we have had in mind in our report and in making our recommendations is that there should be no difference in treatment.

(CIAC, 1964b: 3)

The report then goes onto define the various categories of young blacks which policies had to deal with: those who arrived when they were of school age, those that were very young when they arrived, and those born in Britain of black parents or of mixed parentage (*ibid.* 4–5).In essence it argued that there were 'reasons for concern' about the future prospects of these groups of black youngsters, and that the role of the government should be to ensure equality of opportunity for them and future generations of black entrants into the labour market.

The institutionalisation of measures aimed at the integration of the 'second generation' thus hinged around the same dualistic 'immigration controls plus integrative measures' model that I analysed earlier. But it was also clear that the 'problem' of the black school leaver entering the world of work was seen as a particularly acute test of the prospects for the achievement of greater equality of opportunity in the future. Even if the broad consensus at this time was that the problems of black youngsters in finding work were not beyond resolution, there was an underlying fear that the changing economic situation could produce greater problems in the future. Thus bodies such as the Commonwealth Immigrants Advisory Council and related institutions saw it as their duty to sensitise both official and public opinion to the dangers ahead, in order to encourage urgent action to remedy existing inequalities and protect against the danger of creating a class of 'permanent second-class citizens'.[16]

The institutionalisation of the 'immigration controls–integrative measures' amalgam also resulted in a somewhat contradictory shift in the orientation of state policies away from measures aimed at their assimilation into mainstream culture. This shift became clear during Roy Jenkins' tenure as Home Secretary in the mid-1960s, when he and his department developed a more pluralist notion of integration. This was codified by him in a famous speech on race relations during 1966, when he argued forcefully that any moves towards integration needed to be based on a wider programme of equality of opportunity:

> Integration is perhaps a loose word. I do not regard it as meaning the loss, by immigrants, of their own characteristics and culture. I do not think that we need in this country a 'melting pot', which will turn everybody out in a common mould, as one of a series of carbon copies of someone's misplaced vision of the stereotyped Englishman. I define integration, therefore, not as a flattening process of assimilation but as equal opportunity, accompanied by cultural diversity in an atmosphere of mutual tolerance.
>
> (Jenkins, 1966)

Whatever the contradictions that were to become apparent when this model of cultural pluralism was implemented (Lea, 1980; Solomos, 1987: 30–53; Solomos, forthcoming: parts 2 and 3), it represented a shift in focus from a preoccupation with immigration *per se* towards the morphology of domestic 'race relations' as defined from a liberal perspective. Indeed the subsequent development of policies in a number of areas cannot be fully understood if we do not contextualise it against the background of this ideological shift. Examples of such policies, apart from the issue I am looking at in this book, are educational, employment, urban and social welfare interventions in relation to black minorities. In all these areas the notion of integration, as defined by Jenkins and others subsequently, exerted an important influence.[17]

(b) Social deprivation and second-class citizens

The issue of whether a 'cycle of deprivation' along the American model was emerging among the black communities became a matter of concern from the early 1960s, although it did not become fully articulated until after the American race riots had taken place (see for example the coverage in *IRR Newsletter*, June/July 1967, and subsequent issues). But the period from 1964 to 1966, did see a number of officially inspired attempts to analyse this question in detail and to draw conclusions for policy. The public debate on this issue took place in a number of contexts, including voluntary agencies, race relations bodies and government departments. During March 1966 for example the National Committee for Commonwealth Immigrants organised a conference on 'The Second Generation' which discussed the educational, employment and social prospects of the growing number of young blacks either born in Britain or newly arrived who were going through the main institutions of society.[18] The Department of Education and Science set up the Hunt Committee in December 1965, with the following terms of reference: 'To consider the part which the Youth Service might play in meeting the needs of young immigrants in England and Wales and make recommendations' (DES, 1967: 1). At a local level there were investigations of the position of young blacks in a number of cities, including London, Bradford and Birmingham. The Birmingham study was in fact a re-study, since another study of black children and young blacks had been carried out in 1961 by Westhill College of Education. The second study, completed in 1966, was entitled 'Operation integration two: the coloured teenager in Birmingham' and contained recommendations about the need for local initiatives (Milson, 1961, 1966).

All of these studies were far from taking place in a vacuum, since the position of black youngsters was seen as intimately linked to a number of other issues:

(a) the broader question of the social position of black minorities in British society;
(b) the transformation of inner city areas through changes in the economy, labour markets and demography;
(c) the development in certain localities of 'twilight areas of special need'; and
(d) the combination of disadvantages associated with bad housing, old schools, poor amenities, and limited occupational opportunities.

It was perhaps not surprising that the press coverage of this issue during this time concentrated on such issues as the danger of creating a permanent class of 'second-class citizens' and the dangers that this could pose for society as a whole and for 'good race relations' in the future. *The Times* reported from Birmingham in February 1967 that young blacks were becoming more marginalised from society and not less, and warned that 'if nothing is done, nobody knows how to stop Handsworth producing second-class people by the thousand' (14 February 1967). Metaphorically, arguments such as this were saying that unless urgent action was taken to deal with the immediate problems of discrimination and disadvantage, the medium- and long-term prospect was that feelings of anger and injustice could explode into political opposition or violent protest.

The analysis of the Hunt Report, which was published amid much publicity and political debate in July 1967, is perhaps the most gloomy and the most interesting. The Committee which produced the Report was chaired by Lord Hunt and included both academics and practitioners as members.[19] It took evidence from government departments, voluntary agencies, pressure groups and individuals with some knowledge of the issues faced by young blacks in relation to the youth service, but also as regards schools, employment, parents and voluntary services, mixed marriages, and the general question of 'integration'. After looking in some detail at the substantive policy issues and the history of the 'second generation' the report came to a number of conclusions that were to stir up some controversy both in the press and in policy circles. Arguing that the basic issue was 'a question of attitudes' it warned that (a) there was evidence of growing feelings of injustice among young blacks, and (b) there was a need for action if 'race riots' were to be prevented. In what were to prove to be prophetic terms it warned that 'Tomorrow may be too late' (DES, 1967: 66–7).

Controversy about the Report started almost as soon as it was published.[20] It was criticised for being a partial view of the situation of young blacks, and for talking of 'race riots' and disorder as an inevitable consequence of current trends. But in ethos the Hunt Report was a concise statement of the view that there was a need to shift attention away from immigration *per se* and look more seriously at the social condition of the 'black British'. It was in many ways a report based on Jenkins' formula about integration and mutual tolerance, which I have referred to above. Thus its concluding paragraph summarised its basic arguments in the following terms:

> The second and succeeding generations of coloured Britishers, fully educated in this country, will rightly expect to be accepted on equal terms, and to have the same opportunities as the rest of us. Within ten years there will be enough of them to make their voices heard. Will each one be accepted on his own intrinsic merits, as one of us? That is the crux of the matter.
>
> (*Ibid.* 67)

The basic framework of this, and other reports of the mid- to late sixties is organised around the liberal notion of 'integration': meaning in this context equal opportunity for 'black Britons' with their white counterparts.

(c) 'Between two cultures'

The third element in debates about the 'second generation' during this period was the question of how they could be 'helped' to adjust to their existence 'between two cultures'. Again, this was not seen as a question of dealing with the present situation as such, but of taking measures to integrate future generations of black youngsters into British society and culture. Throughout the early and mid-1960s this question was widely discussed in both official reports and in media coverage of black children in schools and black school leavers.

This is not to say that there was a uniform definition of the question of 'cultural conflict', or that it was a concept with clear policy consequences. In both theory and practice the notion that young blacks were somehow caught between two (sometimes contradictory) cultural contexts was not fully thought through, and it was often used in a common sense fashion.[21] Indeed, throughout this period the notion that there was a cultural transformation going on within the younger members of the migrant communities bore several meanings.

At its most basic level the idea of 'between two cultures' implied the idea that young blacks were the bearers of the cultural values of their ethnic identity and the cultural values of the 'host' society. As the Hunt Report succinctly put it, the young black could not 'afford to weaken the ties with his own family and ethnic group, yet at the same time he cannot remain immune from the other social influences with which he now comes into contact in his daily life' (DES, 1967: 20). Diagrammatically expressed this notion implies that the cultural influences on young blacks look something like the drawing on p. 69. The 'situation of the second generation' was thus compared to that of groups living on the margin of two cultures, and thus facing problems of 'integration' into both cultures.

Another level at which the 'cultural conflict' argument was used during this period was that of the family. In relation to such issues as discipline, educational aspirations, religion and social contact, it was argued that the changing attitudes of 'black Britons' could come to diverge significantly from those of their parents.[22] The influences of teachers, friends and outsiders could work against the maintenance of the values of the ethnic community and thus cause conflict within the family.

Yet another common sense element in notions about cultural conflict was that young blacks, particularly those disillusioned by life in Britain and the realities of discrimination, could drift into the cultural values of 'twilight' areas, 'hanging around street corners' and becoming a member of a socially defined 'problem group' of second-class citizens.[23]

A number of attempts were made by voluntary agencies and official race relations agencies to increase public awareness of the experiences faced by young blacks in English society. Conferences were organised on this issue nationally and locally, to discuss such issues as 'Immigrants and the Youth Service', 'Are these teenagers really different?', and related themes. Indeed Anthony Crosland, the Secretary of State for Education and Science, encouraged local authorities, churches, employers, trades unions and social workers to take joint action to tackle the problems of 'young immigrants' (DES, 1967: iii). Similar calls for action emanated from other sources and became more common towards the end of the 1960s.[24] There were even some attempts to look beneath the surface of

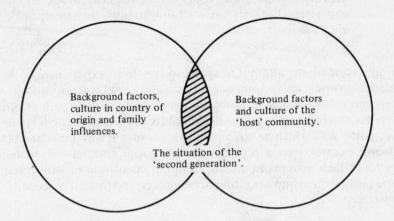

Background factors, culture in country of origin and family influences.

Background factors and culture of the 'host' community.

The situation of the 'second generation'.

the black youth phenomenon and ask deeper questions about the reasons why this group within the black communities was being increasingly singled out for special attention.

In 1967 the National Committee for Commonwealth Immigrants published a pamphlet by Stuart Hall, a radical black academic, which tried with sympathy to understand the predicament of young blacks growing up in British society. Hall compared the situation which he had witnessed as a teacher in London in 1958, when the Notting Hill riots took place, to the mid-1960s. He concluded that there had been little progress towards greater equality and awareness of the needs of black communities, and indeed he saw evidence of a retreat from some of the high expectations of the 1950s. His account of the situation of being young and black in mid-1960s Britain is worth recalling.

> The lived experience of the immigrant teenager is a little like that of the traveller whose routes in and out of home take him along extended bridges across deep and dangerous chasms. Already the young immigrant is trying to span the gap between Britain and 'home'; trying to make some sense of the striking contrasts in climate, environment, tempo of life, and social position. These are not abstract ideas to him, they are two lived identities. There is the identity which belongs to the part of him that is West Indian, or Pakistani or Indian and is continually affirmed in the home and reaffirmed in his relation with his family, in the language he speaks with them, in remembered experiences, in relations he left behind. But there is also the

identity of 'the young Englander', towards which every new experience beckons him – school, friends, the street, work and England itself.

(Hall, 1967: 10)

Hall's sympathetic attempt to speak to the 'lived experience' of young blacks growing up in, but not necessarily being part of, Britain was republished a number of times and was widely quoted both in official reports and in broader public debate.[25] Its particular strength lay in the sympathy with which he attempted to show how it was not young blacks themselves who were a 'problem', but the social, cultural and ideological factors which marginalised them from the mainstram of British society and pushed them into a position of being seen and treated as second-class citizens:

> The problems of the young immigrants are the problems of the marginal men and women of British society. Britain's new second-class citizens. Few people have begun to understand the stresses placed on them or their complex needs and expectations or their particular vulnerability. Before we try to find 'solutions' to their 'problems', we must imagine ourselves in their place. We must try to understand what it is like for them, standing at the point of conflict and intersection between two worlds – one world which carries echoes, associations, memories and ideals of the past and another carries the promise – but also the threat and the danger of the future.
>
> (*Ibid.* 14)

The very definition of the 'problems' of young blacks from the outside, Hall argued, carried with it the danger of a second 'marginalisation'. As well as being excluded from equal participation in economic and social institutions, they are defined as a 'problem' in schools, work, and as potentially violent and criminal.

As argued above, these three elements did not, by any means, constitute a monolithic ideology about the 'second generation'. But they did help bring about during the 1960s a situation whereby public and policy debates about the position of young blacks was thought through the ideological arguments I have just outlined. This was an important development in itself, for it had taken less than a decade for the issue of the 'second generation' to emerge as one of the main axes around which debates about race relations policies revolved. In the latter part of the sixties the full consequences of this shift in policy and practice were to become even more apparent.

The question of black school leavers

The future of black school leavers, or more generally the position of young black workers in the labour market, became a focus of official concern as a result of two main factors. First, there developed through the 1960s a concern that unless government could prevent such a development young blacks could drift into a cycle of deprivation and exclusion which could result in the creation of an underclass with deep resentments against the majority society. Second, the outbreak of violence in the black ghettoes of the United States during the mid-1960s raised the question of a link between violent forms of protest and the existence of a section of society that was economically, socially and politically marginalised. A number of the studies produced in the United States had suggested a correlation between riot participation and age and employment status (Fogelson, 1971: 26–49; Lipsky and Olson, 1977: 1–36 and 107–47). This concern with the possibility of young blacks drifting into a cycle of deprivation and violent protest in turn linked up with a fear articulated both within and outside government circles that riots and violence could result if no effective remedies were found for racial inequality and racialism.

Underlying both these concerns was the wider question of how a fundamental change in the employment picture could affect black workers, and young blacks seeking work more specifically. Worries about differential rates of black unemployment date back to the 1950s (Richmond, 1950: 147–65; Reid, 1956: 199–206), but during the early 1960s there were already signs that the full employment of the immediate post-war conjuncture was not a permanent feature of the labour market. The 1964 Commonwealth Immigrants Advisory Council report, for example argued:

> At present there is full employment in this country as a whole and we have received no evidence that immigrant school children are unemployed. We have no reason to think that the larger numbers of immigrant pupils leaving school in a few years' time will not also find jobs, although they might find it significantly more difficult than other boys and girls to do so if there were a change in the general economic situation and more competition for jobs. We are more apprehensive, as regards both the future and the present, that they may have difficulty in finding the right job for their qualifications and abilities.
>
> (CIAC, 1964b: 7)

The concern with unemployment among young blacks was at this stage only emerging, and it was not to mature fully for another decade, but it is significant that it was already a cause for concern both to the government and to local authorities (particularly in some areas such as Lambeth and Birmingham where there was an emerging debate about this issue). Evidence collected by the Hunt Committee, and also by the NCCI, suggested that there was little evidence of high levels of unemployment among young blacks as a whole, but this was not necessarily the case for all localities or for all the different groups of young blacks (DES, 1967: 15–25; NCCI, 1967b: 29–33). Moreover, the prospects for maintaining full employment as a national policy objective did not look good and a likely consequence of rising unemployment seemed to be a growth in levels of unemployment among both young and older black workers.[26] The growing national importance of the question of black school-leavers and their prospects was indicated by a debate in Parliament in December 1966, initiated by David Winnick. Pointing to mounting evidence that there was increasing incidence of discrimination against them in a number of cities, and that government policies on immigration and race did not address their situation, Winnick argued that unless their present and future prospects were considered seriously, the issue of black school leavers was likely to emerge as a 'new problem' in the race relations field. He referred to evidence from the Campaign Against Racial Discrimination and the Inner London Education Authority[27] which showed that 'colour bar' was operating against black youngsters in certain sections of employment, particularly white-collar work (*Hansard*, vol. 737, 1966: cols. 1715–18). From this he concluded that unless the government and other agencies responded to the challenge posed by the threat to the employment prospects of black school leavers, it could result in growing bitterness and disenchantment among them; creating feelings of injustice which might be difficult to overcome.

The government's response to Winnick's intervention is interesting on two counts. First, for what it tells us about the perception of this issue within government circles. Second, for what it does not say. Shirley Williams, as parliamentary secretary to the Ministry of Labour, delivered the government's response. On the first point Williams' response stated that all the evidence showed that 'the problem of unemployment among immigrant children is at present slight', though she did concede that they may not have all got jobs which were equivalent to their abilities (*ibid.*: col. 1721). On the second point, however, the response was less illuminating since it said little about what the government was planning to do about the prospect that the situation could change when the overall employment position was transformed. Neither did the government respond to the evidence from CARD and the ILEA about the extent of discrimination against young blacks on their entry into the labour market. This despite the fact that both sets of evidence pointed to the pervasiveness of discrimination against young blacks, particularly in (a) white-collar jobs, (b) apprenticeships, and (c) jobs involving contact with the public. The official view seemed to amount to saying that such issues were minor problems. But what is interesting about the CARD evidence is that it showed that among employers there were stereotypes linking colour to lower-grade work, apprehensions about customer and staff reactions to black workers in white-collar jobs, and direct racism against black youngsters (*IRR Newsletter*, September 1966: 2–3).

Perhaps the most interesting aspect about the emergence of this concern with the black school leavers during the period 1966–8 was that the situation in general for school leavers was favourable. As Colin McGlashan noted in a discussion of this question:

> Employers are desperate for labour. In Central London last year there were two jobs for every boy and girl who left school. More than 300 vacancies for engineering vacancies were left unfilled. The years ahead are less promising: the second post-war birth-rate bulge starts to leave the schools in 1971. And unemployment has started to rise. What happens then to coloured youngsters – most born and educated in Britain – could set the pattern for a generation.
>
> (*The Observer*, 25 September 1966)

The questions raised by McGlashan, and others, pointed to the broad nature of public concern about the future of black school leavers. In this sense they also highlight the distance that existed between such public concerns and official policies, as articulated by Shirley Williams for example. The limited concern expressed by Williams in 1966 was to be rapidly transformed over the next two years, to the extent that in 1968 the newly formed Select Committee on Race Relations and Immigration could devote its first investigation to *The Problems of Coloured School Leavers*.

At the same time a number of academic studies helped to popularise certain explanations for the predicament of black school leavers. For example, David Beetham's (1967) study of Asian and West Indian school leavers in Birmingham argued that they were consistently at a disadvantage in competing for jobs because of (a) their lower level of educational attainment as compared to white youngsters, and (b) their attitudes about the kinds of jobs they aspired to (Beetham, 1967: 10–14). He linked these issues partly to the schools that these children found themselves in, but also their own backgrounds. He saw Asian children as suffering from a lack of proficiency in English, while West Indian children were affected by their home background and personality characteristics. The main conclusion of his study was that the aspirations of immigrant school leavers were 'unrealistic', in the sense that:

> Both in terms of scarcity value ... and qualifications required, aspirations for such jobs could be called relatively high aspirations, particularly in view of the level of educational attainment most immigrants in fact achieve.
>
> (*Ibid.* 1967: 17)

To some extent Beetham's explanation of this phenomenon relied on assumptions about the cultural background of the parents. Talking about the aspiration of many West Indian children to become motor mechanics, engineers or electricians he argued that

> The aspirations of immigrant children ... seem to derive largely from the aspirations their parents have for them. The particular form these aspirations take can best be explained by the employment structure of the country of origin. Notions of what jobs are desirable in Britain are determined by what were seen to be desirable at home, even though the circumstances here are different and the possible choices much more varied. This supposition can certainly be confirmed for the West Indies, which has seen the recent establishment of large numbers of Canadian and American firms, giving rise to a great demand for electricians, mechanics, welders, and so on.
>
> (*Ibid.* 21)

Arguments such as these were to be found outside academic research as well, although Beetham's research certainly helped to popularise and cause some controversy.[28] Around the same time as Beetham's report the head of the Youth Employment Service in Birmingham outlined a similar analysis of the issues (Heginbotham, 1967: 215–17). Other professionals working with young blacks seemed to share and support the validity of such assumptions through their own practices.[29]

Although little research-based evidence has provided support for the 'unrealistic aspirations' argument, it has been a constant theme in popular debates about the position of young blacks in employment (Solomos, 1985: 523–35; Cross, Wrench and Barnett, 1987), and in society generally (Fisher and Joshua, 1982: 129–42; Field 1984: 27–34). The dangers of such a line of argument were pointed out at an early stage by a number of authors (Nandy, 1969: 9–11; Allen, 1969: 235–7). In a forceful riposte to Beetham, Nandy (1969) pointed out that any assessment of what constitutes 'unrealistic aspirations' cannot be seen as value-free or free from assumptions that the 'unrealistic aspirations' of black youngsters were a product of their own cultures – rather than a 'problem' caused by discriminatory practices in employment and schools (*ibid.* 11).

Other studies of the question of the 'second generation' were also influential. The Report of the Institute of Race Relations 'Survey of race relations', which was eventually published amid much debate in 1969 as *Colour and Citizenship*, included a detailed study of the position of the 'British-born children of immigrants' (Rose *et al.*, 1969: chapter 24). Indeed, this was one of the sections of the report that was picked out for special attention by the press, which gave the report as a whole the kind of coverage that was later to be given to the Scarman Report.[30] The Report summarised evidence of the kinds of disadvantages suffered by the second generation in relation to education and employment, pointing out that the higher educational levels and social contact of black children did not seem to reduce discrimination (*ibid.* 483–4). But the Report also looked at the position of young blacks in older settlements, such as Cardiff and Liverpool, where the children were often not second but third generation blacks. Even in such localities it noted that there was no noticeable reduction of discrimination over time, and described their position in such areas as 'dismal'. On this basis it concluded that 'On the evidence of what has happened in Liverpool and Cardiff there is no room for complacency about the future of the second generation of post-war coloured immigrants' (*ibid.* 490).

More fundamentally, perhaps, the future of the 'second generation' and indeed the whole morphology of 'race relations' in Britain had become issues which were inextricably linked in both public and policy debates. Expressions of fear about the future reflected fundamental uncertainties about the present, and perhaps a failure to understand why the position of young blacks had become an increasingly politicised issue. The situation in 1969 and 1970 allows us to explore the dynamics of this uncertainty and the contradictions involved.

The 1969 Committee Report

As mentioned above the first inquiry of the Select Committee on Race Relations and Immigration was on *The Problems of Coloured School Leavers*. This inquiry produced a substantial Report, accompanied by substantial collections of written and oral evidence, in 1969. This Report exercised an important influence on the terms of the debate about the 'second generation' young blacks for some time to come[31] and so it is worth looking in some detail at its main arguments and policy proposals.

The starting point of the Report bears some similarity with the Institute of Race Relations study on *Colour and Citizenship*, which was also published in 1969. They both treated the question of the 'second generation' as a test case for the future of race relations policies as a whole, since if governments were seen as being unable to integrate young blacks into the economic, cultural, social and political fabric of British society, there was little hope that they could achieve their broader objective of 'good race relations'. But the Select Committee's Report, and the published evidence on which the Report drew, went further than the previous studies of young blacks. It attempted to construct a broadly based analysis of the conditions that young blacks faced in British society, and to draw up a comprehensive programme of ameliorative measures. Both aspects of its analysis were to be influential in the coming decade.[32]

On the first point, the Report's analysis of the predicament of young blacks was based on detailed evidence in relation to three areas:

(a)   the position of young blacks in the educational system;

(b)   their role in the labour market, particularly when compared to first generation migrants; and

(c)   the 'complex of disabilities' from which they suffered in British society as members of a disadvantaged group.

It attempted also to analyse other issues, the importance of which was to become even more clear during the 1970s, e.g. relations with the police and other social control institutions, the role of local authorities and the question of alienation.

The Report linked all these areas of disadvantage and discrimination together, though the emphasis in the analysis lay more on the 'complex of disabilities' than any other issue. The underlying logic of this notion is interesting from the perspective of what it tells us about the policy implications of the Report, which I shall discuss later. While it warned early on of the 'dangers of particularisation', i.e. of seeing all the problems of young blacks as deriving from 'race' or discrimination, it was substantially devoted to the 'special problems' which were faced by young blacks because of their colour (Select Committee, 1969, Report: 13–15). The Report explicitly endorsed the evidence which was submitted by the Community Relations Commission which argued among other things that

> The difficulties encountered by coloured school-leavers in this country are not of a simple easily distinguishable kind. They arise from a complex of disabilities to which social deprivation, deficiencies in education, psychological stress and racial pre-

judice all contribute. Colour is no doubt the main and common factor running through this complex of disabilities, but it would be an over-simplification to present the problem exclusively or even perhaps essentially in terms of colour.

(Select Committee, 1969, Evidence: vol. II, 240)

Among the other factors in this complex of disabilities were such problems as bad housing, poor schools, educational deprivation and family problems.[33] The substantive part of the Report was therefore devoted to an explanation of how young blacks experienced 'special problems' in schools and employment, and the consequences of such problems on their levels of attainment.

How did the Report explain the genesis and perpetuation of these problems which were faced by young blacks at all levels of society? In essence it did so by referring to the combined impact, over a period of time, of four factors: (1) discrimination against young blacks in their search for jobs; (2) deficiencies in their education; (3) defective social adjustment; and (4) personal and psychological stresses arising from the social position of immigrants and their children. The combined effect of all these factors was as yet unclear the Report concluded, but the dangers were there to be seen in the growing expressions of anger and resentment (Select Committee, 1969, Report: 31–2).

The main policy conclusions of the Select Committee were contained in a section entitled 'Special problems need special treatment'. The underlying premise of this section of the report was a reiteration of Roy Jenkins' definition of integration 'not as a flattening process of assimilation but as equal opportunity, accompanied by cultural diversity, in an atmosphere of mutual tolerance'. It asked the government, race relations bodies, local authorities, trades unions, universities and black organisations 'to work together in order to provide special help to young blacks so that they could acquire the economic and social status to which their skills entitle them'. It legitimised this ameliorative approach by comparing policies for black youngsters to other areas of social policy:

> Equality of opportunity does not always mean treating everyone in exactly the same way. All people are not equal. Special problems need special treatment. We apply this principle in many areas. Economically depressed areas at home and overseas get financial assistance. Backward school children are given special attention. Physically handicapped people are given special assistance in both education and employment. This principle should be equally applied to the problems of immi-

grants and especially to those of coloured school leavers. In so far as they are handicapped in competing with other school leavers, then special assistance is needed to give them equal opportunity. However, it must be recognised that such special assistance must be provided fairly with due regard to the needs of the indigenous population, some of whom are also in need of special assistance. Recognition of this point is essential if we are to secure good race relations.

(Select Committee, 1969, Report: 31)

By 'special problems need special treatment' the Committee seemed to mean at least two, somewhat different, things. The first meaning was linked to the call by the Committee to all relevant government departments and agencies to ensure that they took all possible action to ensure that young blacks were able to compete equally for jobs, by overcoming discriminatory barriers and overcoming a lack of knowledge of the problems faced by racial minorities in British society. The second meaning, however, was much more ambiguous both in intention and in effect. Deriving from the notion that black children were 'handicapped' in competing for jobs, in the same way that physically handicapped children were, the underlying assumption seemed to be that welfare and central and local state bodies should attempt to provide 'special treatment' to overcome such deficiencies as existed in educational achievement and personal adjustment.

Quite apart from problems intrinsic to the way in which the notion of 'special treatment' was conceived, the 1969 Report can be seen as an essentially limited analysis of the social and economic position of young blacks. Though much of the evidence, written and oral, suggested that the processes of racial discrimination in the labour market against black workers generally were fundamental to understanding the position of the 'second generation', the Committee Report mentions discrimination as only one of a number of factors. In this sense, the role of *The Problems of Coloured School Leavers* in shaping public debate about young blacks reflected a broader tendency in official thinking about 'good race relations'. Rather than linking personal and family dilemmas to a wider social context 'structured by racism' (Hall, 1980), the policy model of the Report was based on the assumption that racism was merely one 'handicap' out of a number which confronted young blacks.

I shall return to this point in the next chapter, where I shall analyse the development of policies during the 1970s.

The educational system and black children

The location of some of the first attempts to tackle the 'problems' faced by second generation blacks can be traced to a number of educational initiatives during the 1960s. It was in the field of education that much of the early policy initiatives in relation to black children were located (Mullard, 1982; Troyna, 1982; Arnot, 1986). Troyna and Williams (1986) among others have provided detailed historical studies of policy change in this field, and the interplay between such policies and wider issues in the 'race' area.[34] There is no need to go over this question in any detail, but we do need to look at some aspects of educational policies and how they influenced policies towards the 'black youth' question more generally.

As noted above, the new 'pluralist' approach to integration was first developed in the educational system from the early to late sixties. A number of reports by official bodies and by black political groups had singled out education as an area where urgent action was necessary to meet the special needs of black children and to overcome the opposition of white parents to the entry of black children into schools. In these early stages, therefore, the role of the state was seen largely in terms of action to change attitudes to race within the school system. The new integrationist perspective differed from the early assimilationist arguments in emphasis, rather than in content. Rather than locating the whole 'problem' in relation to black children, it was implied that society as a whole needed a greater understanding of race:

> White people in the host community should try to understand coloured people and immigrants, and coloured immigrants should try to understand the problems of the host people. But the main obligation for improving race relations rests with the indigenous people in this country, if only because they are by far the majority. The central problem of race relations in Britain today is that of colour. Difficulties arise from people's attitude towards colour. Here again is an educational challenge.
> (Select Committee, 1969, Report: 20)

In addition to the 'educational challenge' of changing society's attitude towards colour, it was implied that the schools themselves could perform a useful role in changing the attitudes of white and black children by providing more teaching about different religions, cultures and customs. It is from these early shifts that the multicultural education movement of the seventies and eighties grew into a fully-fledged response to the presence of black children in schools. As is clear from the above quotation, however, this response contained within it two, sometimes conflicting, elements.

The first was the recognition that the special needs of black children had to be given more priority than hitherto. These needs were seen largely in terms of language, culture, family backgrounds and identity. The second element was seen as the discrimination from which black children suffered on the basis of colour. This second question, however, has tended to play on a minor part in official discussions of education, and most central and local state agencies have chosen to concentrate on special arrangements to meet the 'needs' of ethnic minority pupils. But how have these needs been defined? What assumptions have been made in formulating policy options?

Two major assumptions were made by the pluralists in the way they defined the needs of black children in schools. First, it was accepted that black children would not be assimilated in a linear fashion, and that for some time to come they were likely to retain specific characteristics which had to be allowed for. The fourth Report of the Select Committee on Race Relations and Immigration was on education and one of its main conclusions was that

> The presence of fairly large numbers of immigrant children in this country makes special demands on many local education authorities. The children themselves must have special help if they are to compete on equal terms in a technologically-advanced, multi-racial society. They will continue to come here for many years, a large number of them ill-educated, most of them illiterate in English. Even many of those born here, of all ethnic groups, will be handicapped by language difficulties, family backgrounds and different cultures.
>
> (Select Committee, Report: 53)

Second, it was assumed that if racialism was educated away then equal opportunity would begin to flourish. In addition, the development of a more culturally diverse curriculum in the schools would provide a launching pad for a more racially harmonious society. Education was seen as central to producing such a situation because it was a process through which every individual had to pass. Within the broad ideological common sense of multiculturalism the objective was to produce more understanding of racial issues through the reform of the educational system.

Against the background of fears about the political implications of the alienation of black children from the dominant culture and political institutions, the extension of the curriculum was also seen by policy-makers as a way of keeping the lid on the pressures arising from black community groups and the children themselves for more 'relevant' teaching. It was a means of incorporating the teaching of 'black studies' within the schools, but at the same time depoliticising its content. In relation to pressures from the West Indian community to transform the education system to meet the special problems of black children the Home Office recommended that

> For the curriculum to have meaning and relevance now in our schools, its content, emphasis and the values and assumptions contained must reflect the wide range of cultures, histories and lifestyles in our multi-racial society. The more informed teachers become about a wider range of cultures and communities and the more possible it is for all pupils to see their values reflected in the concerns of schools, the less likely is the alienation from schools and indigenous society experienced by some minority group pupils.
>
> (Home Office, 1978: 6)

A number of subsequent official and academic reports have further developed this response in relation to specific local and national issues, but they still retain the basic assumption that cultural pluralism is the only adequate response to the specific needs of pupils of different ethnic origins. This is why among the numerous celebrations of the theory of multicultural education we find little discussion of the social relations of power within which minority and majority cultures exist, or the wider determinants of the educational needs and attainments of black children. The emphasis is on what an ideal multi-racial society should look like, and not why it has so palpably failed to emerge.

To summarise the argument so far: I have argued that in relation to education the pluralist model involved an incorporation of the assimilationist arguments within a more sophisticated concept of complex disabilities, or 'specific difficulties arising from linguistic, cultural, religious and historical differences' (Home Office, 1978: 6). This introduced an emphasis on policies aimed at providing 'special treatment' to compensate for home and cultural backgrounds:

> We must compensate for these difficulties if such pupils are to be given the same range of opportunity and choice as indigenous pupils. Consequently in areas of minority group settlement local education authorities, schools and teachers are involved in responding to the specific needs of pupils of different ethnic origins.
>
> (Home Office, 1978: 6)

In terms of policy this response, despite all the talk about 'special needs', has certain similarities to the old assimilationist framework. It identifies the special needs as a 'handicap' from which black children have to be extricated, and therefore places the onus of adaptation on the children themselves. In addition, even when discrimination is seen as a problem, it is not the conditions in urban areas that reproduce racism which are put under scrutiny but the attitudes and behaviour of black children.

The bias towards policies that attempt to ameliorate the position of black children and control their responses is not a mere accident. Recent research on the implementation of multicultural education has shown that it has been applied largely in those education authorities with high and medium concentrations of black pupils, since authorities with low numbers of ethnic minorities thought that teaching about a multicultural society was not a matter for them. The practice of the pluralist approach therefore has little to do with the promise of providing a more adequate response to the problems facing black children in schools as a whole. It can best be seen as a contradictory attempt to keep the responses of black children and their parents to institutional racism in schools under control. It offers token changes in educational practices, but does not question the overall structures of racism within which schools function, or the reproduction of racially specific attainments through the school system. The limited application of multiculturalism is not a mere function of inadequate policies or weak guidance by government. It is a reflection of the common sense and policy notion that black pupils are the target group at which policies should aim, since it is their 'deficiencies' and 'problems' that have to be overcome. Even when clothed in 'progressive' language this notion tends to support the view that it is West Indian or Asian children who cause problems for schools and not vice versa.

Although there have been many changes in the official and common sense ideologies about the position of black children in the school system the pervasiveness of assumptions about the culture of the black migrants remained an important influence throughout the 1960s and 1970s (CCCS Race and Politics Group, 1982: chapters 2 and 3). The broad logic of these assumptions was stated by one of the early reports on the question of the education of black children, produced in 1965 by the Commonwealth Immigrants Advisory Council. It argued that

> The education of children of unfamiliar backgrounds and customs presents real difficulties at a time when classes are already overcrowded. There are problems arising from differing customs, habits and attitudes to learning and to life, which immigrant children bring to school, as well as educational

problems in the more academic sense of the word ... One important need is for clear thinking as to aims. For our immediate purpose, it is possible only to state the assumption on which we are working. This is that a national system of education must aim at producing citizens who can take their place in society properly equipped to exercise rights and perform duties which are the same as those of other citizens. If their parents were brought up in another culture or another tradition, children should be encouraged to respect it, but a national system cannot be expected to perpetuate the different values of immigrant groups.

(CIAC, 1964a: 5)

Arguments such as this were not so clearly expressed during the 1970s, with the increasing rhetorical emphasis on cultural pluralism and multiculturalism, but they remained an important influence at the level of educational policy and practice, as a number of studies have shown (Troyna and Williams, 1986; Brah and Deem, 1986; Williams, 1986). The attribution to black children of 'differing customs, habits and attitudes' remained a constant refrain in the policy documents and reports on educational achievements, education policy and on the employment position of young blacks. More importantly, the common sense assumption that any rights to citizenship required that blacks also bear the equal responsibilities of citizenship helped to legitimise the pursuit of policies which aimed at integrating them into broader 'societal values', as defined by the dominant political consensus.

Defusing the 'social time bomb': the genesis of a policy response

In July 1967 Anthony Lester wrote an article in *The Sunday Times* under the headline 'Why it shouldn't happen here'. Arguing from the background of the American riots he argued that it was wrong to think of the situation in cities such as Detroit or Los Angeles as irrelevant to the British context. Lester argued that the question was not whether there will be violence, but whether the conditions which had driven American blacks to violent forms of protest were being reproduced in areas of London, Birmingham and other cities. Indeed, he warned that once patterns of discrimination were established they would not be easily broken, and that could lead to frustration and violence:

The alternatives are clear. We can provide effective redress for the victim of discrimination, or we can compel him to choose to accept injustice or to take his grievances to the streets. Britain's

coloured population is more likely to put up with injustice in the
next few years than to riot, but does a civilised society have any
choice?

(30 July 1967)

The fear of young blacks taking to the streets was particularly strong,
since it was accepted that in the American riots young unemployed
blacks had played a leading role.[35] But Lester's fear about the 'worst
possible' scenario for the future of black communities in Britain was
widely shared by other race relations lobbyists, politicians and press
commentators. It was around this time too that sections of the police
begun to express their concern about the 'problems' they faced in
policing multi-racial areas (see for example: *IRR Newsletter*, September
1967 and October 1968; Gilroy, 1982). Moreover, the symbolic linkages
with the American situation were maintained through the everyday
usage of comparisons not only between Britain and America, but
between areas such as Handsworth and Harlem and other black localities
across the water.[36]

Throughout the period from 1966 onwards the issues raised by Lester
recurred with some regularity in debates and reports about 'race relations' in general and young blacks in particular. More importantly,
however, they served to fuse the various questions about the second
generation and black school leavers around one central symbol: namely,
the image of young blacks as a 'social time bomb', which could explode at
any time unless it were to be defused by the positive actions of
government and by ameliorative measures. Apart from the press and
race relations lobbyists the usage of this symbolic language can be seen at
the highest levels of governmental policy-making.

As early as 1967 Roy Jenkins, the Labour Home Secretary, included
the following warning in one of his major speeches on race relations:

> The next generation – who will be not immigrants but coloured
> Britons . . . will expect full opportunities to deploy their skills. If
> we frustrate those expectations we shall not only be subjecting
> our own economy to the most grievous self-inflicted wound, but
> we shall irreparably damage the quality of life in our society by
> creating an American type situation in which an indigenous
> minority which is no longer an immigrant group feels itself
> discriminated against on the grounds of colour alone. One of the
> most striking lessons we can draw from experience in the United
> States is that once this has been allowed to happen even the most
> enlightened and determined Government and voluntary action
> cannot avert outbreaks of racial violence . . . It is (essential) to

deal with racial problems before they assume such a magnitude that they become, if not insoluble, then capable of solution only at immense cost and effort, and over a very considerable period of time. What we must ask ourselves, therefore, is whether the action we have so far taken is sufficient to avoid these possible dangers.

(Jenkins, 1967: 216)

The tone of Jenkins' speech, and the uncertainty of his concluding question, reveals the tension which was already beginning to emerge within government circles about the position of young blacks, and most importantly their future prospects of achieving 'equality of opportunity' in the labour market and other economic and social institutions.

Expressions of this uncertainty are also to be found among those practitioners who were involved in day-to-day street-level contact with young blacks. While such expressions of concern were by no means at the same level as those I shall discuss in chapter 3, they did represent a level of policy formation which was to emerge as the dominant focus of state interventions during the 1970s: namely, the issue of how to keep young blacks off the streets and how to avoid them drifting into a vicious cycle of deprivation, alienation and social conflict.[37] The prospect of areas of black settlement becoming 'coloured ghettoes from which the second generation is unable to escape' was seen by the Home Office as the most likely prospect if there was no concerted programme of action, including effective social policies, to prevent the situation from becoming worse (Select Committee, 1969: vol. 2: 5–6).

As we shall see in later chapters the debate about this prospect was not necessarily reflected in effective policies to remedy the situation. But what is clear is that the fear of 'social disruption' if young blacks became a class of permanent 'second-class' citizens helped to politicise their position and to make it into one of the central themes in debates about race relations by the end of the 1960s.

Evidence collected in various localities about the employment position of young blacks gave support to the warnings of the Select Committee and of Roy Jenkins about the growing inequality in the labour market between black and white youngsters. A study in London, carried out during 1969, reported that 22 per cent of the sample of young West Indians it studied were unemployed, that young West Indians as a whole seemed to display a sense of alienation from and distrust of white institutions, and were to some extent being ignored by institutions that were supposed to help them find jobs (Stevenson and Wallis, 1970: 278–80).

Similar evidence was reported by Peter Figueroa to the Select Committee in 1969, which noted that there was a greater likelihood that black boys and girls were (a) more likely to be turned down for jobs and (b) to be more disappointed with the jobs that they eventually got (Select Committee, 1969: vol. 2, 207–13). Evidence to the Select Committee from a number of towns pointed to the same conclusion. Indeed *The Times* report on the 1969 Select Committee report run under the headline: 'Jobs or strife warning on coloured youth' (26 September 1969).

Reports such as these were a sign of things to come in more ways than one. They reflected both the growing number of young blacks leaving school and entering the labour market, and their problems in getting the kind of jobs to which they aspired or were qualified to do. Official concern was thus shifting from the general question of black youth as a whole onto those groups that were likely to be unemployed or find difficulties in getting jobs. Such young blacks were seen as particularly vulnerable to the influence of either politicised black radicals or members of the 'twilight world' of the criminal subculture.[38] The articulation of this fear into a fully-fledged 'moral panic' about young unemployed and 'criminalised' young West Indians in the early 1970s will be analysed in the next chapter.

The pervasiveness of this language in common sense debates and policy circles during the period from 1962–70 does, however, indicate the value of contextualising the developments around mugging in the early 1970s against a broader historical background. The process I have covered in this chapter represents only part of this background, and there are a number of other issues which are beyond the parameters of this book. But in attempting to analyse the genesis and development of the 'second generation' question in policy debates I have laid the basis for understanding the fundamental shifts in policy on this issue that took place in the 1970s and 1980s.

Conclusion

I have been concerned in this chapter with the ways in which the question of the 'second generation' of black British was framed through ideological and policy debates in the 1960s. As we have seen, the terms of discourse and political language used to interpret the 'black youth question' during this period were intimately linked to the broader context of the racialisation of British politics and the growth of problem centred images of the black population. More specifically, the development of ideology and practice in relation to young blacks was based on the twin assumptions of (a) the increasing alienation of this social group from the main institutions of society, and (b) the danger of young blacks engaging in violent protest if their position was not remedied by state intervention. A combination of fears about increasing youth violence in inner city areas and the example of 'race riots' in American cities during the mid-sixties provided the impetus for both policy-makers and analysts to single out second generation young blacks as a potential destabilising factor. In addition to this the stereotype of the young black as enmeshed in a cycle of poverty, cultural conflict, and homelessness/unemployment was beginning to take shape and exercise a major influence on political debate and the presentation of the 'second generation' issue in the mass media.

Given this climate of opinion, it is not surprising that in 1970 a prominent social scientist was moved to argue that 'The most obvious question to ask about the Black British is: will they revolt?' (Halsey, 1970: 472). The increasing prominence of questions such as this in debates about young blacks and their future in British society reflected a major shift in ideology and practice in the space of ten years. But the decade of the 1970s was to see an even more profound politicisation of this issue, and this is the question to which I now turn.

3

Black youth, crime and the ghetto: common sense images and law and order

Introduction

As I have argued above no discussion of the ideologies, policies and forms of state intervention in relation to young blacks can be complete without reference to wider political issues and the general political climate on 'race' questions. The value of this procedure is particularly clear when one looks at the evolution of policies and ideologies during the 1970s, a period during which many of the inputs which went into the racialisation of British political life were mediated via popular and policy concern about the 'problem' of young blacks growing up in 'ghetto environments'. As shown in chapter 2, images of young blacks as 'children of the ghetto' had already become common during the 1960s, but it was during the 1970s that these images reached full maturity.

In this chapter I shall discuss the genesis and evolution of ideologies and policies in relation to young blacks around three issues: (a) the supposed link between 'race', youth and criminality; (b) mugging and street crime; and (c) policing and law and order. The three issues will be used to illustrate the articulation of debates about the black youth question as a highly politicised dimension of contemporary political debates about 'race relations' and the transformation of policy images about black youths. Additionally, however, I shall aim to explore the complex reasons for this change and the contradictions which resulted from it. This will then make it possible to link the history of the black youth question, as a general phenomenon, to the more recent politicisation of the black youth unemployment question and the outbreak of urban unrest during the 1980s.

Before turning to these aspects, however, it is necessary to make a few remarks about the historical context which has shaped the emergence of 'black crime' and 'street violence' as primary concerns in public policy in relation to young blacks.

Crime and 'race'

Ideologies linking immigrants as a general category, and black immigrants in particular, with crime have a long history in British society.[1] This is not to say that these ideologies have been constant throughout this history, or that they were monolithic. They have undergone numerous transformations over the years, and ideologies which link immigrants to crime have not been universally accepted even by those who opposed migration. But it is certainly true that whether one looks at the Irish migrants of the nineteenth century, Jewish immigrants in the period 1880–1914, or other significant groups of migrants the issue of crime has been a common theme in the construction of ideologies and policies towards them (Garrard, 1971; Gainer, 1972; Holmes, 1978; Lunn, 1980).

Black seamen who settled in port towns such as Cardiff, Liverpool and London were similarly stereotyped. The areas in which they lived were seen as localities in which the presence of migrants combined with social deprivation and poverty to produce not only patterns of criminal behaviour but social values outside the mainstream of the majority society. A number of studies of black communities during the period from 1900 to 1940 have noted how important such images were in determining both the form and content of dominant ideologies of the 'Negro problem' within both official circles and local voluntary associations (Little, 1947; Banton, 1955; Fryer, 1984; Ramdin, 1987).

An important early study of St Clair Drake provides a detailed account of the processes through which the Tiger Bay area of Cardiff was constructed in this manner. He shows how the inhabitants of the area were defined as a 'problem' by outside institutions, and how the black inhabitants were seen as a specific 'problem' group. Even though many of the Tiger Bay inhabitants expressed the view that 'the colour-bar is the problem; not the coloured people', the black inhabitants of the area were attributed with characteristics which helped to define them as the 'problem'. Within the general category of the black population of Tiger Bay the younger generation of 'half-caste' children was seen as a particular problem group (Drake, 1954: 69–129).

Other studies have shown how the areas into which post-1945 black settlers moved rapidly became identified as localities with crime-related behaviour and other 'social problems', including decaying housing, lack of social amenities, and low levels of community involvement (Carter, Harris and Joshi, 1987; Harris and Solomos, forthcoming). In areas such as Notting Hill and Brixton in London, Handsworth and Balsall Heath in Birmingham, and in similar localities in other cities the question of rising crime and law and order became intimately identified with the broader question of the impact of black immigration on these areas. Questions about the involvement of specific groups of migrants with criminal activities were asked both in and out of Parliament and became a topic for popular concern in the press (*The Times*, 28 March 1958). Such questions became even more pronounced during and after the 1958 riots in Notting Hill and Nottingham, which helped to politicise the issue of black migration and to influence the direction of both local and central government policies.[2] Indeed during the late 1950s and early 1960s the issue of immigration control was intimately tied to the question of the involvement of black migrants in criminal activities. Even before the 1958 riots a number of pro-immigration-control MPs had attempted to politicise the issue of 'black crime' (*Hansard*, vol. 578, 1957: cols. 743–76; vol. 585, 1958: cols. 1415–26). The political climate in the aftermath of the riots proved to be conducive to those ideologies which blamed the rising levels of 'racial tension' on the arrival of 'undesirables' from the colonies. At the 1958 Conservative party Conference Norman Pannell moved a resolution calling for the deportation of such 'undesirables'; whom he defined as those migrants who were not of good character, not in good health, or lacked sufficient means to avoid becoming a liability on public funds (*The Times*, 13 October 1958).

Along with the broader processes of racialisation which I have already analysed in chapters 1 and 2, the 1960s saw a growing politicisation of this question, and continuous attempts by the police and by government to deal with the danger of conflict between the police and black communities. The concerns at this stage were about the growing number of complaints of racial discrimination by the police against blacks, the future of younger blacks if their social and economic position deteriorated, and the fear that an American-type situation of racial violence and disorder could be reproduced in major cities.[3] In July 1967 the Home Office issued a circular to all Chief Constables on *The Police and Coloured Communities*, which advised them to appoint, particularly in areas of black settlement, liaison officers whose task would be to develop better relations with black communities and educate the police themselves on the dilemmas of policing such areas.[4] This was followed by a number of consultative meetings to discuss the policing of particular localities and to analyse the long-term prospects of future conflict between the police and black communities. In the period from 1967 to 1970 a number of articles appeared in specialised journals which discussed the policing of multi-racial localities, the specific problems faced by young blacks and accusations of discriminatory behaviour by the police in relation to the black communities in areas of London, Birmingham and other localities.[5]

The police themselves began to recognise, somewhat hesitantly, the need to develop an understanding of the context of policing in multi-racial areas. In 1970 a conference of US and British specialists and practitioners was held under the auspices of the Ditchley Foundation to discuss 'police–community relations' on both sides of the Atlantic (Clarke, 1970). Other meetings and seminars were also held to discuss this issue, and from 1970 onwards the annual Reports of the Commissioner of Police of the Metropolis contain some discussion of the specific issues related to the policing of multi-racial localities (Reports of the Commissioner of Police for the Metropolis, 1970–86).

In this context an article written by Robert Mark, who was then Deputy Commissioner of the Metropolitan Police provides an enlightening insight into the emergent ideology of the police on the question of 'race'. While being quite clear that 'there is no evidence to show that migrants commit a disproportionate amount of crime', Mark argued that a minority become involved in frequent contact with the police. He linked this to two issues:

(1) the involvement of a small number of migrants in prostitution, gaming and the fringes of criminal activity; and

(2) the involvement of other migrants in public order offences, family disputes or noisy parties (Mark, 1970: 4–5).

For Mark such situations of conflict were partly the result of the newness of the migrants and their socio-economic position in British society, but also the result of a failure by the police and other institutions to deal with the 'special problems posed by migrants' (*ibid.* 5). But he saw the situation as one which would not damage relations between the police and the migrant communities on a permanent basis:

> Traditionally the protector of all groups and classes, irrespective of race, colour or creed, we believe that we, the police, have done no less than any other public service to promote the welfare and security of the migrant in his transition from his homeland to an alien highly industrial, urban society; and we are not unduly discouraged that we should be attacked and criticised by representatives, self-appointed or otherwise, of the very people that we are trying to help.
>
> (*Ibid.*)

The implicit optimism about the effectiveness of 'positive action' by the police was not shared, as Mark points out, by a growing number of critics of the overall strategy and tactics of the police in policing multi-racial areas. In fact it was partly in response to increasingly trenchant criticisms of the police role from both within and outside the black communities that the police began to develop and articulate an ideological legitimation for their policies in relation to 'black areas' (Lambert, 1970; Humphry, 1972).

This debate was carried forward in the national media, as well as in specialised 'race' journals like *Race Today*, which was at the time published by the Institute of Race Relations.[6] The public nature of the debate helped to politicise the question of 'race and policing' to a new level during the early 1970s, particularly as pressure mounted from within the black communities for investigations into cases of harassment by the police, and for 'greater equality before the law' (Nandy, 1970; John, 1970; Hall *et al.*, 1978). It should also be remembered, of course, that it was during this period that the question of 'immigration and race' came to occupy a central role in debates about domestic social policies at both a national and a local political level (see chapter 1). This broader process of racialisation helped to increase the impact of the policy debate about the inter-relationship of crime and 'race', since this issue served to give further credence to the Powellite warnings that immigration was undermining the whole of the social fabric of inner city localities. The imagery of black involvement in criminal activities and in public order offences helped to fuel and give a new direction to the increasingly volatile public debate about 'race relations'.

For the purposes of this chapter I will not explore in detail this wider context of the interplay between images of 'race' and images of crime, since my main concern is with the issue of how a particular category of the black community, namely 'black youth', came to be seen as caught up in a vicious circle of poverty, homelessness and criminal activities. The roots of this phenomenon lie in the wider process I have touched on above, but this need not prevent the analysis of the politicisation of the question of the involvement of young blacks in crime from the early 1970s onwards in its own particularity. This is particularly important since, while a number of general accounts of the interplay between 'race and policing' have been written, the specific nature of the black youth question within this process has not yet been analysed in much detail.[7] It is to this question that I now turn.

Black youth, crime and ghetto life

The convergence of images of criminality and delinquency with the wider set of concerns about the future of young blacks in British society has already been touched on in chapter 2. Throughout the late 1960s fears about the increasing alienation of young blacks from the mainstream of British society were regularly expressed in the media and policy documents, and became a constant refrain in both academic and policy writings on the subject.[8] But by the early 1970s it became clear that this was not merely a passing phenomenon which would disappear with the 'integration' of young blacks into the mainstream institutions of British society.

This was so for at least two major reasons. First, it became clear that the calls for action to help 'coloured school leavers' gain equality of opportunity in employment and other arenas did not necessarily result in the development of effective policy measures to put such calls into practice. Evidence of high levels of unemployment, low levels of attainment in schools and homelessness among young blacks continued to accumulate during the early 1970s. The evidence tended to show that, even in the space of a few years, the picture painted in *The Problems of Coloured School Leavers* in 1969 had been overtaken by events. Far from the positive measures which had been called for in this Report, the net result of the intense debates during the 1970s seems to have been inaction and a deterioration of the socio-economic condition of young blacks.

Second, by the early 1970s it also became clear that the condition of young blacks was rapidly becoming one of the central concerns within the black communities. In various forums, both locally and nationally, black political activists were discussing issues such as education, employment and policing in relation to young blacks. They were also questioning the failure to take positive measures to tackle the root causes of racism and racial inequality.[9] Such political debates from within the black communities helped to emphasise the centrality of this issue within the context of racialised political debates, and to force state institutions to review the nature of their interventions.

At a symbolic level the commitment to the principle of equal opportunity was still part of the climate of political opinion. The Conservative Home Secretary, Robert Carr, restated this commitment in context of the debate on race relations issues at the 1973 Conservative party Conference:

> Our principle is that there should be no second-class citizens in Britain. Everyone who was born here or has come here legally should be equal before the law and not only that but they should be treated equally in the practices of everyday life. I know we do not live up to that perfectly but that is our commitment and that is what my colleagues and I will do our best to achieve.
>
> (*The Times*, 11 October 1973)

But such symbolic promises did not answer the fundamental question which was raised by the reproduction of young blacks, along with their parents, as second-class citizens: namely, why and how were the inequalities and problems faced by the first generation of black migrants being reproduced within the second generation? What were likely to be the medium- and long-term consequences of this process both for young blacks and for society as a whole? Symbolic promises of future action did not touch upon the substantive issues, but deflected attention onto the prospect of a 'better future'.

The reality of the situation in the early 1970s, however, was made clear in a number of reports which highlighted the dismal prospects for young blacks and the potential of conflict with the police.[10] In 1970 Gus John published his influential study of Handsworth called *Race and the Inner City*, and in the same year John Lambert published a study of *Crime, Police and Race Relations*. Both studies attracted attention because they came out at a time when the issues of relations between the black communities and the police and the involvement of young blacks in crime. During the period from 1969 to 1973 a number of feature articles and reports in the press discussed various aspects of the growing tension between the police and the black communities, both at a national level and in relation to specific communities.[11] The complaints against the police by the black communities themselves, which had been articulated as early as 1966 in Hunte's *Nigger Hunting in England*, reached new levels during the early 1970s and were rapidly becoming a political issue.[12]

John's study of Handsworth was a particularly important document in this growing debate. Written by a black researcher who had spent some time living within the black community in Handsworth it highlights the question of policing and the position of young blacks as the core concerns of local residents. It was written at a time when the police themselves were discussing their role in the policing of multi-racial inner city areas and formulating their ideologies and practices on this issue (Humphry, 1972). Additionally, media coverage at the time talked of the growing tensions between the police and black communities, and 1969–70 saw a number of minor street confrontations with the police in areas such as Notting Hill.[13] John began his account of Handsworth with an analysis of the area and the contrasting perceptions offered by local residents of the changes in its social structure and population make-up during the post-war period. But the core of his report, and the issue which gave rise to a full debate in the press, is the description which it offers of relations between the local black community, particularly younger blacks, and the police.[14] John reports that one police official had pointed out to him that the 'growth of black crime' in the area was the work of a 'hard core' of forty or fifty youngsters (John, 1970: 20). But his own perceptions of the situation were more complex, and he summarised them as amounting to three main issues:

(1) the prevalence of rumours, fears and explanations of black involvement in criminal activities;

(2) a tendency by police to blame the 'hard core' of young blacks for 'giving the area a bad name'; and

(3) deep resentment by older and younger blacks with their social position and the discrimination they had to endure.

Additionally he warned that there were signs of 'a massive breakdown in relations between the police and the black community', and that if nothing was done the situation was likely to lead to confrontations between black residents and the police and outbursts of urban unrest:

> In my view trends in Handsworth are a portent for the future. A decaying area, full of stress and tension, which also happens to be racially mixed, is going to find it increasingly difficult to cope with the root problems because racial animosities and resentments have taken on an independent life of their own. The problem is not, and can never be, simply one of law and order.
>
> (*Ibid.* 25)

It was this context, argued John, which explained why both young blacks and the police saw the situation in the area as one of open 'warfare' (*ibid.* 28–9).

Some aspects of John's account of relations between the police and the black community were criticised as overstated and impressionistic. Yet there is a certain symmetry between his account of the situation and that described later on in the 1970s by John Rex and Sally Tomlinson in their detailed empirical analysis of the political economy of race and class in Handsworth (Rex and Tomlinson, 1979). Additionally other studies of the interplay between 'race' and policing during the early 1970s indicated that the relationship between young blacks and the police was becoming an issue of public concern in other areas similar to Handsworth.[15]

Evidence from black communities across the country highlighted three particularly contentious issues. First, complaints by young blacks that they were being categorised as a 'problem group' by the police, and that they were therefore more likely to be questioned or arrested. Second, allegations that the police used excessive physical violence in their dealings with black suspects. Finally, it was argued that such attitudes and forms of behaviour by the police were helping to fuel popular rumours about the involvement of young blacks in crime, and to drive a wedge between the police and the black communities.

Perhaps most significantly in the context of my general argument is that the shifting emphasis on young blacks as a problem category for the police and for society as a whole was being framed increasingly around the question of 'police–community relations'. This shift became particularly clear when (a) the question of policing was investigated by the Select Committee on Race Relations and Immigration during 1971–2, and (b) popular and media debate focused on the involvement of young blacks in forms of street crime which were popularly defined as 'mugging'.

As argued above, the politicisation of the question of crime in relation to young blacks is best seen within the broader context of official and public concern with the interplay between ghetto life, the social position of young blacks and criminal activities. The Select Committee on Race Relations and Immigration investigation of *Police/Immigrant Relations*, which was carried out during 1971–2, represents a useful starting point for understanding the concerns of the state, the police and the black communities in relation to policing and law and order.[16]

The Committee's Report, two substantive volumes of evidence, and the government response to its recommendations (which was published in 1973) were, in effect, the first coherent official statement on the inter-relationship between race, crime and policing.[17] Young blacks were a central issue in the deliberations and the conclusions of the Committee, since it was the younger generation who were both popularly and officially seen as the 'source of the problem'. The Committee took evidence from community groups, police officials, local authorities and government departments on the causes of 'growing tension' between the police and sections of the black communities. Although the popular press and John's report on Handsworth had shown that police on the ground perceived a section of blacks disproportionately involved in criminal activities, the Committee concluded that this claim was not supported by the evidence:

> The conclusions remain beyond doubt: coloured immigrants are no more involved in crime than others; nor are they generally more concerned in violence, prostitution and drugs. The West Indian crime rate is much the same as that of the indigenous population. The Asian crime rate is very much lower.
>
> (Select Committee, 1972, Report: 71)

It did point out, however, that there was one major source of conflict between the police and black communities: namely, the 'explosive' relations between the 'younger generation of West Indians' and the police. The source of this conflict was seen as lying in a combination of factors, most notably in the situation of young blacks themselves and the attitude of the police (*ibid.* 68–9).

The Committee's Report saw young West Indians as becoming increasingly 'resentful of society' and expressing their anger and frustration against the police because they were an obvious authority symbol. It explained this situation as arising from three factors:

(1) pressures faced by young blacks in competing for jobs and housing;

(2) the nature of West Indian family discipline, which although 'Victorian' for younger children did not extend to the West Indian youngsters aged between 16 and 25; and

(3) conflict between the younger and older generations of West Indians (*ibid.* 69).

The Report did accept that there were problems of discrimination faced by young blacks, but significantly it did not prioritise these processes in its explanation for growing tension between them and the police. It pointed out that much of the evidence presented by black community groups argued that there was a process of 'nigger hunting' and a tendency for 'the police to pick on black youths merely because they are black'. But it balanced this out by adding that the evidence of the Metropolitan Police showed that 'in London black youths are stopped and/or arrested proportionately no more than white youths'.

On the question of allegations that policemen were engaged in practices ranging from harassment, assault, wrongful arrest and detention, provocation, fabrication, planting of evidence and racial insults, the Committee was much more reticent to come to any conclusions. It accepted that much of the evidence by various black groups or individuals, and the evidence submitted to it by the Community Relations Commission, contained claims that such practices were common in many localities (Select Committee, 1972, Evidence: vol. II: 65–8; vol. III: 716–35; vol. III: 765–71). While accepting that these claims were believed by many black people, it found it impossible to 'prove or disprove' them, with the truth lying somewhere in between the claims of the police and their critics (Select Committee, 1972, Report: 20–1). Rather, it saw these claims and counter-claims as the natural outcome of a lack of communication between the police and sections of black youth. This lack of communication helped to build stereotypes and to reproduce situations of conflict. The Committee explained this process thus:

There are examples throughout our evidence of the way in which a simple situation builds up to a confrontation. A policeman's mode of address is resented by a black youth sensitive to insult; the youth replies with what the policeman sees as insolence, often accompanied by gesticulation; the policeman counters with what the youth sees as hostile formality. Neither understands the other's point of view; each sees the other as a threat. The youth says he is being picked on because he is black and the policeman is immediately in a dilemma. If he takes firm action he can be accused of racial bias by black people, if he doesn't he is open to the same accusation by white people.

(*Ibid.* 69)

The Committee recommended that a programme of action should be implemented to improve communication, including more training and schemes to improve relations with the black communities in 'problem areas' (*ibid.* 92–5). It concluded that such a positive programme of action could ensure that better relations were re-established between young blacks and the police:

If the best examples of leadership in police and immigrant relations prevailed throughout forces in the United Kingdom, many of the difficulties we have dwelt upon would, within a reasonable space of time, diminish. In some places they could wither away.

(*Ibid.* 92)

From this perspective the situation in some localities, although 'explosive' and dangerous, could be defused if the pressures which produced tension between young blacks and the police were dealt with.

This was a hope that was to remain unfulfilled throughout the 1970s, since the production of the Select Committee's Report on *Police/ Immigrant Relations* coincided with a marked politicisation of debates about black youth, and police and crime during the period 1972–6. This politicisation, occurring as it did at a time of upheaval about 'race and immigration' more generally, was reflected in frequent media reports, official documents, and speeches by politicians, police officers and other opinion leaders.[18] From the summer of 1972 it focused particularly on the supposed involvement of young blacks in forms of street crime popularly defined as 'mugging'.[19]

'Mugging', social control and young blacks

The social construction of the question of 'mugging' and black youth during the early 1970s represents perhaps the clearest example of how the politicisation of this issue came about. The genesis and development of official, police and media ideologies about 'mugging' has been analysed and commented on from a number of angles during the last fifteen years, and I do not want to retrace the steps of existing accounts. In this section I shall focus on one aspect of this phenomenon; namely, the interplay during the early 1970s of images of 'black youth' and 'mugging' and the consequences of this process for policy and practice in relation to young blacks.

As I have shown in chapter 2, during the 1960s the political debate about the 'second generation' of young blacks became synonymous with images of alienation, despair, a lack of equal opportunity and urban disorder. The concern by the early 1970s, as we have already seen in the previous section, was beginning to shift towards the involvement of young blacks in 'muggings' and other forms of street crime.[20] This shift reached its peak during the period from 1972–6, when the 'moral panic' about the mugging issue was at its height in both the press and in official discourses, reaching the point where Enoch Powell could publicly declare mugging to be essentially a 'black crime' (*The Guardian*, 12 April 1976).

The history of the media and popular response to the 'mugging' issue has been analysed in some detail by Hall *et al.* in *Policing the Crisis* (1978). The premise of this study is that the construction of black communities as 'social problems' was the ideological bedrock on which the black youth/urban deprivation/street crime model of mugging was constructed during the early seventies. Mugging as a political phenomenon, according to Hall *et al.*, became associated with black youth because they were seen as:

(a) a social group which suffered the most direct impact of the cycle of poverty, unemployment and social alienation which afflicted inner city areas; and

(b) suffering from the added disadvantage of belonging to a racial group with a 'weak' culture and high levels of social problems, such as broken families and lack of achievement in schools (Hall *et al.*, 1978: chapter 10).

The power of these images according to this study derived partly from popular common sense images about 'race' and the 'inner cities', but also from the feelings of uncertainty which were developing within British society as a whole about the position of black communities and their role within the dominant institutions (*ibid.* 346–9).

This contradictory response to the growth of permanent black communities in many inner city areas coincided with growing concern about 'inner city problems' and the impact of multiple deprivation on the residents of localities with a combination of problems arising out of:

(a)   the rising levels of crime and violence which afflicted particular areas of cities;

(b)   the emergence of racial disadvantage and inequality as a particular aspect of the social conditions of inner city areas; and

(c)   the development of 'ghetto areas' with distinct cultural values and attitudes towards law and order and the police.[21]

Such concerns about the changing character of the inner city areas were intrinsically imbued with racial overtones as well, since the localities which were defined as particularly problematic – in terms of poverty, poor housing, lack of jobs, broken families and crime – were those of high levels of black settlement. Problems of the 'inner city' were therefore often synonymous with questions about 'race'.

Hall *et al.* note, for example, that even in areas where young blacks were a small minority of the total youth population, the issue of crime on the streets became intimately tied with the category of 'black youth'. This ideological construction became possible because during the period from the early 1970s onwards a dominant concern about the 'ghetto areas' focused on the supposed drift of young blacks into a life of crime and poverty. According to Hall *et al.*,

> For all practical purposes, the terms 'mugging' and 'black crime' are now virtually synonymous. In the first 'mugging' panic, as we have shown, though 'mugging' was continually shadowed by the theme of race and crime, this link was rarely made explicit. This is no longer the case. The two are indissolubly linked: each term references the other in both the official and public consciousness.
>
> (Hall *et al.*, 1978: 217)

This convergence of concerns about race, crime and the 'ghetto areas' onto the category of black youth thus involved a combination of images which linked particular areas to specific types of crime, and these crimes to a specific category of the local population. The definition of 'criminal areas' in everyday police practices thus gained a clear racial dimension, which was in turn further accentuated by the wider social and economic processes which confined black communities to inner city localities and excluded them from equal participation in the labour market and in society more generally.

The politicisation of the 'mugging' question occurred with reference to a number of issues which preoccupied both government agencies and the police. Chief among these were: (a) a breakdown of consent to policing in certain areas; (b) confrontations between the police and young blacks; and (c) a concern that Britain was becoming a 'violent society'. I shall comment on each of these themes in turn before moving to the broader question of the racialisation of crime and the threat of urban disorder.

(a)   Breakdown of consent and 'problem areas'

A glimpse of the everyday confrontations and conflictual situations between the police and sections of the black community can be found in the evidence collected by the Select Committee during 1971–2 on *Police/ Immigrant Relations*, the press coverage of this issue during the early 1970s and the activities of various groups within black communities which prioritised the issue of policing as a central complaint. But it was during the period of 1972–6 that the issue of declining consent to policing and the development of volatile problem areas became a major theme in public debate about policing (Humphry, 1972; Alderson and Stead, 1973; Cain, 1973; Pulle, 1973). This was a theme also in the government's response to the Select Committee Report, which was published in October 1973. After noting that the question of policing black communities was not just a problem for the police, it went on to argue that

> The police are of course only one element of the society which is confronted by this challenge. While part of the test is the extent to which coloured people are treated by the police on the same terms as white people, any failure of the rest of society, in employment, in housing and elsewhere, to accept coloured citizens on equal terms would undermine the efforts made by the police and leave them facing forms of discontent which spring from causes outside their control.
>
> (Home Office, 1973: 5)

This image of wider forces at work which delegitimised the role of the police pervades the government's response, although it also makes the point that only a 'small minority' of young blacks were opposed to the police, while the majority were 'law-abiding'.[22]

At a more popular level this issue of a lack of consent to the police role was regularly mentioned in press coverage in both the popular and the serious press.[23] The imagery of American writings on the black ghettoes was transposed onto the British situation – with areas such as Brixton, Notting Hill and Handsworth being compared to the streets of

Harlem, Watts and other black ghettoes.[24] The questions being asked amounted to asking: Why are young blacks being driven to crime? How can they be re-socialised into the dominant values of society?

Within the terms of this debate the central preoccupation was how to reverse past patterns and ensure that the growing tensions between young blacks and the police did not result in them becoming permanently 'alienated' from British society and its values. Indeed one writer argued that the alienation of many black youngsters from the police was already complete, and that it would require a fundamental programme of positive action at a national level to reverse the situation.[25] Writing in the *New Statesman* in October 1972 Colin McGlashan, a perceptive journalistic observer of the race relations scene, commented that

> It is hard not to feel that race relations in England are at five minutes to midnight. The 'second generation' of black teenagers, born in this country or formed by it, are starting to have children of their own. Far too often they are growing up without fathers, in areas that are not racially exclusive but which in most other ways increasingly resemble in their institutions and attitudes the US ghettoes. Having been left outside most of society's benefits, their morality does not involve staying inside its rules.
>
> (McGlashan, 1972: 497)

In the numerous official, political and media references to 'community relations' and 'police/immigrant' relations this concern about the consequences of growing black 'alienation' and exclusion for society and for public order remained an underlying theme. Whilst not necessarily stated in these terms the main fear was that the growth of black disadvantage, and the involvement of sections of the black community in criminal and semi-criminal activities, would produce a political response from both the black communities and the white majority that would threaten social stability and order. This was seen to be a particularly important phenomenon in certain localities where the factors I have discussed above had produced tension between young blacks and the police.

The issue of 'mugging' was therefore intimately linked to wider conceptions about the social problems faced by young blacks in areas of the country that were popularly and officially identified as 'problem areas'.

(b) Confrontations between young blacks and the police

During the early 1970s it also became clear that everyday confrontations about minor issues could easily escalate into open conflict and acts of collective protest on the streets. This phenomenon had already been noted in media coverage and in the Select Committee's 1971–2 Report, but the level of tension mounted during 1973–6 in a sequence of incidents which can now, with the benefit of hindsight, be seen as presaging the larger-scale disturbances during the 1980s.[26] This included the widely reported confrontation in June 1973 between black youth, the police and the wider black community in Brockwell Park, south London. The events were widely reported in the popular and serious press, and in black journals such as *Race Today*.[27] One of the features of the reporting of this event centred on the image of the events as a 'race riot' and as a sign of larger riots and disorders on the horizon. This theme became more pronounced once it was clear that the Brockwell Park incident was not merely an isolated incident, and that outbreaks of a similar kind were becoming part of the everyday experience of many inner city localities.

The immediate causes for such outbreaks were often small incidents which escalated through rumour and counter-rumour, leading to the arrival of more police and more young blacks to join in the fray.[28] But the underlying conditions which helped to create the basis for such confrontations were a much more complex issue. As early as 1970 John's study of Handsworth had noted that 'the massive breakdown of relations between the police and the black community' held the potential for violent unrest. Attempting to describe black feelings about the local police he says:

> The police station in Thornhill Road is one of the buildings most dreaded and most hated by black Handsworth. It is commonplace to hear references made to 'the pigs at Thornhill Road', or 'Babylon House', or 'the place where the thugs hang out'.
>
> (John, 1970: 22)

Attitudes such as this helped to create a climate of opinion in areas such as Handsworth where the actions of the police were being questioned and at times actively resisted both by young blacks and older members of the community. At the same time the police themselves were adopting in practice a belligerent attitude to all forms of black cultural and social activity which could be described as either 'alien' or 'deviant'. Thus, during the period from 1969 onwards there were numerous reports in the media of confrontations between the police and young blacks and the police in places such as youth clubs, restaurants and other locations which had become identified as 'trouble spots' or as places where criminal activities thrived. Notable examples include the confrontations at the Mangrove restaurant in Notting Hill and the Metro youth club in the same locality.[29] Confrontations between young blacks and the police were also reported in places such as Brixton, Chapeltown in Leeds, Handsworth in Birmingham, Liverpool, and Moss Side in Manchester.[30]

While the extent and scale of the confrontations cannot be compared to the post-1980 riots (which I shall discuss in chapters 6 and 7) their impact was sufficient to produce a sharp debate on the issue of police–black relations and the policing of inner city localities in both the national media and in black journals and police journals.[31] The underlying themes in much of this debate, which to some extent continue to influence perceptions of this issue today, revolved around three fundamental questions:

(1)   What factors explained the increasingly volatile and confrontationary relationship between young blacks and the police?

(2)   What were likely to be the medium- and long-term consequences of this confrontationary situation?

(3)   How could the causes of this situation be tackled so that the likelihood of future violent confrontations be reduced?

The highly politicised nature of these questions, however, meant that the answers provided to these questions by different interests reflected differing interpretations of the reasons why the confrontations between young blacks and the police were becoming more evident on the streets of inner city localities. Thus, while the police journals tended to emphasise such issues as lack of communication and the influence of politicised black groups, the tenor of comments in the black journals and newspapers focused on such issues as police harassment or maltreatment and the racism of British society more generally.

Such contrasts and conflicting interpretations of the relations between young blacks and the police were themselves a reflection of wider preoccupations about the future of 'race relations' in urban localities that were experiencing major transformations in their economic, social, political and cultural institutions (CCCS Race and Politics Group, 1982; Gilroy, 1987). During this time the racialisation of political debates about urban policy and social policy more generally was reaching new heights through the interventions of Enoch Powell and the articulation of public concern about the immigration of Ugandan Asians. It was also during this period that the imagery of 'violence' and 'decay' became synonymous with those inner city localities in which black migrants had settled and established themselves.

(c)   Towards a 'violent society'
The final factor which helped shape the politicisation of the 'mugging' issue was the wider picture of societal concern about the 'growing

problem' of violence, disorder and a breakdown of law and order in British society. Although this phenomenon was not always linked to popular and official perceptions of 'race, crime and policing', the volatile racialisation of political debate during the early 1970s helped to bring the two issues together in popular discourse.[32]

In an important debate on the Queen's Speech to Parliament at the height of the public debate about 'mugging' the linking of arguments about 'black crime' to this wider concern became apparent. The debate was ostensibly on the general theme of 'social problems' and was called by the Labour opposition. But as Shirley Williams pointed out in her opening remarks, this was one of the few sessions when the House of Commons had discussed in detail 'the future directions in which our society is moving', particularly the 'crisis in the cities' (*Hansard*, vol. 863, 1973: col. 315). For Williams the situation in many inner city localities was the most critical in over a century, particularly in relation to policing, social deprivation, housing, education and juvenile delinquency. The centrality of youth to this scenario was made clear by the remark that

> Young people, white and black, in increasing numbers (are) moving into cities such as Birmingham and London, often in desperate and futile pursuit of better pay, amenities and conditions. They have themselves become a large floating element among the homeless and ... an element that is particularly disturbing to the police, because it is this reservoir of homeless youngsters who, unless emergency action is taken, will become the young criminals of the next decade.
>
> (*Ibid.* col. 320)

This was a theme taken up throughout the debate by MPs from all political parties, and also by sections of the media covering this and other debates in parliament during this period.[33] Indeed the Home Secretary, Robert Carr, emphasised the importance of ensuring that law and order was maintained in the inner city localities, and that disadvantaged groups were not allowed to drift into a vicious circle of disadvantage, alienation, violence and crime (*ibid.* cols. 327–9).

In most of the speeches during this, and related debates of the time, the connection between the 'growing problem' of violence and disorder with 'race' was established in coded terms: largely through references to 'urban problems' and 'pressures on services'. But some MPs, most notably John Stokes and Ivor Stanbrook, linked the growth of violence to the issue of immigration and their impact on urban localities. Stokes used a number of examples from his West Midlands constituency to show how 'mugging' and growing violence were linked to the admission of 'very large numbers of coloured immigrants', a phenomenon which he saw as fundamentally changing the cultural values and relationships that had shaped such areas over the centuries. He warned that if successive governments uprooted indigenous people to make way for 'new, quite alien peoples', that the country would lose the basis of its national identity and cultural fabric (*ibid.* cols. 371–2).

Views such as these, along with those of Powell, were still not acceptable to the main ideologues of the Conservative party, and were certainly a minority viewpoint.[34] But within the wider public debate the questions of immigration and crime became closely interwoven. 'Jobless young blacks' became a powerful symbol that helped link the issue of 'race' to crime and violence, and a politically sensitive symbol as well. In sharp contrast to the reporting of riots during the 1980s, for example, the BBC report on the Brockwell Park incident of June 1973 omitted to mention that the youths involved were black. In response the Monday Club accused the BBC of trying to cover up a 'race riot' in order to avoid open debate about the 'consequences' of immigration. Describing the situation in Brixton during the aftermath of the Brockwell Park incident Paul Harrison described local black leaders as seeing the events as 'an outbreak of spontaneous anger at what appeared an obvious injustice' (Harrison, 1973: 672). After cataloguing the examples of injustice which were reported to him by local residents, including the tactics of the local police of the Special Patrol Group, and the 'harassment' of young blacks, Harrison prophetically concluded that 'there will certainly be more confrontations, more unnecessary arrests, and more tension. It is a self-fuelling process' (*ibid.* 673).

By the mid-1970s therefore, confrontations on the streets between the police and young blacks had become a central feature of the political agenda about race.[35] Yet, the consequences of this politicisation remained to be worked out in practice.

Policing, racialisation and 'black crime'

The question of the involvement of young blacks in 'mugging' and other forms of street crime remains very much a current issue in political and policy debates. This can be seen partly in the regularity with which stories in the media about mugging refer either directly or in coded terms to the involvement of young blacks.[36] But since the 1970s the issue of 'mugging' *per se* has been overdetermined by other preoccupations about 'black crime', which involve broader issues about 'race relations' as well.

At least two processes seem to be at work. First, the growing politicisation of debates about the social and economic conditions within the black communities has broadened concern out from a preoccu-pation with young blacks as such towards the wider communities within which the younger generation lived. In this sense debates about 'black crime' signify concern about the crisis of the 'urban black colonies' (Hall *et al.*, 1978: 338–9). Second, the period since the mid-1970s is one in which the question of 'black youth' has become intimately tied to the broader issues of disorder and violent protest, particularly in localities of high levels of black settlement.

The period from 1974–8 saw a number of examples of the material importance of these shifts in political language. The most important were the attempts by Enoch Powell and other politicians to politicise the debate about 'black crime', and the occurrence of small-scale riots in areas such as Notting Hill in 1976 and 1977, and in other localities from 1977 onwards.

(a) 'Black crime' and the political agenda

As we saw earlier the 1971–2 Select Committee Report on *Police/ Immigrant Relations* had concluded that on balance 'coloured immi-grants are not more involved in crime than others'. But it seems clear from John's research in Handsworth and from much of the evidence in the Report's appendices that a stereotype of areas of black settlement as 'criminal areas' was already deeply entrenched in police mythology. The Report itself notes that despite the lack of evidence to support a link between blacks and crime

> There seems to be a fairly widespread feeling, shared, as we found in informal discussion, by some police officers, that immigrants commit more crime than the indigenous popu-lation.
>
> (Select Committee, 1972, Report: 22)

The public debate about 'mugging' helped to amplify and popularise the perception, and the issue of 'black crime' was firmly placed on the poli-tical agenda. A number of stages in this process were particularly important.

First, the release in January 1975 by the Metropolitan Police of figures from a study of victims' descriptions of assailants in the Brixton area of London. This claimed to show that 79 per cent of robberies and 83 per cent of offences of theft from the person were carried out by black people.[37] This study was widely reported in the media and helped to attract attention to the 'growing problem' of black involvement in crime and the destabilising role of young disillusioned blacks.

Second, in May 1975 Judge Gwyn Morris jailed five young West

Indians for 'mugging' offences in south London. In sentencing them he commented:

> These attacks have become a monotonous feature in the suburbs of Brixton and Clapham, areas which within memory were peaceful, safe, and agreeable places to live in. But immigration resettlement, which has occurred over the past 25 years has radically transformed that environment.
>
> (*The Guardian*, 16 May 1975)

He went on to argue that youngsters such as them were collectively a 'frightening menace to society', and that they represented 'immense difficulties' for those interested in the maintenance of law and order.

Third, and perhaps more important in terms of its public impact, Enoch Powell's speech of April 1976 about 'mugging' being a 'racial phenomenon' helped to articulate a wider undercurrent of concern about the inter-relationship between 'race and crime'.[38] Powell's speech was in turn linked to the evidence submitted by the Metropolitan Police in March 1976 to the Select Committee on Race Relations and Immigration. The committee was investigating *The West Indian Community*. In its evidence to the 1972 Select Committee Report on *Police/Immigrant Relations* the Metropolitan Police had not raised black crime as a major problem, but the intervening period had obviously transformed their image of this issue. In the very first paragraph of its evidence the Metropolitan Police mentioned the 'uneasy nature of the relationship between police officers and young blacks' in some localities. Although the memorandum did not argue for a direct link between crime and 'race', and it mentioned the social disadvantages which were common in such areas, it went on to argue that:

> It is not part of our position that there is a causal link between ethnic origin and crime. What our records do suggest is that London's black citizens, among whom those of West Indian origin predominate, are disproportionately involved in many forms of crime. But in view of their heavy concentration in areas of urban stress, which are themselves high crime areas, and in view of the disproportionate numbers of young people in the West Indian population, this pattern is not surprising.
>
> (Select Committee, 1977, Evidence vol. 2: 182).

Whether surprising or not this analysis was to prove extremely controversial, and was directly criticised in the evidence submitted by the Community Relations Commission, to which the Metropolitan Police responded with additional evidence to support their claims.[39] The public debate over these statistics helped to push 'black crime' onto the political agenda in a way which gave legitimacy both to popular concern about crime on the streets and to the arguments of politicians such as Powell who called for 'repatriation' as the only solution to crime and disorder.

(b) Riots and violent disorder

As argued above the symbolic threat of violent disorder was a theme in official political language about young blacks from the late 1960s onwards. But in August 1976 it became a material reality, on the streets of Notting Hill. During the annual Carnival in the area a major confrontation took place between young blacks (and to some extent young whites) and the police.[40] Although not on the same level as the events in St Paul's, Brixton, Toxteth, Handsworth and Tottenham during the 1980s the symbolic significance of this event was clear at the time and has been reiterated with some regularity ever since. In a recent speech, for example, Kenneth Newman has argued that the events at the 1976 Notting Hill Carnival were at the time a unique phenomenon, and represented an important watershed in the severity of public disorder that the police had to deal with (Newman, 1986: 9). He argues:

> In relation to public disorder, the major changes over the last decade can be easily followed. In 1976, following the riot at the Notting Hill Carnival, defensive shields were introduced; five years later, after petrol bombs were used, we added flameproof clothing and metal helmets; and last year, after the police were shot at, plastic baton rounds were deployed, but not used.
>
> (*Ibid.* 9)

The unstated issue which links all these events together was that the confrontations mentioned all involved young blacks in one way or another. Other less major confrontations also took place in November 1975 in Chapeltown (Leeds), and in other localities. During this period police activities under the 'sus' legislation and through the Special Patrol Group often led to frequent instances of lower level confrontations between the police and young blacks (Demuth, 1978; Hall *et al.*, 1978; AFFOR, 1978). More broadly the concern with the 'growing problem' of black crime helped to make the police on the ground suspect of all black youngsters, and particularly those who congregated in groups. The imagery of violent street crime combined with that of violent street disorders and confrontations to make every young black, or particularly groups of them (such as Rastafarians), a potential suspect in police eyes. They were suspect not only because of social perceptions about their involvement in street crime, but because they were black, because of the areas in which they lived, their style of dress and social contact, and their leisure activities. This is certainly how an increasing number of younger blacks, along with their parents and independent researchers, saw the situation in many inner city localities – particularly those that were seen as 'immigrant areas'.

It was because of this 'growing problem' that Robert Mark, the Metropolitan Police Commissioner, chose to highlight in his annual Report for 1975, even before the Notting Hill disturbances, the fact that there was a tendency within black communities 'for groups of blacks people to react in violent opposition to police officers carrying out their lawful duties' (*Report of the Commissioner of Police of the Metropolis for the year 1975*, 1976: 12). This was a theme taken up in articles in police journals and by official police documents during this period. The widely publicised Metropolitan Police evidence to the Select Committee investigation on *The West Indian Community* stated the official police wisdom and common sense on the subject when it noted that

> Recently there has been a growth in the tendency for members of London's West Indian communities to combine against police by interfering with police officers who are affecting the arrest of a black person or who are in some other way enforcing the law in situations which involve black people. In the last 12 months forty such incidents have been recorded. Each carries a potential for large scale disorder; despite the fact that very few situations actually escalate to the point where local police are unable to cope. Experience indicates that they are more likely to occur during the summer months and that the conflict is invariably with young West Indians. They can occur anywhere in the Metropolitan Police District, but are of course more likely in those areas which have a high proportion of West Indian settlers.
>
> (Select Committee, 1977, Evidence, vol. 2: 178)

This perception was repeated across the country in the areas where confrontations between young blacks and the police, and growing tension between them, had become a major local issue. Within this context references to urban disorder and street violence became a synonym for confrontations between young blacks and the police.

During 1976 and 1977 other widely reported incidents helped to fuel public and policy debate about the policing of multi-racial areas, particularly in a context of growing tension between young blacks and the police. First, the killing of an Asian youth, Gurdip Singh Chaggar, in Southall during June 1976 sparked off concern about a lack of concern by the police about racial attacks on young blacks as opposed to their preoccupation with 'black crime'.[41] Second, the 1976 Carnival violence was repeated again in 1977 and led to public concern about whether such outbreaks of violent disorder were becoming a regular feature of 'police–black youth' confrontations in inner city localities.

Third, in August 1977 confrontations took place in the Ladywood area of Birmingham and the Lewisham area of London. Both these disturbances involved clashes between the National Front and anti-fascist groups, but it was the involvement of young blacks and the police that became the central issue.

These three incidents helped to ensure that public debate about 'black crime' and 'street violence' in predominantly black localities reached a new crescendo during 1977 and 1978. In Lewisham, for example, the National Front claimed that they were demonstrating against 'mugging', claiming that the local police had long known that the area was a centre of 'black crime'.[42] Indeed they referred to the fact that in October 1976 the police in Peckham had issued a statement which drew attention to the rise in 'muggings' carried out by young blacks. In the case of the 'Ladywood riots' press coverage drew attention to the underlying issue of 'the gradual souring and separation of black youth and authority' (*The Observer*, 21 August 1977).

Apart from the national trends discussed above, it is also clear that the response of the police in areas such as Notting Hill, Brixton, Handsworth and Moss Side further accentuated the stereotype of young blacks (or at least a section of them) as members of a 'criminal subculture'. At a common sense level the everyday contact between young blacks and the police was interpreted through police ideologies as involving a clash between the cultural values of the majority community and those of the minority communities caught up in a web of poverty, unemployment, racial disadvantage and alienation. But such notions about the nature of the 'racial problem' which the police faced in many urban localities were in turn supported by common sense notions about the localities in which the black communities tended to be concentrated in, and the socio-economic conditions which confronted young blacks in inner city localities. This helped to create symbols which the police could easily identify as the source of the problem, whether at the individual level (in terms of 'criminal' young blacks) or at the level of geographical localities ('criminal areas'). This process in turn helped to give further support to the notion that the source of the problem lay in the culture and attitudes of young blacks, with racism and discrimination seen as playing only a subsidiary role.

Gus John, to whose 1970 study of Handsworth I referred earlier, has characterised this position as one in which there is an ascription of certain fixed attributes onto the category of 'black youth'.

> The state, the police, the media and race relations experts ascribe to young blacks certain collective qualities, e.g. alienated, vicious little criminals, muggers, disenchanted, unemployed, unmarried mothers, truants, classroom wreckers, etc. The youth workers, community workers, counsellors and the rest, start with these objective qualities as given, and intervene on the basis that through their operations they could render young blacks subjectively different, and make them people to whom these objective qualities could no longer be applied. When this is done in collaboration with control agents themselves, as in police–community liaison schemes, or instances in which professional blacks collaborate with schools in blaming black kids for their 'failure', it is interpreted as progress towards 'good community relations'.
>
> (John, 1981: 155)

Such categorisations of young blacks helped to deflect attention from the legitimacy of any grievances that they actually had about the police, about racism, or other aspects of their daily lives and focus policy concern on their characteristics or the 'problems' caused by their communal or family backgrounds. During the period of the mid- to late 1970s this process became clear in relation to young blacks who adopted the style and cultural values of Rastafarianism, and who in areas such as Handsworth and Brixton became an easy target for police stereotyping and attracted the attention of other central and local government agencies.[43] Some observers had argued forcefully that the central question about young blacks was not what is wrong with them, but what is wrong with the society which denies them justice and equal rights (McGlashan, 1972; Humphry 1972; Moore 1975). But such arguments about the origins of the problem in social inequality and unequal power relations were easily lost in the maelstrom of common sense images and explanations about the 'problem of criminal and unemployed young blacks'.

The situation in Handsworth during 1976–7 is an example of the impact of such debates on particular localities. The police in the Handsworth area had for long been at the forefront of initiatives which aimed to improve relations between young blacks and the police. In the evidence submitted by the Birmingham Police to the Select Committee investigation on *Police/Immigration Relations*, the police had noted that they did not believe an 'isolated police effort' could deal with the young unemployed West Indians of Handsworth, and they recommended an 'integrated social resources' approach (Select Committee, 1972, Evidence, vol. 2: 446–7). Yet the area became known as Birmingham's 'angry suburb', and as an area with a massive potential for disorder and conflict. In a series of articles during May 1976 on Handsworth the *Birmingham Evening Mail* analysed the tensions below the surface of the area, the plight of unemployed young blacks, and the everyday tensions between young blacks and the police.[44] A year later, in the aftermath of the 'Ladywood riots' *The Observer* provided the following vivid description of one confrontation between young blacks and the police:

> Birmingham's Soho Road at half-past nine last Monday night: fluid groups of edgy young blacks on the pavements. A blue-and-white police Allegro cruises over the traffic lights. With a sudden jagged movement, a group hurls bricks, sticks and bottles at the car, crunching into the windows and bonking on the metalwork
> . . .
>
> Missiles clatter on shop doors and one shatters plate glass. The car slews to a stop and half a dozen youths bombard it from 15 feet. 'Babylon' yells a voice, and the blacks dart outwards, sprinting around corners as a police squad with riot shields and the occasional dustbin lid moves to the stranded panda car.
>
> (*The Observer*, 21 August 1977)

At the same time the local press in Birmingham during this period is full of stories about young West Indians confronting the police in the Bull Ring Shopping Centre and other localities.[45] Such events helped to create a climate in which the local police became centrally preoccupied with the issue of 'young unemployed blacks'.

This concern was in turn fuelled by the study carried out in 1977 by John Brown into the question of relations between young blacks and the police in Handsworth. Published in November 1977 under the title *Shades of Grey*, the essence of the study was an analysis of the issues of crime and violence in the area, particularly as they related to a group defined by Brown as consisting of 200 or so 'Dreadlocks' who 'form a criminalised sub-culture' and whose actions helped to create and reproduce tensions between the black community and the police (Brown, 1977: 7–8). For Brown the activities of this group of 'criminalised' youngsters needed to be counteracted by a combination of improved police contacts with the local communities and wider social policy measures. One result of the study was the strategy of 'community policing' developed by Superintendent David Webb during 1977–81, which aimed to create through direct police intervention more peaceful contacts between the local black communities and the police.[46] But perhaps its broader impact was to help popularise the notion that the 'Dreadlock' minority of black youth was the source of the problem. In their detailed sociological study of the Handsworth area John Rex and Sally Tomlinson commented that *Shades of Grey* fitted in with the popular image in the media that British society was being threatened by a 'menacing group of strangers', and that they found no evidence in their study for the existence of a group of 200 'Dreadlocks' who terrorized the area and committed crimes (Rex and Tomlinson, 1979: 231–2). Such reasoned critiques of Brown did not prevent his sensational account of Handsworth from gaining wide coverage in the press and thus helping to popularise dominant police stereotypes of the situation.[47]

Brown's sensational account of the Handsworth situation notwith-standing, the late 1970s saw a further escalation of concern about police–black youth relations – particularly in the context of growing black youth unemployment. Tensions were reaching new levels and the evidence of conflict and violent confrontations was becoming more clear as time went by.

Describing the situation in areas such as Brixton and Handsworth during October 1972, Colin McGlashan painted a gloomy picture:

> Relations between police and black youngsters in some areas where the SPG and similar local squads have been repeatedly employed are now poisonous to a degree that is truly frighten-ing; two moderate and unexcitable community workers separ-ately described them to me as 'warfare'.
>
> (McGlashan, 1972: 497)

If anything the scenario during the late 1970s was one of even more open hostility and conflict. The depth of opposition to police intervention in 'problem areas' was reaching the stage where violent urban unrest was widely accepted as both inevitable and perhaps necessary by sections of the black communities.

A local resident of Handsworth described the groups of young blacks and other residents marching on Thornhill Road police station as 'more pleased than if they'd won the pools' (*The Observer*, 21 August 1977). Such a depth and intensity of opposition to the police was only partly overcome by the 'community policing' approach adopted by the local police in Handsworth from the mid-1970s onwards. Indeed, as we shall see in chapters 6 and 7 the background to the violent unrest of the 1980s lies precisely in this history of tension and confrontation between young blacks and the police in many localities. The 1970s may not have experienced violent protests of the same level as we have recently seen but the foundations for the breakdown of relations between young blacks and the police were laid during this period.

'Race', crime and statistics

The 1970s then witnessed a complex process by which young blacks came to be seen as intimately involved in (a) particular forms of street crime and (b) confrontations with the police which represented a challenge to the maintenance of law and order. I shall explore the further development of debates about the second issue in chapters 6 and 7. For the moment, however, a few remarks are necessary about how the early 1980s marked a further politicisation of the 'black crime' question.

The early 1980s were an important period in the racialisation of debates about law and order, crime and policing in at least two ways. First, the politicisation of the black youth unemployment issue helped to focus attention on the inter-relationship between unemployment and crime. Second, the riots during 1980–1 forced the issues of 'black crime' and violence on the streets onto the mainstream political agenda. The widespread coverage given to the issue of 'race' in connection with the riots helped to open up a wider debate about issues such as 'mugging' and 'black crime' under the wider concern of 'the future of British society'.

In the aftermath of the 1980–1 riots in Bristol, Brixton, Toxteth and elsewhere, one of the most important public debates about 'race and crime' took place during 1982–3. It followed the decision of the Metropolitan Police in March 1982 to release a racial breakdown of those responsible for street robberies, a statistical breakdown which it had not published previously, although it had been collating such statistics for some time (Scotland Yard, *Press Release*, 10 March 1982: *The Guardian*, 11 March 1982). The police statistics showed a marked rise in street robberies, but the crucial statistic which the press and the media picked on was concerned with the 'disproportionate involvement' of young blacks in street crimes such as 'mugging', purse snatching and robbery from stores. The press reaction to the press release varied from sober commentaries on the nature and limitations of the statistics, sensational headlines about 'black crime', to *The Sun*'s 'The Yard blames black muggers'. But a common theme was the argument that the statistics, along with the riots during 1980–1, were further evidence of the consequences of letting in alien communities to settle in the very heart of Britain. *The Daily Telegraph* articulated this argument succinctly:

> Over the 200 years up to 1945, Britain became so settled in internal peace that many came to believe that respect for the

person and property of fellow citizens was something which existed naturally in all but a few. A glance at less fortunate countries might have reminded us that such respect scarcely exists unless law is above the power of tribe, or money, or the gun. But we did not look; we let in people from the countries we did not look at, and only now do we begin to see the result. Many young West Indians in Britain, and, by a connected process, growing numbers of young whites, have no sense that the nation in which they live is part of them. So its citizens become to them mere objects of violent exploitation.

(11 March 1982)

Such an argument amounted to a direct link between 'race' and 'crime'. A similar tone was adopted by papers such as the *Daily Mail* and *The Sun*, which went even further in their use of images of 'mugging' – harking back to Powell's 1976 definition of mugging as essentially a 'black crime'. A year later the intervention of Harvey Proctor, the right-wing Tory MP, helped to secure the release of similar figures by the Home Office and led to a similar wave of articles in the press about the 'rising wave' of crime in areas of black settlement'[48] Since then the Metropolitan Police have been much more reticent about publishing such statistics (although they continue to be kept), because of their potentially volatile political impact.

Not surprisingly, however, the issue of the involvement of young blacks in criminal or quasi-criminal activities remains a key area of concern for the police and other institutions, both locally and nationally. Because of this climate of official concern the issues of 'crime' and 'violence', which I have analysed in some detail in this chapter, remain central to the full understanding of how contemporary ideologies about young blacks as a social category were formed and how they are being transformed.

What is clear is that the successive shifts in political language about the black youth question throughout the period since the early 1970s have involved the issues of policing and 'black crime' as a central theme. Whether in terms of specific concerns about 'mugging', 'street crime', or with more general concerns about the development of specific subcultures, such as Rastafarianism, among young blacks, the interplay between images of 'race' and 'crime' has remained an important symbol in political language. Since the late 1970s, and particularly after the 1980–1 riots, political debates about the 'black crime' issue have also been overdetermined by the phenomenon of urban unrest and civil disorder. But even within this context the issues of 'race, crime and the ghetto' which I have analysed in this chapter remain the bedrock for the shifts in official ideologies and public debate about 'black youth'.

This also helps to explain the increasingly politicised nature of the response to the two issues which I shall analyse in the rest of this book: namely, black youth unemployment and violent urban unrest. The ideological construction of the involvement of young blacks in mugging and other forms of street crime provided the basis for the development of strategies of control aimed at keeping young blacks off the streets and keeping the police in control of particular localities which had become identified both in popular and official discourses as 'crime-prone' or potential 'trouble-spots'. It also helped to bring to the forefront a preoccupation with the social and economic roots of alienation and criminal activity among young blacks. This was reflected in the debate about the impact of unemployment on young blacks, which I shall analyse in detail in chapters 4 and 5. But it was also reflected in the increasing preoccupation of the police and other social control agencies with particular localities where relations between the police and sections of the black community were becoming tense and politicised. This issue will be analysed in chapters 6 and 7, particularly in relation to the experience of urban unrest since 1980.

Conclusion

What, then, was the nature of the concern with the 'problem' of the increasing involvement of young blacks in 'crime'? To recap briefly, it has been argued in this chapter that throughout the 1970s there was a tendency to pin down the dangers posed by specific groups of the black population: particularly the young, the criminalised, the militants, the Rastafarians, and finally the unemployed. While recognising in some form the relevance of deep social inequalities and urban decay as factors determining the position of young blacks, a continuing preoccupation throughout the 1970s was the connection between deprivation and supposedly pathological or weak black cultures which produced 'special' problems for young blacks. This ideology had the effect of externalising the source of the 'problem', and locating it firmly within the black communities themselves. The net result of this process of externalisation was that official thinking and policy initiatives were constructed on the basis that young blacks were a 'social problem', which was taking shape within the very heart of the major inner city areas. The phenomenon of street crime, particularly mugging, was a symbol of a broader process through which young blacks were constructed both in policy and popular discourses as caught up in a vicious circle of unemployment, poverty, homelessness, crime and conflict with the police. This was encapsulated in Enoch Powell's statement in 1976 that mugging was a 'racial crime', with black youth as the main actors.

By the late 1970s the image of the areas of black settlement as urban ghettos which bred a culture of poverty, unemployment and crime came to dominate both official reports and media coverage of black youth questions. In the short space of time between the late 1940s and 1970s the question of young blacks had shifted from a marginal item on the policy agenda of state and other institutions to become a major preoccupation of the main race relations institutions, government departments, the police, local authorities and a number of voluntary agencies. But this transformation was to be superceded by the substantive changes in (a) the employment prospects of young blacks from the late 1970s onwards, and (b) by the massive transformations in the politics of racism and urban unrest during the decade from 1976 to 1986. It is to these issues that the rest of this book will be devoted, since they tell us much about the articulation between class, 'race' and youth issues in contemporary Britain, as we move towards the 1990s.

PART THREE

The politics of black youth unemployment

4

The social construction of black youth unemployment and state policies

Introduction

In parts one and two I explored the genesis, development and contradictions of policies and practice in relation to young blacks until the 1970s. As I have already shown, the question of youth unemployment and social disadvantage played an increasingly important role in debates about young blacks from the late 1960s onwards. But it was only with the massive growth in levels of adult and youth unemployment from the late 1970s that the issue of unemployment moved to the forefront of debates about black youth.[1]

This and the following chapters will examine the processes which produced a politicisation of this issue, the nature of state responses, and the explanations offered for the high levels of unemployment among young blacks. In particular I shall seek to explore two questions. First, how and why was the increase in the numbers of young black unemployed constructed into an important policy issue, and what impact did this have on the policies pursued both by central government and by the regulatory agencies set up to manage the social and political impact of unemployment? Second, what inputs went into the production of policies in relation to the young black unemployed, and how did these connect with or diverge from the ideologies which predominated during the sixties and seventies?

Taking these two questions as a focal point the chapter will analyse the processes which brought about a particular political response during the late 1970s and 1980s to the question of black youth unemployment. Chapter 5 will then take the analysis a step further by analysing the development of policies by the Manpower Services Commission and other bodies which aimed at providing greater 'equality of opportunity' for young blacks in the labour market.

The question of black youths' employment position is now widely recognised to be a central issue in relation to the question of urban unrest and disorder. This has helped to link the question of unemployment to wider political and policy questions, such as the ones that will be discussed in chapters 6 and 7. But this issue also has to be understood as a specific policy area, with its own policy network and processes of political mobilisation and intervention.[2]

Young, unemployed and black

As I argued in chapters 2 and 3, the phenomenon of high levels of unemployment among young blacks was an issue throughout the 1960s. The 1969 report of the Select Committee on Race Relations and Immigration on *The Problems of Coloured School Leavers*, and a number of subsequent reports, had highlighted the youth unemployment issue as one to which the state had to respond if it was to maintain 'good race relations'. Additionally the debate about 'mugging', policing and crime during the early 1970s had been at least partly constructed around images of young unemployed blacks roaming the streets, excluded from the mainstream of society.

However, what interests us here is the history of how and why the image of 'angry unemployed black youth' became the core symbol in political language about this group in the period from the late 1970s to the early 1980s. It should be clear from the above analysis that there is no simple explanation for this shift. Rather, I shall argue that there were in the late 1970s a combination of factors which worked together to produce a 'moral panic' about the social and economic consequences of black youth unemployment.

In fact the focusing of official concerns about black youth on the issue of unemployment took time to develop fully. Despite the accumulated evidence of relatively higher levels of unemployment among young blacks as compared to young whites from a similar socio-economic background, and protests by young blacks themselves that they were dissatisfied with the kind of jobs that were available to them, a direct political response to black youth unemployment took time to develop.[3]

This delay in producing a direct political response to black youth unemployment resulted partly from the assumption that there was no need for direct measures to deal with discrimination in employment. The emphasis in policies remained on the need to respond to the special needs of young blacks through the youth service and through measures aimed at reducing the risk of conflict with the police (Fisher and Joshua, 1982; Solomos, 1985; Davies, 1986).

The fear that high levels of youth unemployment may help to create more tension in the area of race relations linked up with earlier debates about whether the second generation of young blacks was likely to participate in 'race riots' and develop political attitudes that questioned the legitimacy of the polity (John, 1981; Gutzmore, 1983; Gilroy, 1987; Ramdin, 1987). But the politicisation of debates about this issue during the 1970s helped to give the earlier debates a new form, both at the level of ideology and of practice. This was partly the result of the striking deterioration in the unemployment prospects for black youths during this period, but it was also the outcome of a wider debate about the causes, impact and possible outcomes of black youth joblessness. This debate was evident in media, parliamentary and political debates about 'race relations' during this time. The 'black youth unemployment problem' became a political symbol for a broader set of concerns: about the future of black communities; the impact of employment restructuring on the inner cities; the inter-relationship between rising unemployment and crime; and the social and cultural impact of declining employment opportunities for young people generally.

In the political climate of the 1970s, with increasing attention being focused on the involvement of young blacks in crime, the issue of unemployment served as an important explanatory symbol for the growing anger and 'alienation' of black youths. As early as 1972 the Home Secretary, Robert Carr, asked the Community Relations Commission to enquire into two issues:

(a) the high rate of youth unemployment among young blacks; and
(b) any possible relationship between this phenomenon and involvement in crime (*The Guardian*, 29 November 1972).

At around the same time there was widespread coverage in both the media, and the Select Committee's 1972 investigation of *Police/Immigrant Relations*, of the social and economic situation of young blacks, as well as their deteriorating relations with the police. Within this environment the public political agenda about black youth unemployment was dominated by a concern with the drift of unemployed and 'angry young blacks' into either criminal activities or radical political action.

At a local level it was also dominated by concerns about the emergence of tension between young blacks and the police in localities where 'black youth unemployment' was perceived to be a problem (Humphry and John, 1971; Hiro, 1971; Hall *et al.*, 1978). Whereas in 1969 the Select Committee Report on *The Problems of Coloured School Leavers* had warned of 'jobs or strife' (*The Times*, 26 September 1969), by 1971 the Community Relations Commission was stating that in a number of localities this prediction was already reality and that if allowed to progress the 'alienation' of black youths from the mainstream of British society could become a danger to the stability of society as a whole (CRC, *Annual Report*, 1971). The swiftness of the developments during this period partly reflected the transformation of inner city localities as a whole, but it was also the outcome of the patterns of discrimination in the labour market to which I have alluded in previous chapters. Under the headline 'The growing danger of the jobless young blacks' *The Sunday Times* warned in July 1972:

> Unemployment among young West Indians in Britain is twice as bad as among their white and Asian counterparts. Community workers fear that this is a recipe for crime and racial discord.
>
> (23 July 1972)

The weight of evidence showing a higher rate of black youth unemployment was thus interpreted as a sign of growing conflict, and was used repeatedly to argue that 'something must be done'. Some commentators used the example of tensions between young blacks and the police to exemplify the kind of dangers that lay ahead, while others emphasised the 'alienation' of groups of black youths from society as a whole. Some of the evidence used to support this argument was anecdotal, but there was also a limited amount of research evidence that highlighted growing tensions in areas such as Handsworth and Brixton.[4]

The CRC investigation on employment among black youths thus formed part of a broader wave of concern about the interplay between youth unemployment, crime and racial conflict. At the same time, the continued racialisation of debates about immigration and inner city policy helped to place on the public political agenda the future of the 'politics of race' (Freeman, 1979; Miles and Phizacklea, 1984). In April 1973 the Central Policy Review Staff was asked to look at the issues of 'race and discrimination' and advise the Prime Minister on (a) the nature of 'the problem that needs attention', and (b) what long-term strategies could be adopted to implement policy change (*The Sunday Times*, 1 April 1973). When the Labour party came to power in 1974 it launched a review of the policies pursued by successive governments on race and discrimination, and started the process which led to the passage of the 1976 Race Relations Act.[5]

These two processes were closely connected. Indeed the rethinking of race relations policies during this period was intimately related to public and policy concern about the 'growing problem' of jobless young blacks. The highly political nature of debates about 'race' as a whole pushed the specific issue of youth unemployment onto the public policy agenda. It is interesting to note, for example, that the CRC's investigation into black youth unemployment was opposed by a number of black community groups on the grounds that any information about the drift of unemployed young blacks into crime could be misinterpreted by racialists and used by the police to support tough policing tactics in relation to black youths (*The Guardian*, 1 April 1973). This opposition reflected tensions about the political response to black youth unemployment by the state and other political institutions, but it also symbolised the depth of concern among sections of the black community about this issue. In March 1973 *Race Today* called the proposed survey of black youth unemployment and homelessness dangerous, and represented it as another way of blaming young blacks themselves for their social position (*Race Today*, March 1973). By December 1973 the same journal was warning that, taken together with other state sponsored studies of the race relations situation, the CRC survey was best seen as an exercise in 'social control', which would help to legitimise common sense ideas of black youths as 'alienated' and 'unemployable' (*Race Today*, December 1973: 324). Such criticisms were linked to a growing suspicion from within sections of black political groups and organisations that the main concern of the state was not to help young blacks find employment but to keep them under control, with the overall objective of defusing a potentially explosive situation. During this period the CRC noted that

> Reactions from a significant section of the black community were, therefore, mixed but hostile: irrelevance of the survey, concern about the use of the results, anxieties about their implications and hostility to some of the questions were all present.
>
> (CRC, 1974: 15)

While eventually the CRC was able to carry out a modified survey, the politically sensitive issues which it highlighted continued to be discussed in both the black and mainstream media during this period.

The report of this investigation into black youth unemployment was finally produced in May 1974 under the title *Unemployment and Homelessness*. Press coverage was immediate, and this emphasised the topical nature of the questions which the report covered.[6] The essence of the report itself consisted of an analysis of the background to unemployment among black youths, its causes and the link between unemployment and homelessness. Although the report accepted that the actual numbers of unemployed were relatively small, it also warned that there was a likelihood that the trends which it had uncovered could lead to the issue of black youth unemployment becoming more central in the future.

It also estimated that about half of the young black unemployed were not registered with careers offices or employment exchanges, and were therefore not in contact with the institutions which were supposed to help them find employment. It concluded that

> The evidence . . . leads to the conclusion that unemployment among young black people is substantially higher than among their white contemporaries; that it is connected with homelessness; that each represents a social problem; that the interaction between the two makes the problem more acute. Unemployment may lead to homelessness and vice versa. When combined they create a vicious circle which it is difficult to break. Individuals who find themselves in this situation – unemployed homeless, or both – unable to fulfil their aspirations legitimately, may be tempted to resort to unlawful means.
>
> (CRC, 1974: 56)

The report therefore recommended that a concerted programme of action needed to be developed by central and local government, race relations institutions, the youth service, the police and by voluntary agencies to help break this 'vicious circle' (*ibid*. 57–61).

The context in which the report was produced was one in which public and policy debates about unemployed black youths was centrally concerned with two main issues. First, the role of youth unemployment in generating frustration and anger among young blacks. Second, the possibility that such anger could be expressed in the form of violent confrontations with the police or in the form of increasing involvement in criminal activities. While it was recognised that not all young blacks were involved in this 'vicious circle', a consistent theme in official reports and in the media coverage during this period was the growing conviction that the crises facing a section of black youths could develop into a more generalised problem in the 'ghetto areas' of Britain's inner cities, and threaten both social and political stability.[7]

These early stages of the politicisation of black youth unemployment can be seen as setting the terms for the public debate and policy responses that were to follow during the late 1970s and 1980s. The 'problem' of unemployment among black youths had been a public issue since at least the late 1960s, but the effect of both media coverage and official reports on this issue during the early 1970s was to amplify the spectre of unemployed black youths as a threat to public order and stability. This period was thus central to the future development of a particular ideological and political response to this issue, for at least two reasons. First, inquiries into the nature of the 'problem', particularly those sponsored by the state, tended to reflect the dominant perception that 'black youth' were a destabilising factor. Second, even at this early stage in the political debate about black youth unemployment there was a growing conviction that the state had to play an active mediating role in managing the consequences of growing numbers of young blacks being excluded from the labour market.

The manifest concern of the state, as stated by Robert Carr for example, was with the improvement of the position of young blacks in the labour market through the extension of 'equal opportunity'. Beneath this manifest goal, however, particularly in the case of 'alienated' young blacks, was a more fundamental and determinant concern – the control of the politically and socially destabilising consequences of the marginali-sation of young blacks from the mainstream of British society. The contradictory relation between this underlying concern and the manifest ideology of state interventions in relation to young blacks will be analysed in more detail in chapter 5. But for the moment what I want to emphasise is the fact that we need to distinguish between the manifest concerns which are used to legitimise state policies and underlying concerns which are not so easily detectable but equally important to any rounded analysis of the development of policies and programmes which deal with a particular 'problem'. This feature of policy change has been noted by a number of writers, but is easily ignored if one only looks at the stated objectives of state policies (Offe, 1984: 88ff; Alford and Fried-land, 1985: chapter 1; Katznelson, 1986). The rest of this chapter will examine the manifest and latent themes which went into the construction of black youth unemployment as a 'cause of concern' which required a particular type of political and policy response.

The politicisation of black youth unemployment

The processes outlined above explain why from 1976 onwards the question of youth unemployment came to the forefront in debates about black youth. Indeed the period from 1976 to 1980 marked a turning point in the politicisation of the black youth unemployment issue. Black youth unemployment began to occupy the attention of government agencies at central and local government levels, and to dominate public and media coverage of 'race relations' nationally and in specific localities. During this period there was hardly any debate about race relations, employ-ment policy, policing or inner city policy which did not touch on the question of young blacks and their role in British society.[8]

One measure of this increased politicisation can be found in the report of the Select Committee on Race Relations and Immigration report on

The West Indian Community. I have already discussed this report's account of the growing conflict between black youths and the police, but perhaps the central theme in the report was the deteriorating social and economic position of young blacks in inner city localities. Much of the evidence submitted to the Committee highlighted the bleak employment prospects of young blacks as the main problem for the future, particularly when combined to rising tensions between this group and the police (Select Committee, 1977, Report: xxv–xxvii). The Committee summarised its view of the situation along these lines:

> The young blacks present a critical challenge to all those waiting for the improvement of race relations. The alienation of the young blacks cannot be ignored and action must be taken before relations deteriorate further and create irreconcilable division. The problems of the young blacks are those of the West Indian community at their point of greatest tension and strain.
>
> (*Ibid.* xiiv)

At the same time as the Committee's Report was published, concern about the impact of unemployment on young blacks and the political dangers represented by their 'alienation' was being expressed by agencies with everyday contact with particular groups of young blacks.[9] Media attention also helped to generate popular public concern about the dangers of young unemployed blacks 'roaming the streets' and engaging in anti-social activities. From this stage concern with black youth unemployment became part of the political agenda of 'race relations' in contemporary Britain.

This increased politicisation was the result of a number of factors, including the following: (a) the linking of 'mugging', crime and disorder to youth unemployment; (b) the growth of youth unemployment and the emergence of youth training programmes run by the Manpower Services Commission; (c) the growing number of black school leavers unable to find jobs; (d) an emergent official concern with the social and political consequences of youth unemployment; and (e) growing pressures from within the black communities for action to help young blacks. I shall comment briefly on each of these factors, before analysing the overall rationale of policies and practices which resulted from these pressures.

All these processes taken together can be seen as constituting an explanation as to why the issue of unemployment among black youths was placed on the political agenda.

(a) 'Mugging', crime and disorder

The concern with 'mugging', crime and disorder linked up with black youth unemployment in two ways: first, because high levels of youth unemployment were seen as one of the underlying conditions which breed social unrest and violence; second, because it was widely accepted by policy-makers and by practitioners that the prospect of sustained long-term unemployment for young blacks would lead to disillusionment with the established order and enhance the likelihood of them actively participating in criminal activities and alternative ways of making a living.

It was the prospect of such a development, with its consequent impact on policing and social policy, that came to preoccupy the policy agenda on young blacks from the late 1970s onwards. Not only the police but also bodies such as the Commission for Racial Equality and the Manpower Services Commission showed signs of becoming very concerned at the prospect of young blacks becoming a permanent 'underclass' which was rejected by society and which in turn developed hostile attitudes to dominant values.[10]

As the black youth unemployment figures in many urban localities started to reach 'crisis proportions' towards the late 1970s a discussion document produced within the CRE about black youth warned that

> The black youngsters we are describing are an alienated gener-
> ation and, unless we do something positive . . . this will become
> a progressively stronger racial alienation. By this we mean that it
> cannot be supposed that this is a temporary experience, a phase
> these young people go through. It must be making a permanent
> mark on them in such a way that it is hard to imagine them ever
> settling down satisfactorily in the inner cities which they gen-
> erally inhabit . . . The fact that the vast majority of those who
> immigrated have, to a greater or lesser degree, managed to
> integrate, to assimilate, must not blind us to the fact that an
> increasing number of black people, who have been exposed to
> all the integrating services of our society from birth, seem to be
> moving naturally into a style which is positively alienated. It
> even starts to evolve its own justification for alienation.
>
> (CRE, 1979: as quoted in John, 1981: 151–2)

There are several aspects of this argument that are worth emphasising. The term 'alienated generation' carried with it the image of a whole group of young blacks becoming separated from the main institutions of society and withdrawing into their 'racial' identities. The contrasts between those who have 'integrated' into British society, and those who have become 'positively alienated' emphasises the two choices which are seen as open to the black communities in contemporary Britain; and suggests that it is the role of state intervention to ensure that 'integration' takes place, for the good of society and black youngsters as well.[11]

From this perspective the 'problem' of youth unemployment among black youths is not just a question of labour market policy, since the very construction of the problem resonates with wider questions: about 'alienation', 'integration' and the relationship of young blacks to British society. This was partly because, as I showed in chapter 3, growing youth unemployment in black communities was seen as one of the precipitating conditions for urban unrest, just as it had been in the United States (Jackson, 1985: 107–24). But it was also because young blacks had already been stereotyped as a group which was drifting into a 'vicious circle' of poverty, unemployment and crime. The images of young blacks which developed during the 1970s were in response to the growing tensions with the police, but youth unemployment was a constant underlying theme.

In some ways, of course, the linking of black youth unemployment to 'mugging' and crime was not new. Nor was the fear of violent conflict resulting from jobless young blacks becoming bitter and 'alienated' from the dominant social norms and values. *The Sunday Times* had warned as early as 1972 that West Indian youngsters were becoming bitter and angry and that ignoring this reality could only fuel conflict and disorder:

> Young blacks could be forced to accept unemployment as a normal life-style and if there is a spark of conflict pent-up black anger could spill over into violence and be met with violence.
>
> (*The Sunday Times*, 23 July 1972)

But during the late 1970s and early 1980s three processes helped to emphasise the links between unemployment and crime and disorder. First, there was the outbreak of violent confrontations between black youths and the police during 1975–7 and from 1980 onwards; second, there was the rise of unemployment among black youths, particularly in inner city localities; and third, there was the continuing public and media coverage of the 'race and crime' issue. The latter element played a particularly important role, since it served to emphasise the impact of the 'growing problem' of unemployed young blacks in specific areas and to popularise common sense images of the threat posed to 'ordinary people' by this social group.

The tangled imagery on which such images relied can be traced in the media coverage of areas like Handsworth. A regular columnist for the *Birmingham Post* wrote an article about the area in November 1977 under the headline 'The stark truth about Handsworth'. After describing it as 'a place where our new multi-racial society sprawls drunkenly with all its conflicts raw, all its squalor exposed', he singled out the black youths in the area as a major problem. His description is worth repeating because of the intermingling of common sense images which it exposes:

> While these people exist in rabbit-warrens of lawlessness, the police are hog-tied. How can we expect a force, one fifth under strength, to restore civilisation to no-go streets and outlaw's alleys while politicians refuse to face the fact that, with one and a half million unemployment and a tangle of social stresses, coloured immigration at the present rate of 1,000 a week is fuelling the furnaces of lawlessness?
>
> (*Birmingham Post*, 30 November 1977)

This point of view was, of course, not expressed universally by all the media during this period. However, such media images were important vehicles for the politicisation of the black youth unemployment issue because they served to highlight the supposed role of unemployed black youths in the 'growing problem' of crime and lawlessness in areas such as Handsworth, on which an increasing amount of national attention was being focused. In so doing the media, along with politicians and decision-makers, helped to structure the political agenda for dealing with the growing reality of high levels of unemployment among black youths.

(b) Youth unemployment and the Manpower Services Commission

While we have to look at the context of public and official concern about 'mugging' and crime for part of the explanation of the higher profile of 'black youth unemployment' it is also important to look at the role of the changing nature of the labour market and of political interventions in the field of employment policy. During the period from the mid-1970s onwards there was a noticeable rise in levels of both adult and youth unemployment, and a gradual recognition that the politics of full employment were being superseded by the politics of mass unemployment (Crick, 1981; Showler and Sinfield, 1981; Richardson and Henning, 1984). At the same time a massive apparatus of policies and agencies was being set up by the state to manage the issue of rising unemployment, particularly among the young. With the formation in 1974 of the Manpower Services Commission, there emerged a highly politicised arm of the state which was charged specifically with the making and implementation of new policy initiatives on unemployment, and with the management of the restructuring of the labour market

(Moon and Richardson, 1985; Jackson, 1985; Ashton, 1986; Cross and Smith, 1987).[12]

State intervention to manage the youth unemployment issue involved three processes. First, there was the manifest concern to be seen to be 'helping' the young people who were unemployed. Second, special programmes were developed to translate the stated objectives of state policy into practice. Third, there was an underlying objective of defusing the potentially destabilising impact of youth unemployment by the use of such programmes.[13] But all three processes were tied in to the overarching concern to manage the 'problem' of unemployment through political measures aimed at eradicating the possible dangers to

(a) public order and social stability which could result from high levels of youth unemployment; and

(b) the smooth functioning of the labour market resulting from the exclusion of large groups of young workers from participation in the productive process.

At the same time the state's role in the reorganisation of the labour market was conceived as part of a wider economic policy of restructuring the economy as a whole through the reassertion of the primacy of competition and profit maximisation. This became the dominant theme in state policies towards the labour market after the 1979 victory of the Conservative party on a platform based largely on neo-Conservative free market principles. Thus even when the manifest objective was stated as 'helping young blacks' or 'regenerating employment opportunities in the inner cities', the underlying philosophy of state interventions incorporated a concern with reshaping the labour market along free market principles while promoting social order and stability.

In general terms the emergent political concern with the growth in levels of unemployment during the 1970s did not produce a major change in the limited-intervention stance which successive governments had adopted in relation to the labour market. But during the late 1970s there was a marked increase in political concern and debate about unemployment both in Parliament and other political arenas, and the rise of the Manpower Services Commission after 1974 marked a new stage in both the form and function of state intervention to manage the politics of unemployment. Significantly the main preoccupation of political debate about unemployment during this period was the question of youth unemployment. Increasing state intervention was in response to growing evidence both locally and nationally of the serious social and political disruption resulting from high levels of youth unemployment (Gleeson, 1983; Moon and Richardson, 1985: 63–89; Davies, 1986: 41–65). This preoccupation with the consequences of youth unemployment was reflected in the implementation of special employment measures for the young unemployed, from the Job Creation Programme, the Youth Opportunities Programme to the Youth Training Scheme (Jackson, 1985: 78–106).

All these schemes were managed by the Manpower Services Commission, which expanded rapidly during the late 1970s to become the main government agency managing the 'growing problem' of unemployment. The MSC had set itself as early as 1976 the task of ensuring that all young people aged 16–18 and with no job and who were not engaged in further or higher education should have a chance of participating in a training or job creation programme (MSC, 1976). As a result it set up a working party on how to implement this task, and this produced a report on *Young People and Work* in May 1977, which articulated a programme of action based on the principle that special measures were necessary to tackle the 'hardship and waste' that lay behind the youth unemployment figures. The report argued that

> These young people are at a crucial stage in their personal development. More important than the large sums paid out to them in supplementary or unemployment benefit is the frustration accompanying unemployment. Unless some constructive alternative can be forced, the motivation and abilities of a substantial proportion of the working population may be prejudiced for years to come. The time has now come to turn a major problem and cost into an opportunity and a benefit.
>
> (MSC, 1977: 7)

The task was therefore to 'help' those who were unemployed to deal with their situation and to compete more equally for jobs. The danger was that if nothing was done for the young unemployed their 'frustration' might lead to anger and political destabilisation.

Given this wider context of concern for the question of youth unemployment as a whole it is not surprising that state interventions were also concerned with the issue of unemployed black youths; since young blacks were widely perceived as suffering most from unemployment and frustration, and were seen as a potentially volatile group who were becoming increasingly criminalised and 'alienated' from society as a whole.

(c) Growing black youth unemployment

I have already pointed out that there developed during the early 1970s a focusing of official concern about black youth around the issues of

  (1) the high levels of unemployment among young blacks, particularly in declining inner city localities; and

(2)   the supposed consequences of this phenomenon for public order and the involvement of young blacks in crime.

But by the late 1970s the politicisation of this phenomenon was proceeding to a new level, with increased official and public concern about the anti-social and destabilising consequences of the exclusion of young blacks from any meaningful equal participation in the labour market.[14]

A discussion paper produced by the Department of Employment in October 1977 noted that although for over a decade the manifest objective of government policies had been to ensure equality of opportunity for black youth in employment, the reality was somewhat different:

> Young people from the ethnic minorities are one of the groups of young people who are suffering disproportionately from the high levels of unemployment. This is partly because they have more than their share of the disadvantages which adversely affect job prospects. They also have however, problems specific to their group. Inner city decay disproportionately affects young people from ethnic minorities because of the pattern of immigrant settlement. In particular significant numbers of young blacks are enmeshed by poverty, homelessness and unemployment, and are alienated from the official agencies which should be helping them.
>
> (Department of Employment, 1977: 3)

During the late 1970s and early 1980s the issue of unemployed black youths, and the 'problem' they represented was to emerge as a consistent theme in political debates and policies dealing with youth unemployment.

A measure of this shift can be found in the language of the Select Committee on Race Relations and Immigration Report on *The Problems of Coloured School Leavers*, which was produced in 1969 and its Report on *The West Indian Community*, which came out in 1977, at the height of public concern about the relationship between black youth and the police. As we saw in chapter 2, the discussion of unemployment in the 1969 Report was tempered by the wider socio-economic context of full employment, although it did contain some limited discussion of the dangers that could be posed to 'good race relations' if unemployment rose significantly. By 1977, however, the Select Committee had come to a more pessimistic conclusion. Already in its 1974 investigation into discrimination in employment it had highlighted the growth of unemployment among black communities as a 'cause for concern', particularly in the context of economic decline (Select Committee, 1974,

Report). In its report on *The West Indian Community* it was more direct, and it linked the 'problems' faced by young blacks to their employment position. Commenting on the 'abnormally high level of alienation among young blacks from the institutions of British society' it saw this as the outcome of a cycle of disadvantage which determined their social position:

> On leaving school, black youth, often confronted by discrimination, educationally ill equipped and in fierce competition with whites, feel insecure and find that being black in British society is a real handicap.
>
> (Select Committee, 1977, Report: xii)

Noting that 'the problems of West Indian school leavers and young people' featured prominently in the evidence submitted to it the Committee went on to note that although there were a wide variety of issues raised in the evidence

> Employment problems are the most serious of the problems confronting young blacks. It is on leaving school that many face the consequences of educational under-achievement. It is on seeking a job that they frequently face rejection seemingly simply because they are black. And these problems are made much worse by large-scale unemployment. In general, unemployment rises disproportionately faster among young people and many young blacks live in areas where unemployment is most acute.
>
> (*Ibid.* xxvii)

The Committee therefore recommended that more positive action should be taken to provide 'special help' to unemployed black youths and to integrate them into the youth training programmes run by the Manpower Services Commission.

Although the MSC did not at this early stage make the question of racial inequality and equality of opportunity a central plank of its policies, it did recognise that it had to pay special attention to the needs of disadvantaged groups. The MSC's 1978a *Review and Plan* stated its position as follows:

> There remains the growing problem of long-term unemployment among adults: and there are many other workers who suffer disadvantages in the search for jobs, for example, because of race or colour. We recognise a special responsibility here. We shall monitor closely the effectiveness of our programmes and

will take new initiatives within resources available as we gain experience and new opportunites to act effectively open up. We are particularly anxious to work with bodies which promote equal opportunities and good race relations.

(MSC, 1978a: 6)

To this end when the MSC started the Youth Opportunities Programme in 1978 it made some limited provision for the 'special needs' of the young black unemployed within the context of its general ideological commitment towards providing special programmes for the young unemployed.

I shall discuss the development of 'special measures' for unemployed black youths in chapter 5. For the present, however, it is important to note that the ideology of 'special needs' helped define the 'problem' of black youth unemployment as the outcome of

(1) the social and personal disadvantages and handicaps of black youths; and

(2) the difficulties of responding to the 'special needs' of young blacks in schooling and employment.

During the late 1970s, and even in the early 1980s, it was still common practice in official documents to see the 'special needs' of black youth discussed alongside 'the handicapped and other disadvantaged'; 'ex-offenders' and related groups.[15] The assumption seemed to be that the 'problems' of the young black could be equated, in policy terms at least, to those of the physically and educationally disadvantaged groups. This elision between the idea of 'special needs' and the idea that young blacks were somehow 'handicapped' can be seen as partly the outcome of earlier stereotypes of young blacks as entangled in a web of personal and communal handicaps, but it was also the result of the notion that the reason why young blacks were more likely to be unemployed was not the structure of British society but the result of their own 'problems'.

(d)   Social and political consequences of youth unemployment

A major preoccupation of both practitioners and politicians in relation to high levels of unemployment, particularly among black youths, was the question of what effect persistent patterns of economic exclusion may have on the legitimacy of the polity as a whole.[16] This concern tended to focus on both local and national issues, ranging from the impact of youth unemployment on law and order and policing to broader issues about the moral and psychological impact of persistent mass unemployment among the young. While the importance of this issue was only fully realised in the aftermath of the political debates surrounding the riots in 1980, 1981,

1985 and 1986 (Benyon, 1984; Benyon and Solomos, 1987), it became an important issue in debates about youth unemployment from the late 1970s onward.

Here it is worth recalling Edelman's (1977) argument that politically sensitive issues are typically dealt with by the state and by political institutions through the manipulation of political symbols which help to explain (a) how the 'problem' emerged, (b) what caused it, and (c) what needs to be done to resolve it. It is notable that youth unemployment became a major political issue during the late 1970s through the use of symbolic political language about the social and political threats which it poses: ranging from crime, social problems, welfare dependency to the issue of violent urban unrest. The mobilisation of such threats to help explain the need for government action reflected the belief among both decision-makers and practitioners that the issue of youth unemployment was as much a political question as an economic and social one. The increasingly important role of the Manpower Services Commission during the late 1970s reflected the common assumption that young people on the dole were likely to prove a volatile group, and that if they were going to be kept under some form of social control, then it was necessary for the state to mediate their transition from school to work through training schemes (Moon and Richardson, 1985; Davies, 1986: 55–64; Showler 1981).

Concern about the social and political impact of youth unemployment underlay the development of 'special programmes' for the young unemployed by the Manpower Services Commission, particularly in the aftermath of the 1977 *Young People and Work* Report. The Commission's special concern for the 'special problems' of the young unemployed was part of a broader political debate about the consequences of high levels of youth unemployment for

(1) social cohesion and the maintenance of law and order in urban localities;

(2) the personal well-being of those who had suffered prolonged periods of unemployment; and

(3) the growth of despair, anger and violent behaviour by young people.

In one of the most important parliamentary debates on this issue during the late 1970s, in the aftermath of the *Youth People and Work* Report, these three issues were raised as the most consistent themes which the government had to consider in attempting to manage the social and political consequences of youth unemployment (*Hansard*, vol. 932, 1977: cols. 1221–1332). The manifest concern at this stage was with how to develop temporary measures to deal with what was still perceived as a phase through which the economy was going and from which it would emerge stronger and in a healthier position.[17] But as youth unemployment grew and remained a central aspect of the deteriorating employment situation after 1979, the issue became not one of temporary measures but of how to manage the possible dangers of youth unemployment on a long-term basis.

The outbreak of violent urban unrest in the St Paul's area of Bristol in April 1980 pushed this issue onto the national political agenda. The growth of urban violence and unrest during the 1980s involved mostly young blacks and whites, living in particular localities with high levels of unemployment.[18] Though it was never clear what the precise relationship between the riots and youth unemployment was, the issue occupied an important role in political and policy debates about the riots. The analysis of the Scarman Report was particularly influential, particularly the section of the Report which argued that there was a strong link between the violent disorder in areas such as Brixton and

(1) the overall political economic and social context in these areas;
(2) the high levels of youth unemployment; and
(3) the complex of social and racial disadvantage which determined the life chances of young blacks and other groups in the local communities (Scarman, 1981: 14–15).

During the period from 1981 onwards such issues became part of a widespread political and policy debate about the causes and remedies of violent unrest in British cities. In the period from 1981 onwards it is notable that in a series of parliamentary debates about such issues as urban unrest and employment policy the question of the social and political consequences of youth unemployment played a prominent role. It became the subject of heated political dispute and vociferous debate both inside and outside Parliament.[19]

The debate in the Scarman Report in December 1981 is a case in point. Although the government was keen to dismiss any possible connection between its employment policies and the riots (see chapter 6 below), Lord Scarman's implicit endorsement of a link between youth unemployment and disorder helped to spur a lively debate about the inter-relationship between social and employment conditions and urban unrest. John Fraser, in whose constituency the Brixton riots occurred, was in no doubt that whatever the government's arguments about the long-term prospects for employment, in the immediate context youth unemployment was having a 'corrosive effect' on the young black and white people in his area:

> While relations with the police are a crucial factor, if I had to rate the causes of what happened in order of importance unemploy-

ment would rank second. The figures are extremely high. They had increased dramatically before the riots, and they have increased dramatically since. As unemployment rises crime will also rise. What worries me, however is that unemployment so corrodes the attitudes of young people in particular that when the level of unemployment falls there may be no corresponding fall in crime and anti-social behaviour. The young people cursed by long-term unemployment may have their entire lives destroyed rather than just the period of loss of income.

(*Hansard*, vol. 14, 1981: cols. 1042–3)

This prospect of pent-up social pressures and injustices producing a generation that saw violence and crime as a way out from the present situation was also a theme in the media coverage of the riots.[20] So even though the official government responses to the riots was to portray them as having little to do with youth unemployment, public and political debates helped to place this issue firmly on the political agenda, as we shall see in chapters 5 and 6.

(e) Black community pressures

What is particularly striking about the issue of black youth unemployment over the past decade is the anger it has aroused within various sections of the black community. A number of black groups and individuals have persistently argued that the employment position of black youth and, most importantly, the high levels of unemployment which they have experienced, represents a crucial test case of the commitment of the state to equal opportunity and racial equality. In evidence to a number of official investigations this has been one of the most consistent themes which black organisations have raised.[21] The same can be said about the coverage of this issue in the black media, which played a central role in sensitising both the black communities and official opinion-makers to the 'problems' facing black youths. The direct impact of such demands on the decision-making process is difficult to assess, but it can be said that such expressions of concern by the black communities themselves could not be wished away.

As I showed in chapters 2 and 3 a number of black groups and individuals had drawn attention to the social position of black youths, including the issue of youth unemployment, during the 1960s and 1970s. But by the late 1970s such calls for action were focused on two issues:

(1) the high levels of black youth unemployment and the accumulated disadvantages resulting from the deteriorating economic situation in many inner city localities; and

(2)   the stereotype and identification by the police of black youths as 'criminal' and 'violent'.

The two concerns were intimately linked, since the police were seen as targeting a particular group of young blacks for 'special treatment'. In a number of local contexts, therefore, black community campaigns were organised around the question of the 'police harassment' of young blacks and the lack of effective action to tackle racism and racial inequality (Ramdin, 1987; Gilroy, 1987).

In the context of local situations such pressures were particularly important. In Handsworth, for example, black parents and community groups had played a central role in drawing attention to the plight of black youths from the early 1970s onwards (John, 1970; Rex and Tomlinson, 1979). The same process was taking place in other localities, either in relation to specific issues (e.g. confrontations between black youths and the police) or in the context of wider issues about the politics of race in each area. During 1975–9 a regular theme in journals such as *Race Today* was the issue of the 'black wageless' and the response of the police and the state to this issue.[22] The evidence from black political and community groups to the Select Committee investigations on *The West Indian Community* (1977) and *Racial Disadvantage* (HAC, 1981a) resonate with calls for positive measures to widen job opportunities for young blacks and to help them overcome the barriers imposed by racial discrimination and racism.

Black youths themselves were increasingly and vociferously articulating their own calls for action, and questioning the official definition of their 'problems' by official government and race relations bodies, by social workers and by the police. In a special section of *Race Today* in May 1975 called 'The black youth speak', a young black from Brixton argued that the preoccupation with the 'problem' of young blacks was not neutral but aimed at imposing an official definition of the situation:

> All that they have been telling us about the black youth, I tell you it's all lies. It's all lies. They say they are giving the black youth this and that, it's all lies man. It's all lies I tell you. They have a project like this and when they want to find us they just come here. The project can be a good thing but they still make it so that it is an advantage to them. They must see things coming that's why they give the money. They build up things like the West Indian youths have a whole heap of problems . . . We go on more problems than what they have. Because they have the same problems too . . . They make it sound that the West Indian

youths have a whole heap of problems. Which problems we have that they don't have? Its problems that they put on us.

(*Race Today*, May 1975: 80)

A number of similar criticisms of official policies from both black youths and parents were articulated during the late 1970s and early 1980s. Black academics and radical researchers were also active in questioning both the overall rationale and the specific practices of state interventions in relation to black youths.[23]

Such demands for radical action to tackle the roots of racism in relation to black youths could not easily be integrated into the mainstream of the political agenda. But at the same time they could not altogether be ignored, since they helped to articulate a vociferous and politicised opposition to the dominant approaches of government policies on this question. Certainly as the Community Relations Commission found out when attempting to carry out its survey on *Unemployment and Homelessness* during the early 1970s, oppositional voices from within the black communities could produce a negative impact on the ability of government agencies to impose their definition of the 'problems' facing black youths. In a wider sense black community pressures can be seen as playing a role in questioning some of the stereotypes which I have analysed above and in helping to keep on the agenda of public discussion a wider set of questions about the fate of unemployed black youth, and providing a challenge to the official construction of the 'problem'. I shall return to the implications of such pressures when I discuss the policies of equal opportunity and black youth unemployment in chapter 5.

Black youth unemployment, social control and state policies

Throughout this chapter I have attempted to explore the processes through which public and policy debates shaped the political construction of black youth unemployment. I have shown how the ideologies and practices pursued in relation to this issue were determined by specific demands and pressures from within and outside government institutions. Additionally, I have shown that the beliefs on which these policies were based were not neutral and relied on definitions of the problems which were themselves political.

The whole ethos of the political debate about the consequences of unemployment among young blacks was deeply influenced by the ideologies that had developed over the previous two decades about the 'problem' of the second generation. Thus the emergence of youth unemployment as the central 'problem' did not result in the abandonment of earlier concerns. Rather, these earlier preoccupations became part of the ideological models used to explain and rationalise the high levels of unemployment among young blacks. The debate about the 'special needs' of the black unemployed is a case in point. Whilst at one level the notion of 'special needs' was used to argue that more action should be taken to help young blacks, it also served to reproduce the stereotype of young blacks as suffering from social and cultural deficiencies. This is an issue which I shall analyse in greater detail in chapter 5.

This links up with the analysis of Murray Edelman, who has looked at the American programmes for the unemployed and shown how the ideologies on which these policies were based helped to focus attention on some issues while at the same time deflecting attention from others:

> A reference in an authoritative statement or in a Social Security law to 'training programmes' for the unemployed is a metonymic evocation of a larger structure of beliefs: that job training is efficacious to solving the unemployment problem, that workers are unemployed because they lack necessary skills, that jobs are available for those trained to take them. Because each component of this interrelated set of beliefs is dubious, job training has been largely ineffective as a strategy for decreasing unemployment. But people who are anxious to fight unemployment and eager to believe the problem can be solved without drastic social change are ready to accept this kind of reassuring cue.
>
> (Edelman, 1977: 16)

Other studies have shown how policies which are aimed at helping especially disadvantaged groups also help to popularise stereotypical images about their situation (Halsey, 1972; Stone, 1981; Troyna and Williams, 1986). In so doing, such policies construct definitions of the problems to be tackled which exclude certain issues from serious consideration.

It is this inter-relationship between the larger structure of beliefs and the fears about the social and political consequences of high levels of unemployment among young blacks that helps explain the genesis and development of policies and practices about unemployed young blacks. The impact of such ideological constructions on the practices of government agencies such as the MSC will be analysed in chapter 5. But what I want to emphasise here is the fact that the question of unemployment among black youths becomes a cause of public concern largely because of its supposed effects on society as a whole, rather than because of its impact on young blacks themselves. The same can be said about the question of youth unemployment as a whole (Mungham, 1982; Finn, 1983; Jackson, 1985). The overall question of youth unemployment created a situation in which the supposed links between black youth unemployment and crime and disorder became an established part of the political agenda, even though the precise nature of this linkage was the subject of heated debate among researchers and practitioners.[24] This was because whatever the 'facts' behind the supposed linkage, it was widely believed by both policy-makers and by practitioners that high levels of youth unemployment formed part of a 'vicious circle' which represented a danger to social order and stability, and that state intervention should be aimed at dealing with this danger.

The most consistent theme to emerge in the policy debates about this issue from the late 1970s onwards was the arguments that the role of state intervention was essentially one of taking action to defuse the potential for 'alienation' and growing involvement in crime. As early as November 1977 the Home Office Research Unit had proposed a survey of the 'views, attitudes, beliefs and intentions' of black youths, with a view to exploring their attitudes to political and related institutions, to employment, to the police, and their own version of their future within British society. This concern with the social and political attitudes of young blacks became even more acute during the period from 1977 onwards, with increasing public and media debate about the 'separation of black youth from society' and the politicisation of outbreaks of violence between young blacks and the police during the 1976 and 1977 Notting Hill Carnivals.

Within this context the question of social control came to the fore in debates about the young black unemployed, at both a local and national level. Thus the question of policing in areas such as Handsworth and Brixton became tied, in both the public and the official mind, with the question of young unemployed blacks. Similarly, the outbreak of violence on the streets of Notting Hill was seen as expressive of the 'vicious circle' within which black youths were inextricably caught. The question of what should be done to deal with the issue of black youth unemployment came to be seen as a measure of the success or failure of policies aimed at developing 'good race relations'.

Conclusion

What I have tried to show in this chapter is that even when policy initiatives to tackle black youth unemployment were legitimised on the basis that they were helping young blacks achieve greater equality of opportunity in the labour market, a central concern of the state remained the issue of social control and law and order. It is this wider concern with the role of the state in managing and controlling the young black unemployed which explains the high profile of youth unemployment in debates about this issue from the late 1970s onwards, rather than the specific issue of high levels of black youth unemployment as such. Evidence that young blacks suffered from specific forms of exclusionary practices and discrimination had existed for some time before the question of black youth unemployment achieved a central position in public policy debates about 'race', let alone produced effective measures to tackle its root causes. What made unemployment among black youths a highly politicised issue by the late 1970s to early 1980s was the particular combination of pressures from within and outside pressures which forced the issue of black youths' employment prospects firmly onto the public political agenda. A central part of this process was the debate which took place about the likely political and social destabilisation associated with continued high levels of unemployment among black youths.

The increasing visibility of black youth unemployment on the public political agenda helped to produce new forms of governmental response and initiatives to tackle the 'problem'. Institutions such as the Commission for Racial Equality and the Manpower Services Commission began to look at their functions in dealing with the phenomenon of black youth unemployment. At the same time public concern and discussion about this issue helped to set the terms of debate around the theme of 'something must be done'. The predominant theme in much of the media debate and in the interventions of the pressure groups, community organisations and local authorities was that there was a need for intervention on a major scale to manage and resolve the social and political consequences of high levels of unemployment among black youths.

How did this consensus on the need to tackle the possible threat to social stability and order which black youth unemployment represented manifest itself in terms of policy outcomes? What impact did state intervention have on the employment condition of black youth? These are the questions I shall attempt to deal with in chapter 5. Before that one final point needs to be stressed: namely the inter-relationship between the politicisation of youth unemployment in relation to wider issues about law and order, policing, urban unrest and inner city policy. I have pointed out already that this is a critical factor. But in subsequent chapters I shall link my discussion of the politics of black youth unemployment to the wider issue of urban unrest, since it seems to me impossible to look at one without reference to the other. Nor can the reproduction of racial inequality be analysed without a detailed analysis of the specific strategies pursued by the Manpower Services Commission and other institutions involved in managing youth unemployment.

5

The politics of youth training and equal opportunity: from 'special needs' to the Youth Training Scheme

Introduction

Chapter 4 provided a detailed account of the processes which politicised the question of unemployment among black youths. It thus linked up with the approach of previous chapters which argued that successive political interventions towards this social group have been shaped by wider ideologies and practices about 'race relations' in British society. Thus although such policies have typically been legitimised as giving some form of 'special help' to enable young blacks to achieve equality of opportunity, they have been formulated and implemented in ambiguous and contradictory ways. Additionally, I have shown that far from overcoming lack of opportunity and racial discrimination against young blacks, such policies have worked in ways which have often harmed the interests of racial equality and reinforced dominant stereotypes.[1]

In this chapter I shall develop this argument further by looking at the specific forms of state intervention which have resulted from the processes analysed in chapter 4. In particular I shall look at policies adopted in relation to youth training schemes, administered by the Manpower Services Commission (MSC), and their impact in providing 'equal opportunity' for young blacks. Such policies are sometimes looked at uncritically as reform measures which are aimed at helping young blacks better their status in the labour market and in society more generally. Certainly the MSC and the government have been at pains over the past few years to defend their record on equal opportunity issues and the MSC's provisions for the 'special needs' of young blacks.[2] What I want to explore in this chapter is the interplay between (a) the rhetoric and language of policy pronouncements, and (b) the underlying ideologies and actual policy outcomes of initiatives taken by the MSC and other government agencies to manage the issue of black unemployed youths.

The starting point of this chapter is the political context of measures which have aimed to integrate unemployed black youths into the youth training schemes run by the MSC and related agencies. This is followed by a detailed analysis of the politics of 'special needs', the development of equal opportunity policies in relation to youth training, and the role of state interventions which aim to manage the continuing crisis of black youth unemployment. This will be followed by a critical appraisal of the contradictory meanings of the policies covered by the general charter-word 'equal opportunity' in relation to black youth. This, and the following two chapters, will complete the chronological account of the genesis and development of policies and practices adopted by the state in relation to black youths.

Political language and policy rhetoric

Even a cursory perusal of contemporary political debates about 'race relations' would show that the language and rhetoric of policy pronouncements bear only a contradictory relation to the actual outcomes of policies and initiatives.[3] A good example of this contradictory relation is the whole issue of 'equal opportunity'. The promise that state intervention can produce 'equal opportunity' for a specific social group does not identify a condition that is objectively definable, at least in the sense that there can be a consensus that it has been achieved (Arnot, 1986; Troyna and Williams, 1986). Rather, it articulates an ideal situation to which the actions of the state or related agencies are supposed to be leading. In this sense the passing of legislation or the development of policy initiatives which promise to tackle an existing or emergent inequality are usually premised on the manifest claims that

(1)   the inequality is caused by factors which can be dealt with by the mediating actions of the state; and

(2)   that the achievement of equality of opportunity for disadvantaged groups could challenge dominant inegalitarian structures.

What seems clear, however, is that there is an inherent difficulty in analysing the achievement of such manifest claims – there is a gap between formal statements which articulate a promise of equal opportunity, and strategies of implementation which can challenge established practices of discrimination and institutionalised racist practices (Feuchtwang, 1982; Jenkins, 1986; Jenkins and Solomos, 1987; Edwards 1987). In this sense there are bound to be ambiguities and contradictions between the publicised goals and the actual benefits of such policies.

More importantly, the meaning of equal opportunity in the context of specific practices of discrimination in relation to employment, education or other arena raises important questions about the objectives of policies aimed at overcoming racial inequalities. The most important of these are: What is the objective of non-discrimination policies, and by what standards can this be judged to have been achieved or not? Is the object of equal opportunity policies in relation to unemployed black youths, for example, equal and indistinguishable treatment or separate but preferential treatment for minorities? What can be achieved in terms of equality of opportunity in relation to a specific issue, such as youth unemployment, if such an accomplishment does not noticeably alter the prevailing pattern of racial disadvantage in society as a whole? These are all issues which are at the core of any rounded analysis of political responses to unemployment among black youths, particularly in relation to the consistent tension between the promises held forth in the manifest claims of government agencies such as the MSC and the CRE, and the reproduction of existing inequalities in the labour market and the emergence of new ones within the very programmes which are supposed to ensure equality of opportunity for unemployed black youths.

In the rest of this chapter I want to explore the policies and practices developed around the manifest promise of helping black youths achieve equality of opportunity in employment. I have already analysed the social construction of black youth unemployment as a political problem, and articulated a critical perspective on this process. This chapter will take this account a step further by examining the policies and practices directed specifically at the category of unemployed black youths. I shall be asking two basic questions: What are the manifest objectives of state interventions in this area? How have these objectives been transformed and legitimised through the actual processes of implementation? These questions in turn imply a number of questions about how the manifest claims of state intervention were formulated, through what pressures, and how they express themselves in policy debates. Additionally, they highlight the way in which an issue such as black youth unemployment enters the political arena already defined as a particular type of 'problem' to be dealt with by a set of policy responses mediated by the state.[4]

This is not to say that I have conceptualised the role of the state in this field as purely reactive, since in this, as in other social policy areas, the role of state intervention can range from preventive to reactive measures (Offe, 1984: 109–14). But as I shall argue in this chapter what seems to be important in the area of policies manifestly aimed at equalising opportunities for black youths are not the stated objectives and mechanisms of state intervention but the capacity to implement policy change within a broader reality of racial inequality and political racialisation.

The theory and practice of 'special needs'

Perhaps the most important notion which has pervaded official thinking on young blacks since the 1960s has been the idea of their 'special needs'. As framed in the 1969 Select Committee Report on *The Problems of Coloured School Leavers* this notion consisted of two basic propositions:

(1) that black youngsters were particularly 'handicapped' by a complex of disabilities and disadvantages arising from social deprivation, deficiencies in education, psychological stress and racial prejuduce; and

(2) that there was a sizeable group of black youths who also suffered from problems associated with their cultural, family and personal backgrounds (Select Committee, 1969, Report: 15 and 31).

I have discussed the articulation and development of this notion in chapters 2 and 3, where I showed how it affected official policies in the period from the 1960s to the mid-1970s. In this chapter I want to explore the development of this notion in relation to the issue of youth unemployment. I shall do this by looking at how the ideology of 'special needs' was used to construct explanations of the 'problems' faced by black unemployed youths.

From the late 1970s onwards a number of policy documents by the MSC, CRE and government departments began to articulate a policy response to black youth unemployment. As we have seen in chapter 4 a number of the main elements of this response were organised around the perceived dangers to law and order, social stability and 'good race relations' posed by the growth of a 'black underclass'. But in the context of growing mass unemployment and evidence of continuing racial inequality the emphasis began to shift to the question of how the broader issue of how to ensure that the 'complex of racial disadvantage' within which young blacks found themselves did not produce a situation in which they found themselves more or less socially, economically and politically excluded from the mainstream of British society.[5]

Significantly, when the MSC and CRE produced a joint report on ethnic minorities and special programmes for the unemployed it was entitled *Special Programmes, Special Needs* (1979). Although this report began with a clear statement that there was no special 'minority' youth unemployment problem which could be solved by 'minority' responses; it then went on to make a number of statements about the needs of black youths which linked the notion of 'special needs' to the inadequacies of blacks and their alienation from British society. Thus the report warned that

> There are a minority of disaffected young people from ethnic minority communities who are losing touch with the statutory services and who are therefore in danger of remaining unemployed for long periods of time.
>
> (MSC/CRE, 1979: 11)

This report was part of a series produced by the MSC on other groups with 'special needs': women, the handicapped, the educationally disadvantaged and ex-offenders.[6] The report was widely welcomed at the time and used by the Home Affairs Committee of the House of Commons as an example of the awareness of the Manpower Services Commission of racial disadvantage and the need to take positive action about black youth unemployment (Home Affairs Committee, 1981a, Report: para. 204).

In a sense the report was important, but perhaps less for the reasons given in public debate than for the fact that it exemplified the tendency to

(1)   compare the position of black youths and their 'special needs' to the position of the handicapped, the educationally disadvantaged and ex-offenders; and

(2)   construct the 'minority of disaffected' and 'alienated' young blacks as the core of the problem.

Within this general tendency the usage of the ideology of 'special needs' did not necessarily exemplify an awareness of racial disadvantage, since it seemed to rely on the notion that the 'complex of racial disadvantage' in which black youths were enmeshed was partly (if not largely) the result of their own inadequacies and problems of adjustment in British society. The Home Affairs Committee's report to which I referred above reflected this kind of argument as well, when it pointed out that racial disadvantage and the unequal position of blacks within British society were only partly the result of discrimination (*ibid.* paras. 28 and 29).

During the late seventies, however, there was still the common perception that the 'special programmes' for the young unemployed were still essentially a temporary measure to help manage the youth unemployment issue before the economic upturn created more jobs and reduced the need for state mediation (Solomos, 1983a; Finn, 1983; Jackson, 1985; Cross, 1987). Thus the 'special needs' of unemployed black youths could be fitted into the overall philosophy of the MSC of providing an equal opportunity for all unemployed youths to participate in its schemes. Thus, in its evidence to the Home Affairs Committee the MSC argued that although many of its schemes were of relevance to black youths

> The policy pursued in the Special Programmes is that minority unemployed should participate to the greatest extent possible in YOP and STEP and that it is not in their interests to treat them as 'special cases' to be segregated into certain types of opportunity.
> (Home Affairs Committee, 1981, Evidence, vol. II: 209–10)

The dominant view from within the MSC seems to have been that as long as young blacks were incorporated into either YOP schemes or locally based 'special schemes' it was fulfilling its major objective of offering equal access to all youngsters, and that it was playing its part in ameliorating the unemployment position of black youths. But there were clearly some concerns about the distribution of black youths on MSC schemes, and during this period the Commission undertook two research projects on the issue, analysed the local context of black youth unemployment, and investigated the possibility of co-operation between itself, the CRE and local black community groups in developing schemes for the young black unemployed.[7]

In its annual report for 1980–1 the MSC pointed out that the aim of its programmes was to help all the unemployed, but that 'a number of Commission programmes were designed to serve a range of jobseekers, ethnic minorities (including recent immigrants), and people who are re-entering the labour market after long periods of illness or after bringing up families' (MSC, 1982: 31). It also noted that as a way of encouraging black community groups to sponsor projects under YOP the Commission had allocated a number of 'enabler' posts to 'areas of high ethnic minority concentration'.

In a report which reviewed services for the unemployed the MSC clearly articulated this aspect of its approach to 'race' issues:

> The needs of the ethnic minority unemployed are related partly to their having a relatively greater share of certain characteristics than the general population (e.g. more young people, unskilled), and partly to problems specific to the ethnic minorities (language skills, educational disadvantage, racial discrimination). The first type of disadvantage can be alleviated by services made available to the unemployed generally . . . and the ethnic minorities do not seem to find it harder to gain access to these services than others. The second type of disadvantage

requires measures more specifically geared to the needs and problems of this group.

(MSC, 1981: 13)

What the MSC seemed to be advocating was a dualistic approach to service delivery for black youths, but within a context of manifestly proclaiming the broad objective of providing equal access to its schemes. These early steps in the formalisation of a specific approach to black youth unemployment by the MSC not only reflected images of social unrest and political instability but also served to show the importance of the disorders in Bristol and other localities in forcing the question of how to manage unemployed young blacks within a context of growing urban unrest onto the policy agenda.[8] This underlying consideration was evident in the articulation of state intervention during the early 1980s by the MSC and related agencies.

The context of state intervention

Apart from the contradictions outlined above, one of the central problems in the common usage of the language of 'special needs' is the tendency to construct the problems of black youth as 'their own fault'. This was pointed out in the CRE's influential Report on *Youth in Multi-Racial Society*. Produced in 1980, just prior to the Bristol riots of April, it argued that

> It is sometimes easy for those in authority to regard young people as 'the problem'. To do so is to confuse cause and effect. The real 'problem' lies in the inadequacies of society and the inability to respond to the needs and challenges of new generations of young people – especially those with different ethnic backgrounds, colour and/or culture.
>
> (CRE, 1980a: 10)

The CRE additionally pointed out that there was still a strong body of official opinion which saw higher levels of unemployment as being caused by young black people's attitudes to work, language difficulties, educational disadvantage, and the double disadvantage of being concentrated in deprived inner-city areas.

The very notions of 'special needs' and 'racial disadvantage', which are the terms commonly used by the government and agencies such as the MSC to define the position of black minorities, contain assumptions about these groups that have helped to reproduce a problem-oriented approach which seems to reproduce the American-type situation of 'blaming the victim' (Ryan, 1976). A report by the Home Affairs Committee of the House of Commons on *Racial Disadvantage* (1981a) contains the most articulate statement of this approach. The report argues that racial inequality is produced by the twin processes of *racial discrimination* and *racial disadvantage*. The first process was seen as not necessarily the prime factor, because

> Racial disadvantage is a particular case of relative disadvantage within society. With the exception of racial discrimination, the disadvantages suffered by Britain's ethnic minorities are shared in varying degrees by the rest of the community. Bad housing, unemployment, educational under-achievement, a deprived physical environment, social tensions – none of these are the exclusive preserves of ethnic minorities.
>
> (Home Affairs Committee, 1981a, Report: para. 12)

Within this model the context of discrimination is seen as another 'handicap' from which blacks suffered, and one that could be dealt with by legal measures against discrimination. According to the Committee the central problems of the 'complex of racial disadvantage' were (a) newness and problems of social and cultural adjustment, (b) the geographical location of minorities in inner city areas, (c) language and literacy problems, and (d) educational disadvantage (*ibid*. paras. 14–24). By locating 'discrimination' as a discrete category which can be understood separately from 'racial disadvantage', arguments such as this helped further to marginalise the questions of racial inequality and racism from the main political agenda about unemployed black youths.

The popular association of the riots with young blacks did, however, push the issues of law and order and racial inequality more directly onto the political agenda. This was particularly the case in the aftermath of the Scarman Report, which prioritised the issues of racial disadvantage (along the lines of the Home Affairs Committee Report) and black youth unemployment. This has produced a contradictory mixture within official and policy thinking about unemployed black youths; on the one hand it continued to see them as a problem category because of their 'special needs' and disadvantages and on the other it saw its role as one of compensating for broader social disadvantages resulting from the position of young blacks as a deprived minority in British society and ensuring the maintenance of law and order if such compensation did not work.

(a) The 'problem' of black youth unemployment

The first approach is quite evident, for example, in the responses of the Manpower Services Commission since the riots of 1981.[9] Writing about the events in Bristol, Brixton, Liverpool and numerous other urban areas during 1980 and 1981, the MSC's Corporate Plan for 1982–6 contains the following interpretation:

> Last year saw an explosion of unrest and violence in some of our inner cities which has focused public attention on the problems of these areas, and, in particular, those of the ethnic minority groups who are concentrated in them. The ethnic minorities in these areas suffer a double employment disadvantage; registered unemployment among ethnic minority groups is particularly high, and the unemployment and social problems of many inner-city areas are also acute. This represents one of the most difficult challenges in the field of social, economic, environmental and employment policy, and the programme of development for Merseyside announced by the Secretary of State for the Environment indicates the range of problems and remedies under consideration.
>
> (MSC, 1982c: para. 5.20)

What is interesting about this quotation is the way it combines some recognition of wider social and economic issues with an emphasis on the 'double disadvantage' faced by blacks in inner city areas. The Report then goes on to outline the ways in which the MSC was responding to this challenge, and in the process summarises its own philosophy of the 'problem':

> Our approach has been based on the view that over a wide area of employment the problems of ethnic minority groups in inner cities and elsewhere are similar in kind, though often much more acute in degree, to those of the labour force generally . . . Through our planning system we try to concentrate our services on areas where labour market needs are greatest and where they can be most effective, and ethnic minorities in inner cities benefit from this.
>
> (MSC, 1982c: para. 5.21)

The Commission's claim that minorities suffer from a 'double employment disadvantage' is here balanced against the claim that the problems they face 'are similar in kind, though much more acute in degree'. This means that the issue of racism is hardly mentioned in relation to training programmes for the young unemployed, since it is assumed that young blacks are only suffering from problems more acute 'in degree' than white youth. As noted above the logic of this approach fits in quite well with the thinking of the MSC as a whole about 'special client groups' (e.g.

the disabled, ex-offenders, young girls, and the educationally disadvantaged), which, while making some reference to the processes of
discrimination, tend to negate the importance of this issue by emphasising only the 'special needs' of such groups.[10]

In the aftermath of the growing unrest of the 1980s, however, it was
also evident that the manifest as well as underlying objectives of state
interventions were being transformed by the political debate about the
inter-relationship between youth unemployment and public order.

(b) Racial disadvantage, youth and social order

The outbreaks of urban unrest during 1980 and 1981 do not in themselves, as I have shown above, explain the politicisation of the black
youth unemployment question. But they were certainly important in
defining the political debate about this issue around the specific problem
of law and order. During the early 1980s 'black youth' became synonymous with the phenomenon of urban unrest and emerging political
violence. A number of official reports and inquiries, parliamentary
debates and statements by politicians raised questions about the impact
of unemployment among black youths on the likelihood of urban
disorder and violence.[11] At one level the government did not officially
move away from its rejection of any link between youth unemployment
and the riots and it argued that the main remedy for racial disadvantage
was the 'creation of a stronger and more prosperous economy where new
real jobs are created, existing jobs flourish and unemployment falls'
(Home Office, 1982a: para. 13). But this formal position did not prevent
this issue from being publicly debated, and influencing the policies and
practices of bodies such as the Manpower Services Commission and the
Commission for Racial Equality.[12]

The political dangers of high levels of black youth unemployment were
perhaps best encapsulated in the debates surrounding the 1980–1 riots,
the Scarman Report and subsequent outbreaks of violent unrest. Speaking during the July 1981 riots Roy Hattersley encapsulated one view of
this danger when he compared the situation of 1980s Britain to 1960s
America. He quoted the argument of the Kerner Report that America
was 'a nation of two societies, one black, one white – separate but
unequal' with approval, and went on

> The residents of inner cities did not cause urban deprivation.
> They are the victims of it. But they are the most dramatic
> example of fading hope and rising resentment. As their hope
> fades and as their resentment increases – we must tell them – and
> I shall continue to tell them – that in a democratic society there

are democratic ways of solving their grievances. But I must be honest and say that I have some pessimism about the sort of answer that I am likely to receive from the young man of 16, about to leave school, certain to become and to remain unemployed, and denied any unemployment benefit until the second week in September. If that young man is black, how do the Government think that the answer is affected by the Prime Minister talking on television of other blacks 'swamping' this country and the knowledge that a dozen or two dozen of her Back Benchers want to send that young man home, when he knows no other home than Brixton, Toxteth or Southall.

(*Hansard*, vol. 8, 1981: col. 1409)

It follows from this, according to Hattersley, that the main objective was to show to such groups that 'they have a stake in our sort of society' by developing programmes of ameliorative action which show that 'society is capable of responding to their needs' (*ibid.*).

While Hattersley's assumption was questioned vociferously by other participants in this debate, the 1980–1 riots, and the ensuing political debates about unemployment and public order, did force the MSC and other government agencies involved with black youth issues to give greater priority to the 'problems' of this social group.[13] This was achieved partly through the utilisation of promises that state intervention would attempt to deal more centrally with the question of 'equal opportunity', and that the formulation of employment policy as a whole would advance the interests of black youths and other disadvantaged groups. I shall look at each of these issues in turn, before returning to the general issue of equality of opportunity.

Training for all: racism, youth training and declining employment

The language of 'equal opportunity' has been part of official thinking on the question of black youths from the mid-1960s, as was shown in chapter 2. The pursuit of this principle has, however, been framed around different objectives and it has not been without its ambiguities. Since the late 1970s the declining employment position of young blacks and the emergence of the Manpower Services Commission as the key arm of state intervention in the labour market has meant that a key arena for public and policy debates about equal opportunity has been in the area of youth training and special employment programmes. Since the joint MSC and CRE report on *Special Programmes, Special Needs* which was published in 1979, there has been a massive expansion in state and local government interventions in this field; most notably through the provisions made for unemployed black youths under the Youth Opportunities Programme (1978–83) and the Youth Training Scheme (1983 onwards). This inevitably raises the question about the prospects for racial equality within the broader environment of high unemployment and labour market de-regulation.[14]

It has become a commonplace of official debates about black youth unemployment to argue that training initiatives such as YOP and YTS can help the pursuit of racial equality in the youth labour market. This is argued at two levels. First, in relation to 'special measures' to help unemployed black young people overcome the specific problems they face in entering the labour market, whether these result from their own personal or communal characteristics or from discriminatory processes. Second, it is argued that the creation of a robust economy with 'jobs for the future', even at the cost of high levels of unemployment in the transitional period, will enhance the chances of young workers (including young blacks) securing permanent jobs once they have been trained to meet the needs of a fast-changing economy.[15]

There is however, some ambiguity about the MSC's and the government's commitment to equality of opportunity for black youths. For example, as I have pointed out already, there is often a confusion in official rhetoric between 'special need' and 'handicap', an over-emphasis on the supposed 'cultural' characteristics of minorities, and an under-emphasis on the role of racism and processes of discrimination. Additionally the actual meaning of the 'equality of opportunity' which government interventions are supposed to bring about has never been specified in any but the most general and often contradictory terms. A good example of recent thinking can be found in the Manpower Services Commission's *Annual Report* for 1981–2, which argues:

> In providing services (to ethnic minorities) the Commission's approach has been to maintain and facilitate equality of access by all groups and to establish a number of programmes which deal with particular labour market needs, such as those of ethnic minorities.
>
> (MSC, 1982b: para 5.25)

In practical terms, equality of access (which is used here interchangeably with equality of opportunity) is defined by the MSC as (a) the avoidance of discrimination on its training programmes, and (b) as the provision of special help to minority youth who have special needs (e.g. language, educational disadvantage). What the outcome of such equality of access will be, however, is never adequately defined. Neither do we have an analysis of how the development of equal access to training schemes can help young blacks get jobs in the labour market. It has been argued persuasively, for example, that even when special treatment for minority unemployed is legitimised in terms of improving their training and skill levels, the unintended consequence may be to marginalise the problems they face, while not challenging the failure of mainstream services to tackle the racism and discrimination which prevent black workers from getting jobs (Cross *et al.*, 1983; Cohen, 1984; Means *et al.*, 1985). The consequence of training measures may thus be providing short-term alleviation of a highly politicised issue without producing the structural changes that would be necessary to improve the chances of young blacks finding permanent work.

Lea (1980) has pointed out the inherent problems of implementing 'equal opportunity' in societies which are characterised by deep social inequalities that are over-determined by class, race, and gender: he argues that the conception of equality of opportunity that has dominated thinking on race since the sixties has served to locate unequal opportunity for blacks 'outside the fundamental inequalities and socio-economic structure' of British society, and has thus not aimed to change the structured inequalities from which blacks suffer. It has aimed merely to increase opportunities for mobility of individuals within the structure.

It is thus very difficult to see in what sense the promise of equal opportunity provides a basis in practice for bringing about greater equality between young blacks and whites in the labour market. When combined with the notion that young blacks need 'special treatment' the outcomes have been even more contradictory. Although it may be true that some members of the ethnic minorities need compensatory training or education, it is difficult to see how such measures can actually help all young blacks who are unemployed. Unless, of course, it is assumed that all blacks who are unemployed necessarily suffer from cultural deficiencies which have to be remedied through training provisions. Research evidence from a variety of sources has shown, however, that such an assumption cannot be justified, and that its influence on policies may act to restrict even limited equality of access of black youth to training.[16]

Part of the problem with the current use of terms like 'equal opportunity' is that they have become ideological charter-words which do not necessarily help us understand the root causes of racial inequality. While much of the recent concern with the special needs of groups such as the black unemployed can be said to represent an improvement on a 'race-blind' approach, it seems rather questionable to assume that such special treatment as is provided will overcome the essential problems –

which are that young blacks face strong institutionally racialist barriers in their search for work and that government agencies have not been able or attempted to overcome such barriers. Moreover, if schooling cannot compensate for society (Bernstein, 1971) it is doubtful if training will be able to compensate for the long-standing discrimination against the second and third generations of young blacks in their search for work.

The first step in any critical evaluation of current policies towards the young black unemployed must be to analyse the differences between unintended and intended consequences. At a minimum the promise of equal access to all types of training provision means little unless it is made clear to what it actually refers – does it mean the recruitment of large numbers of young blacks on MSC schemes, the provision of special assistance, or an attempt to ensure equality of outcomes as between white and black participants on training schemes? A study of training schemes and ethnic minorities during the early 1980s concluded:

> We have been appalled to see just how many times black and Asian youngsters are bracketed with the handicapped and the afflicted. How on earth can groups of normal young people – with all the range of human talents and diversities – develop their potential when they are continually referred to as having 'special needs' analogous to the mentally handicapped, the educationally disadvantaged and the ex-offenders.
>
> (Cross *et al.*, 1983: 32)

The underlying confusion hinted at here is between the generalised notion of 'special needs' and the view of the young black as pathological and in need of remedial treatment. The tenacity with which such notions have maintained their hold over policies in this field suggests that there is widespread confusion between the need to eliminate the deep-seated nature of unemployment among young blacks and the need for specific measures to help those young blacks that have 'special needs'. As a consequence this has helped shift attention away from the pathological institutions to the pathological individuals.[17]

Another problem with the current quest for equal opportunity is the failure to link issues of access to markets (e.g. housing, employment) to outcomes which are a result of participating in these markets. There is a tendency, for example, to separate out questions relating to participation on training schemes from actual participation in the labour market. The success of the MSC in integrating minority youth into its schemes is taken to show that movement towards equality of opportunity is actually taking place. In terms of numbers participating in training schemes this may well appear to be true, but this in itself does not resolve the much more problematic issue of whether such developments have much effect on the structural inequalities resulting from institutionalised racialism, class stratification and age stratification. At best interventions aimed at the 'special needs' of minority youth may help individuals achieve more equality of access while leaving untouched the inequalities which affect young blacks as a social group.

It may well be argued that policies of remedial help must necessarily leave certain inequalities untouched, since the rationale of such policies is to help individuals to overcome disadvantages. This would be at least a plausible answer to the criticisms advanced about the role of training schemes. But the legitimation of current policies towards the young black unemployed rests on the premise that such interventions will render them more competitive, in the long run, with their white counterparts. As has been argued in this book, however, such a development would be a limited success, and one which may do little to alleviate the pressures which produced the 'problem' in the first place. In this sense there is an inherent contradiction between the claims on which recent policies towards young blacks have been based and the actual outcomes, since such policies attempt to define the problems faced by young blacks within strict limits. The consequences of this contradiction may be that the coming decade will witness both an increase in individual mobility among young blacks and a reproduction of the structural inequalities that characterise their everyday experiences in the urban ghettos. This in turn would undermine the broader objective of 'harmonious race relations' which is espoused as the basic policy objective.

Training for what? Labour market de-regulation, economic restructuring and young blacks

It is important to recognise that the development of political and policy responses to black youth unemployment has occurred within a wider process of ideological and political rethinking about the politics of unemployment, and that these wider processes severely constrain the effectiveness of 'equal opportunity policies'.

A mass of research evidence shows that the impact of the wholesale restructuring of the labour market that has been pursued since 1979 on the prospects of equal opportunity has not been good. This research has also shown that, in a period of economic decline and recession, the pursuit of equal opportunity is severely constrained by the pressure on firms to maximise their profitability in order to survive in the national and international markets.[18] When such pressures are combined with political initiatives which attempt to facilitate the creation of a 'strong economy', the likely result will be that black workers (particularly young ones) will not benefit substantially from symbolic equal opportunity initiatives. In fact some research has shown that unless strong and effective ameliorative measures are implemented, their position will deteriorate even further (Jenkins, 1985; Jenkins and Solomos, 1987). It is not, however, simply a matter of the reproduction of existing patterns of inequality; the danger is that the development of a 'strong economy' within a *laissez-faire* framework may help institutionalise new patterns of inequality for groups of workers who are already in a disadvantaged position.

The pursuit of labour market de-regulation as a solution to youth unemployment hinges crucially on the broader belief that the biggest single cause of unemployment is the failure of the jobs market, which has been seen as 'the weak link in our economy' (DE and DES, 1985: 1–2). Thus, when the New Training Initiative was announced in 1981, its central objectives were intimately linked to the government's broader objective of accelerating change in the labour market and shaping training around 'flexible skills' appropriate to the jobs available. Additionally, however, it is important to note that, like most Western governments in the 1980s, the British administration has sought to minimise the political costs of high youth unemployment by being seen to be doing something about the social costs of a highly volatile section of the population being out of work (Cohen, 1984: 104ff; Moon and Richardson, 1985: 91ff).

Both components of this dual strategy have been pursued, with varying degrees of consistency, since 1979. Whenever the blame for specific social or political problems – e.g. the 1980–1 'riots', increasing levels of juvenile crime, hooliganism and general discontent among young people – has been directed at youth unemployment the social policy aspects have been emphasised. But the government has consistently attempted to question the assumption that governments are in some way responsible for high levels of unemployment. This was reflected in the 1983 election, and the period since then, during which the Conservative party has argued that the record levels of unemployment were largely outside the control of the state, and were due mainly to the failure of the job market and the inability of British industry to compete on the world market.[19]

It is in this sense that we can see the various programmes of the MSC since the late 1970s not just as a response to the immediate problem of youth unemployment, but as part of a more complex de-regulation strategy which involves at least three components. First, a move away from the pursuit of the principle of full employment and the acceptance that levels of employment will be determined largely by the jobs available. Second, a conscious attempt to create a 'culture of enterprise' and new job creation by challenging existing industrial relations practices, the power of trade unions and wage levels which prevent people from pricing themselves into jobs. Third, a commitment to break out of the current economic impasse by halting Britain's declining international competitiveness and creating jobs in high-tech new technology industries and low-tech service industries.[20]

Apart from the narrow training objectives, post-1979 neo-conservative youth training policies have inherently contained wider social and political objectives which are associated with the social market principles of the majority group in the Conservative party. The vision of 'jobs for the future' is but one element of these objectives, which are invariably couched in terms of 'investing in vital skills', 'preparing for the real world outside', 'improving the efficiency and flexibility of the labour force' or 'coping with change'. The underlying objective is not only to create a more favourable culture for business and enterprise, but to shed jobs in declining industries and the state-subsidised public sector.[21] The comparison is between 'real jobs' and 'make-work jobs', the former being the product of free enterprise. Explaining his philosophy to the House of Commons Employment Committee Lord Young, then the Minister for Employment, made this point clear:

> My present task includes a number of key areas including policy towards small firms, measures to increase competition, the reduction of controls and regulations, and the coordination of policies to provide the education, training and employment of 14–18 year olds. All of these are in the context of encouraging enterprise. I see that as being at the core of my task. Enterprise is the engine of a strong economy and must be the greatest and most dependable generator of jobs, jobs both for those enterprising themselves and for those they go on to employ. What I am therefore seeking to do is to make it easier for that natural growth to happen.
> (House of Commons, Employment Committee, 1984–5: 1)

Not unnaturally the 'natural growth' which is referred to constantly in neo-conservative political language is never specified in quantitative terms, since it is a symbolic evocation of a future in which job creation will be the endogenous product of market forces. This argument has the further implication that if the state is to be centrally concerned with the employment issues, then its major concern should not be to 'create' jobs but to fan the flames of free enterprise to produce 'real' jobs.

An important example of this logic can be found in the experience of youth training policies, and their utilisation to further the overall goal of reorganising the labour market. Since 1981 a series of reports have attempted to bring about what one commentator has called 'a revolution in education and training' (Lloyd, 1985). The unifying principles behind this 'revolution' have been recently articulated in a number of official documents, most notably the White Paper on *Education and Training for Young People* (DES, 1985) and the MSC's (1985) *Development of the Youth Training Scheme* report. Starting from the twin principles of competence and competition, these reports articulate a strategy for putting Britain on an equal basis with its main competitors, and a strategy for vocational education and training as a permanent feature of the labour market. Under the general heading of improving the 'flexibility' of the labour force and extending the 'responsiveness' of workers to technical change and change in national and local labour markets, these reports offer a commitment to (a) use the current crisis in the labour market in order to develop vocational education and training for young people so that they can compete for the jobs that exist or will be created in the future, and (b) encourage 'responsiveness' so as to ensure that the kind of training provided meets the demands of employers for certain types of 'flexible skills' and competitive wage levels.

In practice this has involved the development of YTS as a two-year training package for 16–18 year olds, a further set of initiatives within full-time education and an attempt to create a new balance between training provisions and the 'jobs of the future'. *Education and Training for Young People* contains a number of passing references to the contribution that youth training can make to 'social well-being' and to 'changing attitudes' to employment and unemployment. These statements are partly an expression of a political intervention on the part of the government to overcome criticisms of its lack of concern over unemployment. But in addition they reflect a belief that 'flexibility' also involves changing attitudes to pay levels, employment protection, trade union rights and business regulation.[22] These concerns link up with the broader attack launched since 1979 on Keynesian consensus policies, and with the pressure to roll back unproductive expenditure and collective consumption so that it does not impinge on profitability.

Perhaps the most important rationale of the employment policies pursued by successive government since the 1970s, and particularly since 1979, has been the need to reorganise the labour market. Since 1979 the policies pursued by the government in relation to the labour market have had four objectives:

(1) to improve the quality of the labour force through education and training;

(2) to improve costs and incentives so that people are neither prevented from pricing themselves into jobs nor deterred from taking them up;

(3) to improve the flexibility of the labour force; and

(4) to increase freedom so that employers are not so burdened by regulations that they are reluctant to offer more jobs.

All these objectives have been seen as strategies for de-regulating the labour market and rationalising the labour force. In practice, however, the government has been equally concerned during the same period with managing the destabilising effects of mass unemployment and economic restructuring. It is the interplay between these two concerns which perhaps best explains the way in which training and labour market policies have developed since 1979.

Lord Young, who was at that time Secretary of State for Employment, neatly summarised the broad contours of government policy in this field when he argued that the main role of intervention should be to encourage 'free enterprise' and the creation of 'real jobs' in expanding productive sectors of the economy, and to enhance the competitiveness of British industry on the world market (House of Commons, Employment Committee, 1984–5). Rejecting suggestions from critics of the government's employment policies, Lord Young forcefully argued that the main objective should be to reinforce the medium-term financial strategy of controlling inflation through a programme of de-regulation, privatisation and commercialisation in order to bring Britain more in line with its main competitors, notably the United States and Japan. Within neo-conservative thought the relative prosperity and robust economic performance of these countries is the result of political, legal, cultural and labour market conditions which encourage profit maximisation, the development of new technologies and industries, and a climate in which individuals rely less on the state and more on self-help (DE and DES, 1984).

Within the logic of this neo-conservative vision the outcome of policies pursued between 1945 and 1979 (particularly in relation to financial, industrial and employment policies) was the creation of a culture against profit and heavy reliance on collective consumption and unproductive employment. The Keynesian consensus politics of this period are seen as largely responsible for the failure to overcome the conditions of economic decline and falling profits which concerned successive governments through the 1960s and 1970s. The central question which the present administration has forcefully posed since 1979 is: Why have the policies of successive governments failed to bring about a fundamental reversal of the spiral of decline which has been evident since the 1960s?

This is a theme which has been central to the debate about employment policy, in which post-1979 neo-conservative policies have effectively attempted to question the possibility of pursuing a full employment policy while attempting at the same time to regenerate the economy and encourage productive employment (Fairley and Grahl, 1983; Jessop, 1986).

From the 1981 White Paper *A New Training Initiative* (MSC, 1981a and 1981b) onwards, a succession of government reports have given expression to this vision of labour market policy. The most notable of these are *Training for Jobs* (1984), *Employment: The Challenge to the Nation* (1985) and *Education and Training for Young People* (1985). Starting from the view that there was no alternative but to abandon the Keynesian consensus policies, all these reports have been premised on the notion that in order to win the battle against economic decline, the basic objective should be 'to create a climate in which enterprise can flourish, above all by removing obstacles to the working of markets, especially the labour market'. From this basic presupposition there follows the dual strategy of using legal and political interventions to replicate the free market conditions which are supposed to exist in other economies (notably the USA) and the gradual rolling back of the boundaries of the state in order to help sustain a market-oriented approach to economic and social change.

The changing contours of official thinking on training and labour market policy are perhaps best encapsulated by the White Paper *Training for Jobs*, jointly produced by the Department of Employment and the Department of Education and Science in 1984. Arguing that past policies had failed to make training work-oriented and responsive to the needs of industry, the paper outlines the 'national effort', co-ordinated by the MSC, which it sees as necessary for the creation of a 'flexible link' between training and jobs. After restating the four objectives outlined above, and the central role of the MSC in guiding change, the paper argues:

> But the responsibility for success goes far wider. It rests above all with those involved at specific practical levels – with employers, with those who provide education and training for work in schools, colleges and elsewhere, and with all individuals who are seeking to acquire or improve the skills needed for work in the fast-moving economy. Successful training is a continuing investment in the most valuable of all our national resources – the energies and qualities of our people. In the past we have not sufficiently recognised its importance. This we must now remedy

and ensure that the skills of our people are fitted for the change of the years ahead.

(DE and DES, 1984: 16).

The linking of training to the needs of industry was not really a new initiative, since it had been a recurring theme in policy debates since the late 1970s (Gleeson, 1983). But *Training for Jobs* represented a move towards a more generalised market-oriented approach in job training, partly signalled by the limited role assigned to government policy as an agent of change. The subject of individual responsibility and the need to fit training to the needs of a de-regulated and fast-moving economy has been further developed in more recent reports. The 1985 White Paper *Education and Training for Young People* announced the move to a two-year YTS by saying that the objective was

> To produce by age 18 a very much larger flow than at present of qualified young workers capable of meeting the skill require-ments of a modern economy either directly or after some further training. In particular, the Government believes it to be right that we should set ourselves the target that all young people should enter the labour market with a qualification, either general or work-related, relevant to employment.
>
> (DE and DES, 1985: 6)

In practice the pressure to take immediate responsive action to deal with the political and social pressures associated with unemployment has not produced a consistent set of policies. As Offe has shown, to be seen to be doing something about the consequences of unemployment can be of more concern than developing a consistent market-oriented approach (Offe, 1985). The experience of youth training and unemployment policy is a good example of how these twin pressures have produced at best contradictory policies and initiatives aimed at massaging the statistics and redefining the sources of high levels of unemployment.[23]

Equal opportunity for young blacks?

In summary, the development of policies in relation to black youth unemployment and labour market restructuring more generally reveals two main points. The emphasis given to the manifest claims that the MSC and other government agencies were promoting equality of opportunity for young blacks resulted from the impact of the 1980–1 riots on the political agenda. Also, the broader policy objective of the post-1979 Conservative administrations in relation to the labour market has emphasised the need for de-regulation and the creation of an 'environment for profit'. Given this broad context, what are the implications for the pursuit of greater 'equal opportunity' for black youths, and other disadvantaged groups?

As we saw above, a major aspect of the post-riot response to black youth unemployment was the development of co-operation between the MSC and the CRE in drafting an equal opportunity strategy for the new Youth Training Scheme and encouraging public and private employment organisations to take on board more 'positive action' initiatives to help young unemployed blacks. During 1982–3 the CRE produced a statement on equal opportunity and YTS, and a broader document on equal opportunity and positive action (CRE, 1983a and 1983b). By January 1983 the MSC itself had adopted a statement on equal opportunity which stated:

> The YTS will . . . be open to all young people within the range of eligibility regardless of race, religion, sex or disability. The scheme will need to comply with legislation forbidding discrimination, but more than that it should provide special help for disadvantaged groups.
>
> (Quoted in CRE, 1983b: 1)

Beyond that the MSC, during the period since 1983, has introduced monitoring by racial and ethnic group within its schemes, supported by a number of research projects on the special needs of minority youth and adopted other positive actions towards unemployed black youths. Increasingly the MSC has been attempting to emphasise its aim of making its programmes open to all 'regardless of sex, ethnic origin or disability', and its related objective of responding to the special needs of the ethnic minorities. When the Youth Training Scheme was instituted in 1983 the MSC developed a four-point programme to promote equal opportunities:

(1) monitoring participation on various types of YTS schemes;
(2) producing publicity, marketing and training material to help promote participation and eliminate racial discrimination;
(3) Area Manpower Boards were asked to co-opt onto the Board someone to represent ethnic minorities and to develop adequate knowledge of the local black employment situation; and
(4) Application of the 1976 Race Relations Act in respect of recruitment to end termination from schemes (House of Commons, Employment Committee, 1986, Evidence from MSC: 48).

The manifest objective behind this programme was to ensure that a 'comprehensive new approach to equal opportunities' became an established part of the MSC's provision for the young unemployed.

At a public level the adoption of this programme of action has been presented as an historic transition; the MSC sees the Youth Training Scheme's pursuit of equal opportunity as a way of challenging the root causes of black youth unemployment through the provision of training in the kinds of skills that would allow young blacks to compete for the kind of new 'real jobs' in expanding sectors of the economy. But the problem remains, however, of how one analyses the actual impact of such measures on entrenched patterns of labour market inequality and racial discrimination.

'The fire this time': the context and limits of reform

The 1980 report by the Commission for Racial Equality on *Youth in Multi-Racial Society* was subtitled 'The Fire Next Time', and it warned that there was a clear risk of creating a 'whole generation of alienated black adults' and laying the seeds for urban unrest unless urgent action was taken (CRE, 1980: 7 and 59). In the aftermath of the St Paul's disturbances in April 1980 the CRE returned to this issue, and used the example of St Paul's to show that such warnings were no longer about the future, but rather about the present:

> There is no definite insurance policy against future occurrences like the events in St. Paul's. However, such events are a conformation of the reality underlying the warnings, too long ignored by policy makers, which have been given by race relations organisations. Bristol should be seen as a barometer of the situation throughout Britain today. If it is still ignored, there will be stormier weather ahead.
>
> (CRE, 1980a: 8)

This analysis is a good example of the transformation in political language used to describe the phenomenon of urban unrest during the 1980s. As we saw in chapters 2 and 3 the fear that the anger and frustration of young blacks would burst out into violence and disorder was an ever-present theme throughout the 1960s and 1970s. Once urban unrest had been placed on the political agenda, however, the question was no longer how to prevent it, but how best to respond to it and how to minimise the chances of it recurring. This new reality was the wider context within which the political responses to black youth unemployment were shaped.

I shall discuss the impact of the riots in more detail in chapters 6 and 7.

Two points are, however, worth emphasising here since they link the arguments of this chapter to the next two.

First, the stress on the part played by black youth in street violence during the 1980–1 period reinforced the pre-existing stereotype of young blacks as a subculture of violence and criminality and renewed the concern with 'riot prevention' which had been a theme of public debate from the sixties onwards. What is clear, however, is that in the aftermath of July 1981 the fear that unemployment among young blacks would lead to street violence became an important influence not only on the police but also came to be accepted as a major rationale for a more interventionist stance outside policing issues. It was no longer seen as inopportune to see youth unemployment as a highly political issue, since even neo-conservative ideologists accepted the need to provide greater support for the unemployed in order to reduce the likelihood of social dislocation and political instability (Mungham, 1982; Croft and Beresford, 1983).

Second, by reinforcing the mythology which links black youth with crime and social unrest, 'the riots' may have, in fact, strengthened the image that they needed help and assistance from the state to prevent them from becoming marginalised from society as a whole. As a consequence of this there are two slightly separate but related issues which have to be looked at in an analysis of the policy impact of urban unrest during the 1980s. First, the direct impact on actual policy outcomes in the period since the 1980–1 riots. At this level the more interventionist stance since 1981 has meant that more resources have been directed at young blacks as a social category. Nevertheless, as I have shown, we cannot simply read into this increase in resources an actual improvement in the position of young blacks in the labour market.

The third issue to be analysed is the ideological interpretation and definition of the riots. Pearson (1983) has argued that the image of the 'hooligan' has performed the function of mobilising 'respectable' fears about youth, and metaphorically about society as a whole. The riots would seem to represent an extreme example of this process, because they concretised fears about a number of 'problems' around the theme of street violence and the breakdown of law and order. Moreover, their representation by the media made them into a national issue, and one which was a political issue. It is this political aspect, which cannot be pinned down simply to policy outputs, which is perhaps the most important aspect of the ideological aftermath of the riots of 1981 and 1985.

The politics of racism and black youth

I have argued in this chapter that the pursuit of equal opportunity in the field of youth employment and youth training has been an inherently contradictory process. First and foremost, while the Manpower Services Commission and the government have manifestly proclaimed the need to give young blacks an equal chance, the consequences of their actions have been more contradictory and ambiguous. This is not surprising if we bear in mind the historical fact that state interventions always interact with wider structures, beliefs and institutions, and that even the most radical policies often produce largely symbolic changes. According to Edelman,

> The actions that governments take to cope with social problems often contradict, as well as reflect the beliefs used to rationalise those actions. While claiming to help the poor, public welfare agencies also control them and take pains to limit the help they offer. While claiming to rehabilitate prisoners and the emotionally disturbed, authorities also constrain and punish them. Governmental rhetoric and action, taken together, comprise an elaborate dialectical structure, reflecting the beliefs, the tensions, and the ambivalence that flow from social inequality and conflicting interests.
>
> (Edelman, 1977: 19)

The 'dialectical structure' of state interventions in the area of black youth unemployment is the result of the complex social and political processes which I have analysed in this and the previous chapter. Chief among these have been a preoccupation with young blacks as a 'problem category', which needed to be managed and controlled as well as 'helped' to achieve some kind of equality of opportunity. This has become a particularly dominant theme in the context of urban unrest and street violence during the 1980s (Benyon, 1984; Benyon and Solomos, 1987).

The legacy of the past fifteen years of state intervention to 'help' young blacks improve their position in employment has served to remind us once again of the difficulty of effectively tackling racism, and other forms of inequality, without challenging the structural basis for their production and reproduction. The general argument of this chapter is that the changes brought about by policy initiatives have been both superficial and symbolic. It is clear, for example, that in a number of crucial policy areas in the broad field of 'race' (education, transition from school to work/unemployment, law and order) there has been a noticeable shift in the ideology and symbolic language used to legitimise state interventions; from a desire to achieve 'assimilation', through a 'race-blind' approach to the stated objective of achieving integration, through the ideology of 'special needs'. Yet it is also clear that in all these areas there is a mismatch between stated objectives and actual outcomes, with the prospects for black youngsters becoming even more bleak as a result of the economic recession and changing political environment (Rhodes and Braham, 1981; Jenkins and Solomos, 1987).

Conclusion

The picture that this chapter has painted emphasises the limits of what has been achieved by policy initiatives aimed at improving the employment position of young blacks over the past decade. Yet it would be too deterministic to argue that nothing can be achieved within the current socio-economic situation and political climate to enhance the life chances of young blacks or their position in the labour market. Limited reforms can be achieved, and to some extent the impact of the 1980–1 and 1985 riots would lend support to the argument that direct and unconventional forms of protest can help bring about some kind of political pay-off (as we shall see in chapters 6 and 7). However, it is also clear that policy initiatives to deal with social problems are not neutral bureaucratic programmes, but comprise (to use Edelman's language) an elaborate dialectical structure, reflecting the tensions, ideologies and ambivalence that flow from social inequality and conflicting interests. There is thus some possibility for pressures resulting from the actions of disadvantaged groups to produce changes in policy orientation, but strictly within limits determined by the balance of political forces (Dearlove and Saunders, 1984; Offe, 1984). Numerous studies have shown that in a capitalist society egalitarian policy goals have a tendency to remain formal and rhetorical while an inegalitarian social structure is allowed to shape the outcome of reform strategies. This is true in all areas of social policy, and perhaps even more so in the area of race and social policy, where the volatility of public opinion has been a central theme guiding political debate on this issue.

From the above arguments it follows that a successful strategy for overcoming racism and discrimination as it affects young blacks in the labour market must take as its starting point the following two issues: First, the role of the state and political institutions in relation to the 'race question' over the past three decades cannot be understood as that of a neutral arbiter between contending interests. The political system is no more separate from the racist structure of British society than it is from the structures of social inequality. Second, the relative powerlessness of black people as a political force must be overcome if there is to be a concerted campaign against racial inequality. The idea that blacks can be 'helped' from the top is both paternalistic and unrealistic in the context of an unequal distribution of power and socio-economic resources.

What is also clear is that within the context of social and economic restructuring drastic measures are required to prevent racial inequality from becoming more entrenched and divisive. The experience of the past decade provides massive evidence against any naive optimism, but the political and ideological struggle against racism in the labour market remains a vital task for those interested in progressive social change in contemporary Britain. As this chapter has argued, however, such change will not be achieved through platitudes about equal opportunities and compensatory training, but by effective measures to tackle racism and unemployment as they affect young blacks and other sections of the black communities. We need to know more about the economic, political and ideological processes which produce too few jobs and security for young blacks, rather than assume that 'special measures' will somehow engender greater equality. The policy response to the crisis experienced by young blacks in the labour market raises important questions about the prospects for achieving radical change in existing patterns of racial inequality without a concerted national political strategy which aims to tackle the roots of racism. The experience of the past decade indicates that such a radical shift in policy orientation is not going to come about without more effective political action to challenge racism at all levels of British society.

Something to which I have already alluded, however, is that the contours of current political debates about black youth employment have been shaped by the experience of serious urban unrest during 1980, 1981, 1985 and 1986. The question of the position of young blacks in British society has come to be seen through the prism of urban violence and regular confrontations between the forces of law and order and black youths. Within this context the concern with black youth unemployment remains strong, as indicated by the policies pursued by the Manpower Services Commission. But it is the interplay between social and economic issues and urban unrest which can help us understand the politics of the black youth question during the late 1980s. It is this interplay that I shall analyse in chapters 6 and 7.

PART FOUR

Urban protest and the 'enemy within'

6

The 'social time-bomb' explodes: urban protest, youth unemployment and social policy

Introduction

Earlier in this book, in chapter 2, it was shown that during the period of the American race riots an important debate took place in Britain around the question: 'Will it happen here?' Reports by official bodies, newspaper features, academic articles and political speeches all touched on this question. In July 1967, for example, an article by the Midlands correspondent of *The Times*, under the headline 'Birmingham is no Detroit, but there are storm signals', argued that

> Race riots in North America raise an anxious question from some people living in Britain's immigrant areas. 'Could it possibly happen here?' Some people who know race relations think the answer is 'Yes'. A West Midlands expert said: 'If nothing radical is done we shall have violence here within seven or eight years'. A policeman commented: 'It is coming, it is coming.'
>
> (27 July 1967)

The article went on to argue that the 'younger or second generation immigrants' were likely to be the main group involved in violence, particularly those 'who are likely to remain in the lower level of society for the rest of their lives'. Although the article concluded that firm remedial action could prevent riots from actually occurring, the 'storm warnings' were clearly heard by others. Throughout the late 1960s and 1970s public and policy debates about young blacks resonated with images of violence and riots. Indeed examples of the drift of young blacks towards both 'criminalised' and 'politicised' violence became a cause for serious public concern.

Yet it was the outbreak of large-scale violence in a number of cities from April 1980 onwards that gave focus to this concern and provided an opportunity for a rethinking of the 'black youth question' as a whole. This chapter will explore the interplay between the responses to the post-1980 riots and the framing of political debate about black youth.

The occurrence of events such as riots does not, of course, give rise to only one kind of response. By the very nature of such events they give rise to popular ideological and political debates, to governmental and non-governmental enquiries, to academic discourses, and to comparisons with events that take place in other societies. The main object of this chapter is to examine the core ideological and policy languages through which the events of 1980–1 and 1985 have been processed, particularly in relation to 'black youth'. After a brief theoretical and historical detour on the comparative context and the emergence of 'race' as a central issue in urban protests in contemporary Britain, the chapter looks in some detail at the chief ideological and policy impacts of the 1980–1 events. Particular emphasis will be placed on the role of political languages and discourses in helping to construct an official version of both the 'causes' of urban revolt and the 'solutions' which are called for. The responses to the 1985 events are then analysed and compared to the 1980–1 events. From this comparison an attempt is made in the concluding section of the chapter to draw out some implications for the development of official policies towards young blacks. It will be argued here that with the emergence of a growing popular and official association betwen 'race', youth and urban violence we may be witnessing the racialisation of British politics along new and dangerous lines.[1] The position of young blacks may well play a leading role in this process, particularly since they are increasingly being seen as a dangerous 'enemy within'.

Responding to violent protest

Before moving on to this central issue, however, it is necessary to outline briefly the theoretical guidelines that will be used to analyse responses to urban protest in the 1980s. This framework will be based partly on the comparative experience of the United States.

There is no space in this chapter to discuss in detail the nature of the US experience of the 1960s and possible similarities and differences with the reality of Britain in the 1980s. Nor do I want to accept the argument that what we are witnessing in this country today is similar to the turmoil of many US cities twenty years ago, and that an American-type programme to tackle the roots of urban unrest can succeed in this country. But it does seem to be of some relevance to explore briefly the question of the comparative experience of collective urban violence and the responses of the state and other public institutions. This is particularly so given the numerous references in the media, official documents and academic research to the 1960s experience of the US and its implications for contemporary Britain.[2]

In an important study of the 1960s riots in the United States, Michael Lipsky and David Olson suggest that there is a distinctive dynamic to the responses which are called forth by the outbreak of forms of violent protest in advanced industrial societies. They identify the core concerns of elite responses to such events as being:

(a) the re-establishment of order and the rule of law on the streets;
(b) the minimisation of the political impact of violent protest through attempts to depoliticise them and interpret them as outbreaks of meaningless violence; and
(c) the promise that where injustices are shown to exist that something will be done about them in the near future (Lipsky and Olson, 1977: 435ff).

Without going into the rich empirical and historical detail which comes through this important study it is important to quote their conclusion. They argue that

> Two associated general processes appear to minimise the per-
> ception of the disorders as political and to reduce their potential
> political impact. One set of responses to the riots reduces the
> sense of urgency with which they are perceived among mass
> publics. A related set facilitates restoration of previously pre-
> vailing political relationships ... In every phase of the black
> protest movement since 1960 (and before), tactics used to
> compel the attention of the white majority have been condem-
> ned as dangerous and irresponsible, and inappropriate to a
> (pluralist) political system and characterised by its beneficiaries
> as exhibiting openness and accessibility to all.
>
> (Lipsky and Olson, 1977: 443 and 459)

I quote this argument at length because it points out succinctly the main issues which will be discussed in this chapter. In particular this chapter will be concerned with the second element of Lipsky and Olson's model: namely, the processes through which riots are depoliticised and catego-rised as caused by one set of factors rather than another. This will in turn link up with the question of the symbolic promises of reform which are generated by outbursts of violent protest and their actual achievements.[3]

The importance of analysing the ways in which responses to riots are structured and how such responses in turn create popular and official images about the meaning of urban unrest has been shown by numerous other US studies (for an overview see Edelman, 1971; Knopf, 1975). A case study of police violence during the Watts, Newark and Detroit riots shows that the language used by the state to describe the events during which violence occurred differed sharply from the perceptions of those who were the victims of such violence (Bergesen, 1980 and 1982).

At a broader analytical level Murray Edelman's study of the symbolic political language used to describe, categorise and make sense of political tensions has highlighted the important role that governments and political institutions can play in shaping policy and popular conceptions of ambiguous political situations. Edelman argues that there is no political reality which can be captured outside the language used to describe political events. In a perceptive analytic statement he points out that

> It is language about political events and developments that people experience; even events that are close by take their meaning from the language used to depict them. So political language is political reality; there is no other so far as the meaning of events to actor and spectators is concerned.
>
> (Edelman, 1985: 10)

In an important study of the racial tensions in America during the 1960s Edelman uses this model to show how outbreaks of violence typically give rise to mythical fears and hopes and the expenditure of vast resources aimed at coping with them. He shows that while black radicals attached a rational meaning to the riots by labelling them 'rebellions', state institutions tended to see them as atypical departures from a political process that is peaceful and rational. From this analysis he draws two basic conclusions: (a) that an event such as a 'riot' gives rise to disparate and incompatible responses to the same situation, and this leads to (b) that responses to political upheavals are not a simple way of granting and withholding substantive demands, but rather a way of also changing the demands and the expectations, of highlighting what one wants to believe and avoiding what one does not wish to face (Edelman, 1971: chapter 6).

The rest of this chapter will, implicitly, explore some aspects of Edelman's arguments and their applicability to the ways in which the post-1980 riots in Britain have been processed. Additionally, this chapter will raise some broader questions about the interplay between reform and social control during the last six years.

The 'social time-bomb' explodes: 1980–1

As shown in chapter 1, the intermingling of discourses of 'race', 'youth' and 'violence' has a relatively long history in Britain. The most notable dates pre-1970 are 1919, 1948 and 1958, when confrontations took place between groups of whites and blacks in a number of localities.[4] The Nottingham and Notting Hill confrontations in 1958 are indeed often seen as an important event in the racialisation of British politics (Miles, 1984). During the 1970s, however, attention had begun to shift from such occurrences of inter-group violence to the phenomenon of confrontations between the police and young blacks, particularly in many of the most deprived inner city areas. Dire warnings were uttered about the consequences of such localised occurrences on 'race relations', law and order and the social fabric of British society (Hall *et al.*, 1978).

As shown in chapter 3 events during the Notting Hill Carnivals of 1976 and 1977, Lewisham in 1977, Ladywood in 1977 and Southall in 1979 seemed to give further credence that violent protest was intimately linked to 'race' issues. Whether as individuals or as communities blacks were increasingly seen as a potentially volatile group, particularly within the wider context of the growth of unemployment, racism, and social inequalities.[5]

But it was the events in Bristol in April 1980 which awakened popular opinion to the dangers, and concretised these fears around the specific form of street disturbances involving violent confrontations with the police. This explains why a sober newspaper such as *The Financial Times* felt moved to warn after the Bristol riots of April 1980 that the events represented 'the worst communal violence experienced in Bristol in living memory' and 'would be repeated if nothing was done by the government and other agencies' (5 April 1980). The further outbreaks of violence in Brixton (10–13 April 1981) and nationwide (July 1981) provided the spur for a fundamental rethinking of the inter-relationship between 'race', youth and street disturbances. Again *The Financial Times* reporting of July 1981 provides a useful reference point for the ways which this linkage was being constructed. Under the headline 'Outbreak of an alien disease' it compared the violent confrontations to an epidemic to which the body politic has no immunity, and then goes on

> Never before has there been an outbreak so widespread, so sudden and so threatening in what, despite the activities of football hooligans abroad, has always been regarded as one of the world's most law abiding and peaceful countries . . . it is in a way all the more disturbing that there are so many conflicting explanations of the past week's violence . . . For if there are so many forces which are capable of sending hundreds of youths on the rampage, youths of all races, and living in relatively prosperous areas such as London, not just those suffering from desper-

ate deprivation – then the problem of restoring order and respect for law may be all the greater.

(11 July 1981)

The image of a 'law abiding and peaceful country' struck down by an 'alien disease' which could not be easily cured, symbolised many of the most dire fears about the future of British society.[6] It encapsulated the linkages which previous outbreaks of violent protest had suggested and provided an easy metaphor through which to make sense of how and why the protest movement signalled by Bristol in April 1980 had become a national phenomenon by July 1981.

The fear expressed by *The Financial Times* and other press reporting, that the very multiplicity of causes represented a problem for those interested in restoring law and order, highlights the complexity to be found in the discourses used to make sense of the riots during 1980–1 and 1985, whether one looks at official reports, the media or other reports on the events. This is why before any comparison can be made between the ideological and policy responses of these two periods it is necessary to analyse the core issues which governed the debates during both of them. It is to this question that we now turn.

Myth, metaphor and ideology

On 2 April 1980 a violent confrontation took place on the streets of the St Paul's district of Bristol between groups of predominantly black residents and the police. This was an event which immediately gave rise to public and political debate about 'racial violence', 'race riots' and the emergence of 'ghetto violence' on the American model (Joshua and Wallace, 1983).

Even the most pessimistic analyses, however, did not predict that the 'Bristol riot' would soon be replicated in various forms on the streets of London, Liverpool, Manchester and numerous other urban localities. Yet this is precisely what happened during the period from April to July 1981. The major events during this period are summarised in table 6.1.

The development of disorderly street violence on this kind of scale raised the spectre of major inner city areas becoming virtual no-go areas to the police, the formation of urban localities where 'criminalised minority sub-cultures' could take root. There was a thin line between images such as these, and the fear that Harlem-type situations were being reproduced in areas such as Brixton and Handsworth.[7] The most immediate problem was how to deal with and defuse the confrontations, but other more important questions were raised which went beyond the

Table 6.1 *Major street disorders during 1981*

Date	Description of event
10–13 April	Violent confrontations in Brixton between police and crowds of mostly black youth, resulting in nearly 200 arrests.
3 July	Confrontation between Asian youth and the police in Southall, over the arrival of skinheads for a performance of 'The 4 Skins'. On the same evening a confrontation took place in the Toxteth area of Liverpool over the arrest of a black motorcyclist.
4–6 July	A series of confrontations took place between the police and groups of black and white youth in the Toxteth area. CS gas used in Britain for the first time.
8 July	Moss Side police station in Manchester is besieged; outbreaks of violence are reported in the whole areas.
9–13 July	Outbreaks of street violence in a number of locations, including various areas of London, Liverpool, Birmingham, Wolverhampton, Leicester, Derby, Nottingham, Leeds and Huddersfield.
15 July	Police raids on Railton Road in Brixton followed confrontations between black youth and the police.
26–8 July	More confrontations in Liverpool, resulting in the death of David Moore, who was hit by a police vehicle.

Source: M. Venner, 'From Deptford to Notting Hill: Summer 1981', *New Community*, IX, (2), 1981, 203–7.

physical aspects of riot control. Why were people engaging in forms of collective violence? How had policies which aimed to deal with the social crisis of inner city areas failed to prevent violent outbursts? Were the events a sign that an 'underclass' of black citizens were so marginalised from society that they could only participate by protesting violently? Did existing social conditions and high unemployment create the basis for outbreaks of violence in the future? What role did the police play in the actual course of the events, particularly in multi-racial areas?

In whatever form they were put these questions raised problems and made both government and opposition politicians feel uneasy about their policy views on a wide variety of issues. For the purposes of this chapter I want to look at four issues which dominated ideological and policy debate about youth during and after 1980–1: (a) violence, disorder and law and order; (b) 'race', youth and violence; (c) youth unemployment and social deprivation; and (d) political legitimacy and participation. By looking at these issues it should be possible to raise questions about the short and long-term impact of the 'riots' of 1980–1, particularly in relation to the area of 'race' and youth policy.

(a)   Violence, disorder and law and order

Perhaps one way of conceptualising the impact of the events in Bristol on 2 April 1980 is to refer to some of the headlines which were used to describe them:

- 'Riot Fury: 19 police injured in pitched battle with black youths' (*The Sun*, 3 April 1980)
- 'Race mob runs riot' (*The Star*, 3 April 1980)
- 'Mob on rampage' (*Daily Express*, 3 April 1980)
- 'Riot mob stone police' (*Daily Mail*, 3 April 1980)

The *Daily Mail* report began with the image of 'mobs of black youths' roaming the streets of St Paul's and making it a virtual no-go area for the police. Images of the forces of violence and disorder challenging the forces of law and order on Britain's streets were constructed in the media, and in Parliament where the Home Secretary was moved to argue that in view of Bristol's history of good community relations 'it was with some regret, and with some surpise, locally and nationally, that this episode occurred' (*Hansard*, vol. 982, 1980: col. 657).

The outbreak of urban street violence had been predicted for some time, but Martin Kettle argues persuasively that the events in Bristol were symbolically important because

> From the moment it occurred, the likelihood of a Brixton riot and a Handsworth riot and a Moss Side riot was immeasurably increased. Bristol was the psychological breakthrough. Bristol created a climate of confidence and emulation without which the more widespread uprising of 1981 could never have occurred.
>
> (Kettle, 1982)

The symbolism went further. Through the television and media coverage of the Bristol violence the imagery of 'violence on Britain's streets' achieved a popular resonance beyond the confines of police ideologies and the warnings of the new right. The actual outbreak of collective violence in an area of supposed good relations between the police and the local communities raised the spectre of Britain becoming a 'riot-torn society' – and not only in inner city multi-racial localities. After Bristol the question was not whether rioting could occur in Britain, but when will it happen again, and where?

As indicated by the list in table 6.1 during 1981 the question was answered affirmatively in Brixton, Southall, Toxteth, Moss Side and numerous other localities. The imagery of an 'alien disease' spreading through the towns and cities of the whole country and undermining the social and moral fabric resonated through the pages of official reports, the press, the coverage on television and the debates in Parliament. A country which 'had always been regarded as one of the world's most law-abiding and peaceful countries' (*The Financial Times*, 11 July 1981) was seen as drifting into lawlessness, hooliganism, racial strife and confrontations between the police and oppositional groups. The spectre of 'ordinary people being allowed to run wild' (Worsthorne, 1978: 151) was seen as taking shape on the streets of Brixton, Southall, Liverpool, Birmingham and other major urban localities.

These streets were no longer part of the England that was peaceful and law-abiding; they were perceived almost as a different country, whose inhabitants lacked the essential characteristics of 'ordinary' English people. They were alien streets not only because of the people who inhabited them but because of the growth of violence and disorder on a level which was seen as completely new for such a peaceful country, despite evidence to the contrary. The relation of such images to 'the facts' was not the central concern, since the raw material for such imagery was much the same whether it held law and order, youth unemployment or 'race' to be the main problem. This fits in with the tendency observed by Murray Edelman among others for political beliefs to be based not on empirical observations but on cognitions about reality. As Edelman argues:

> To explain political behaviour as a response to fairly stable individual wants, reasoning, attitudes, and empirically based perceptions is therefore simplistic and misleading. Adequate explanation must focus on the complex element that intervenes between the environment and the behaviour of human beings: creation and change in common meanings through symbolic apprehension in groups of people of interests, pressures, threats and possibilities.
>
> (Edelman, 1971: 2)

Edelman cites the case of riot responses in the US to highlight his argument that political perceptions are largely based on something 'other than the facts' – with some blaming the ghetto riots on the conditions of the black poor, others seeing them as evidence of the work of outside agitators, and still others as proof of the psychopathology of the rioters (see also the analysis in Lipsky and Olson, 1977).

The imagery of violence and disorder gained a symbolic value beyond the press and the popular media. As argued in chapter 3, common sense images of violence and disorder during the 1970s fed into policy debates about the growth of a 'violent society' and the need to respond to this trend with the strengthening of the police. During 1980–1 the dominant portrayals of the events located the riots as 'mob violence', 'criminal greed' or simply the outcome of the corrupting influence of growing street violence and 'outside agitators' hell-bent on using legitimate social grievances for their own purposes. Elements of such explanations are present in parliamentary debates during this period and in the authoritative account of the Brixton events provided by Lord Scarman.[8] But perhaps the main purveyor of this perspective remained the popular press; a phenomenon noted earlier in relation to the question of crime and policing.

This is not to say that a uniform explanation of how British society, and more specifically inner city streets, had become violent was accepted. Rather, during the 1980–1 riots and their aftermath a number of explanatory variables and metaphors were used to explain the rise of a 'violent society'. Among these were explanations based on the threat posed to the values of a 'law-abiding country' by the counter-values of groups, inner city communities, and outsiders who wanted to undermine the basis of society through a cycle of violence and hard policing responses to violence. Within this framework the violence that was seen on the streets during the disorders was merely the outward appearance of a deeper problem afflicting British society, an 'alien' problem which could easily undermine the whole body-politic.

The furore about the growth of violent protest, and other forms of violence, in the inner city areas was clearly linked to the question of the role of the police as the representatives of order and the defenders of the values of society as a whole. This was by no means a new issue, since the changing role of the police and the problems faced in maintaining order was a common theme through the 1960s and 1970s.[9] By 1981, however, the occurrence of violent disorderly protests in many of the urban localities helped to transform the nature of the debate. The disorders, and other everyday forms of street and criminal violence, were seen as expressions of the social malaise of society as a whole. According to Edward Norman, the Dean of Peterhouse College, Cambridge, the young people involved in violent confrontations on the streets were a product of the changing values of society:

> The young people on the streets – black and white – have been nurtured in a society which offered them seemingly endless expectations of personal and social satisfaction. They were brought up to dwell on their rights ... The expected outcome ought to be social dislocation, increased personal indiscipline, crime and a sort of national anomie. That seems to be exactly what is coming to pass.
>
> (*Sunday Telegraph*, 19 July 1981)

As Norman makes clear this 'national anomie' was not merely the product of 'race' or 'alien cultural values' since it was both white and black youth who were involved in violent disorder. But 'race' was seen as playing an important role in sparking off the disorders, since it was the young blacks who suffered the greatest dislocation in contemporary British society.

In a very real sense, therefore, the dominant fear that emerged through the responses of official discourse, political commentators and the media to the riots during 1980–1 concerned the changing character of law and order in contemporary Britain and the dangers that this represented to the values of society as a whole. To some extent, the issue was intimately linked to related debates about the role that 'race' and youth unemployment had in bringing about the riots. But as *The Financial Times* analysis observed, the problem was not simply one of black youth or the youth of the most depressed areas, it was a national phenomenon.

Nevertheless, the representation of violence as a facet of a generalised crisis of order in British society competed with other accounts which located the source of the problem elsewhere.

One important theme during July 1981 was the question of family responsibility for keeping their children 'under control'. Both William Whitelaw and Kenneth Oxford, the outspoken Chief Constable for Merseyside, made widely publicised speeches during this period which argued that the responsibility for the riots lay with parents who either did not care about what their children did or who could not control them. Reporting these statements *The Times* reported on a plan to involve parents in 'the consequences of offences committed by their children' (10 July 1981). *The Daily Telegraph* reported Mr Oxford as saying

> What in the name of goodness are these young people doing on the streets indulging in this behaviour and at that time of night? Is there no discipline that can be brought to bear on these young people? Are the parents not interested in the futures of these young people?
>
> (8 July 1981)

A number of other stories on a similar theme were published throughout July.[10] Indeed the Prime Minister herself was able to use the arguments of her Home Secretary to counter claims that her government bore a 'social responsibility' for the riots. After all, she was able to argue, if parents cannot control the actions of their children what can the government do to stop them from engaging in 'hooliganism' and a 'spree of naked greed' (*The Times*, 10 July 1981).

Such arguments were not used in isolation. As we shall see in the following section they resonated in important ways with the symbolic use of racial symbols to explain violent disorder, particularly in relation to the supposed pathology of the West Indian family and the social 'alienation' of young blacks.

(b) 'Race', youth and violence

If the imagery of violence and disorder sweeping the country like an epidemic against which the body politic had no defence was the backdrop of much of the debate during 1980–1, it was the issue of racial disadvantage and racism (particularly in relation to young blacks) which quickly came to the forefront, particularly after July 1981. This racialisation of debate about disorderly protest linked the issue of street violence to the specific social conditions of one social group and thus became one of the most controversial aspects of ideological and policy responses to the riots.

During 1980–1 there was much debate in Parliament, the media, official reports and in academic studies about whether the events in places such as Brixton and Toxteth, and other localities, were 'race riots'.[11] The confused nature of this debate was partly the result of a fear that if the riots were labelled as 'race riots' it would increase the likely destabilising role that 'race' could play. But it also reflected a wider ambiguity about the relationship between the growth of street violence in society as a whole and the involvement of inner city black communities in such violence.

A measure of this ambiguity can be gained from the treatment of this issue in the Scarman Report on the Brixton disturbances, which was published amid a wave of publicity in November 1981. Lord Scarman's Report, while denying that the confrontations were 'race riots' as such, provided an influential analysis of the link between disorderly protest and 'race', particularly when it argued that 'the riots were essentially an outburst of anger and resentment by young black people against the police' (Scarman, 1981: para. 3.110). From Lord Scarman's perspective the riots could not be understood unless they were seen in the context of the complex political, social and economic factors which created a 'predisposition towards violent protest', and a central component of this, from his standpoint, was the position of ethnic minorities (and particularly young blacks) in inner city areas.

Leaving aside the somewhat convoluted debate about whether the disorders could be labelled a 'race riot', it is perhaps not surprising that many others apart from Lord Scarman saw 'race' or 'racial disadvantage' as at the core of any rounded understanding of the events. There was of course not one but many attempts to explain the link between 'race' and disorderly protest. These ranged from the pronouncements of Enoch Powell and other right-wing politicians in favour of repatriation to more complex models of how the compounded disadvantages of inner city blacks may lead them to be more predisposed to disorderly protest. In this sense Miles is right to emphasise that outbreaks of violence which involve 'race' are not racialised in a simple fashion, and may involve quite disparate attempts by the government, politicians, the press and other sections of the media, pressure groups and black groups themselves to construct ideological and political interpretations of such events (Miles, 1984: 10–14). But it is also true to say that the racialisation of the riots resonated with themes that were more dominant than others. As opposed to the questions of racism, political exclusion, economic and social inequality, and social isolation the dominant concerns centred on the cultural backgrounds of black people, the social environment in which they lived, and the street cultures and activities of the 'ghetto' life they created.

The treatment of the 'race issue' in the press exemplifies this general point. Recurring images were resonant with such phrases as 'black war on police', 'the devastating spiral of violence and poverty', 'a spree of naked greed', 'profile of a ghetto', 'the race bomb', 'cities of the lost'. Blacks, and particularly young blacks, were seen as the carriers of cultural values and attitudes which partly reflected the depression and chaos of the inner city areas as a whole, but also contained 'alien' values imported into this country through immigration and the concentration in inner city areas of a 'black British'-born population that suffered from unemployment, social and cultural alienation and a 'ghetto mentality'. Such images, which recurred in a number of press stories during 1980–1, seemed to have served two functions. First, they helped to focus attention on the supposed characteristics of inner city areas and their residents without looking at the history of how such areas had developed and the role of political and economic forces in the creation of 'ghetto' areas. Second, they helped to reassure society at large that violence was the product of aberrant conditions in inner city areas with a particular type of inhabitant, in other words that the riots were 'atypical departures from a political processes that is peaceful and rational' (Edelman, 1971: 1).

Lord Scarman's model of the riots as an 'outburst of anger by young black people against the police' was built around a somewhat different assessment of the inter-relationship of 'race' to 'violent disorder'. The brief of the Scarman Inquiry had been to look into the policing aspects of the Brixton disorders of 10–12 April 1981, though this brief was extended somewhat in July 1981 to cover other localities.[12] Scarman identified two views that were commonly held as to the causation of the disorders. The first explained them in terms of oppressive policing, and in particular the harassment of young blacks. The second explained them as a protest against society by deprived people who saw violent attacks on the forces of law and order as a way of calling attention to their grievances. For Scarman both views were a simplification of a complex reality, or at least 'not the whole truth'. He linked the 'social' and 'policing' aspects of the complex reality of places like Brixton in his discussion of the following issues:

(1) the problems which are faced in policing and maintaining order in deprived, inner city, multi-racial localities;

(2) the social, economic, and related problems which are faced by all residents of such areas; and

(3) the social, economic and racial factors which were faced by black residents, especially the young blacks (Scarman, 1981: paras. 2.1–2.38).

He saw the existence of all these aspects together in areas such as Brixton as creating a 'predisposition towards violent protest', particularly among the young blacks who feel the grievances most strongly. Lord Scarman noted that 'many of them, it is obvious, believe with justification, that violence, though wrong, is a very effective means of protest' (*ibid.*: para. 2.38).

While Lord Scarman himself was quite clear in saying that however widely held the grievances of young blacks were this did not provide an excuse for disorder, or excuse the 'criminal offences' committed during the riots, he did argue forcefully that in a situation where young blacks felt neither 'socially or economically secure' more or less regular confrontations with the police may become the norm of their daily experience. Indeed, from his perspective, the weak family structures of the black community helped to make this more likely. He argued that

> Without close parental support, with no job to go to, and with few recreational facilities available, the young black person makes his life on the streets and in the seedy commercially run clubs of Brixton. There he meets criminals, who appear to have no difficulty in obtaining the benefits of a materialist society.
>
> (Scarman, 1981: para. 2.23)

Though he accepted that the drift to crime and 'alienation' was by no means uniform, he did say in his conclusions that without a knowledge of the family, educational, unemployment and discrimination problems faced by young blacks no efforts to prevent further riots would be successful (*ibid.* paras. 8.2–8.12).

The liberal model of the Scarman Report thus relied on a rather ambiguous interconnection between social inequality, racial discrimination and policing to explain the 'predisposition to violence' on the part of young blacks. Its policy impact has sometimes been exaggerated, as we shall see in the concluding section of this chapter. For – with the open or covert support of a number of Conservative MPs, and newspaper columnists[13] – it still proposed a clear racial explanation of the riots and called for repatriation as the only viable solution. In the parliamentary debate on the Brixton events, for example, Enoch Powell linked the riots to the presence of large and growing 'immigrant' communities in the main urban localities of Britain:

> In reflecting upon these events, will the Home Secretary and the Government bear in mind, in view of the prospective future increase in the relevant population, that they have seen nothing yet.
>
> (*Hansard*, vol. 3, 1981: col. 25)

By July 1981 he developed this analysis in his speeches and in the media coverage given to his pronouncement on Brixton. There were three basic elements to the Powellite explanation of the riots. First, he argued that in some areas of inner London and other major cities between one quarter and one half of the population under 25 was from the New Commonwealth. Second, he foresaw that over the next generation this population would double, or perhaps treble. Third, and as an inevitable consequence of the first two elements, Powell foresaw increasing conflict between New Commonwealth people and their descendants and the 'indigenous population'. This would lead to places like 'inner London becoming ungovernable or violence which could only be effectually described as civil war' (*Hansard*, vol. 8, 1981: col. 1412).

A modified version of the Powell argument can be discerned in some of the media coverage during April 1981 and July 1981. Ronald Butt, a regular columnist on race and related issues, argued forcefully that there was a need for more open debate on the social and law and order consequences of immigration.[14] Writing in both *The Times* and the *Daily Mail* he argued that the Scarman Inquiry could do worse than look at 'the evil mischief makers who are so quick to brand us all "white racists" if it wanted to find out the real causes of the riots' (*The Times*, 9 July 1981; *Daily Mail*, 10 July 1981). Butt argued that perhaps the most important reason for violence and disorder was to be found in the impact of immigration on the culture and values of inner city working-class communities. He saw the prospect that the vast majority of 'ordinary decent people' will become utterly resentful of being stigmatised as a 'racialist white society'. The argument that black youth were rioting as a protest against racism and disadvantage was seen by Butt as simply a way of confusing the central question of immigration, with which 'ordinary people' were concerned. 'They have to live with a problem not of their making as a result of which vast areas of their cities have been changed beyond recognition' (*The Times*, 9 July 1981). This 'problem' was the presence of black communities who had different values and cultures from the indigenous 'English majority'. Few of the press commentators, such as Butt, went as far as Powell in calling for repatriation as the only solution. But it should be noted that apart from his parliamentary speeches and the press coverage they received, Powell wrote articles in both *The Sun* and the *Sunday Express* during July 1981 which openly called for a voluntary repatriation scheme.

The complex mixing of images of race, youth and violence do not lend themselves to a simple mechanical view that the riots were racialised only through the language and metaphors which blamed blacks for the breakdown of law and order, the decline of the inner cities and the loss of community. As the discussion above has shown, the argument of the Scarman Report and related liberal discourses utilised the symbols of 'race' and 'black youth' in a somewhat different manner. In addition it should be noted that only a minority of the press or politicians pursued the issue of immigration or 'race' as the central theme, the majority preferring to label the activities of young blacks on the streets as 'mindless' and 'irrational', or as unrepresentative of 'decent black people'.[15] Nevertheless, the riots did act as a major push towards the construction of the question of 'black youth' around the themes of street violence and the breakdown of order on the streets of inner cities. They helped to construct a strong imagery of young blacks as a corrupting influence in inner city areas, as a collectivity which was increasingly seeing itself as outside the moral and legal restraints of the wider society.

(c) Youth unemployment and social deprivation

One of the characteristics of official elite responses to violent protests, according to Edelman, is the contradictory nature of the relationship between political language and political practice (Edelman, 1971). This is well exemplified by the debate during 1980–1 over the role of youth unemployment, and unemployment generally, in causing the riots.

In the immediate aftermath of Brixton in April 1981 the Prime Minister took part in a confrontation in Parliament about the terms of reference of the Scarman Inquiry. Replying to a question from a Labour

MP she questioned the links he made between unemployment and the riots in these terms: 'If you consider that unemployment was the only cause – or the main cause – of the riots, I would disagree with you. Nothing that has happened in unemployment would justify those riots' (Margaret Thatcher, quoted in *The Financial Times*, 15 April 1981). What is interesting here is that while Thatcher is opposed to any idea that unemployment was the main cause of the riots, she also argues that unemployment levels cannot 'justify' rioting. It is perhaps this second element of her intervention which is the most important, since it highlighted the politicised nature of the youth unemployment issue, with the government eager to challenge any idea that by being 'responsible' for unemployment its policies could also be blamed for the riots. But by not excluding unemployment as a small contributory factor, the Prime Minister could argue that the government was doing something about the riots by introducing special measures for the young unemployed and the inner city areas.

The terms of this discourse about youth unemployment were sharpened by the continual references made to this issue after the April riots in Brixton and the riots of July 1981. Despite the attempt by the Prime Minister to distance the 'causes' of the riots from youth unemployment and social deprivation, it became quite clear through 1981, and perhaps even more so during 1982 and 1983, that these issues were popularly seen as important factors in the causal chain that led to the riots.

The comments on youth unemployment and urban deprivation in the Scarman Report referred to above indicate that, apart from the Labour party, a sizeable body of liberal opinion accepted some kind of link between the riots and youth unemployment, and deteriorating 'social conditions'. Indeed, apart from Lord Scarman, both the Labour and Liberal parties and sections of the popular and serious press organised their responses to the riots around the symbols of youth unemployment and the compounded social disadvantages suffered by the residents of the inner cities. The politicised nature of this response was shown in the links made, by Labour in particular, with the post-1979 Conservative policies on unemployment and welfare. But at a broader level the youth unemployment/social deprivation explanations of the riots were representative of fears about the consequences of growing social and racial inequality on the 'rule of law' which were shared by elements of Conservative opinion.[16]

The youth unemployment and social deprivation arguments cannot, of course, be completely separated from the questions of violence and race. Take for example the following editorial from the *Daily Mirror* during July 1981, which began by reflecting Enoch Powell's explanation:

> What is happening in Britain is not Enoch Powell's prophecy of
> 13 years ago coming true. The truth was explained last Wednes-
> day by Ted Heath.
>
> He blamed government policies which cause high unemploy-
> ment among young people, particularly blacks, for increasing
> racial tension and juvenile crime.
>
> A Government that offers no future to youngsters is breeding
> a generation without hope.
>
> And Bristol, Brixton, Southall and Toxteth will just be the
> beginning.
>
> (*Daily Mirror*, 6 July 1981)

This theme of 'high unemployment', 'increasing racial tension and crime'
and 'a generation without hope' resonated in the press, in official
responses to the riots, some of the police responses, and most importantly the Scarman Report.[17] In essence the link between social causes
and violence on the streets was not established by references to the
'disease of violence' spreading through Britain or to 'immigration and
race', but by a more complex framework which saw the riots as the
outward appearance of underlying problems. *The Guardian* talked of a
'cycle of black alienation and insensitive policing' as the root of the
problem, though by no means the only issue (7 July 1981). From this
perspective the hostility of young blacks towards the police was not
simply a manifestation of a broader trend towards violence in society or
the different cultural values of West Indian communities but the product
of social conditions which created a 'generation on the scrap heap' and
resentment among those young people who did not see themselves as
having a future in this society.

Apart from the general form of the 'social causes' explanation, which
rapidly became part of the common sense of liberal public opinion during
1980–1, a specific form was articulated by many figures of the parliamentary Labour party and the Labour movement more generally.[18]
During 1980–1 these included Tony Benn, who asked the Home Secretary after the Bristol riot to look into the causes of disorder in the St Paul's
area from the point of view of 'rising unemployment, social deprivation
and the circumstances in our urban areas which affect our communities
as a whole, not just the ethnic minorities' (*Hansard*, vol. 982, 1980: col.
663). But perhaps the most consistent use of 'social causes' type of
arguments during 1980–1 is to be found in the interventions by Roy
Hattersley, who acted as the main Labour spokesman on the riots and
related issues both in Parliament and the media. During the main
parliamentary debate about the July disorders he developed an analysis

of the riots which began from the premise that the conduct of the police was not the principal issue. Rather he saw the central causal cycles as 'the conditions of deprivation and despair in the decaying areas of our old cities', (*Hansard*, vol. 8, 1981: col. 1408), areas which he saw as sharing the following characteristics:

(1) Housing that is decaying and inadequate, largely through the lack of adequate investment in public housing provision.

(2) Amenities that were inadequate to the needs of such areas, and which did not cater for the specific requirements of all communities.

(3) Inadequate educational provision, particularly remedial education for deprived families and nursery places for deprived children.

(4) High unemployment, particularly among the young, which bred despair and led to outbreaks of violence.

Although he also included in his speech references to the role of the police, racial discrimination and political alienation, he left Parliament in no doubt of what he saw as the fundamental causes of unrest (*Hansard*, vol. 8, 1981: cols. 1408–10). Rather similar interventions were made by other Labour front-benchers and backbench MPs during 1981, and during 1982 in the debate about how best to implement the social policy components of the Scarman Report.

Indeed the search for social causes of disorder around the resonant themes of poverty, unemployment and deprivation is by no means a feature unique to Britain, as the comparative experience of the United States also shows (Lipsky and Olson, 1977). But the term 'social causes' is in fact itself a simplification, since in much of the debate during 1980–1 the symbolic evocation of social deprivation as the main cause of disorder coincided with calls for strong action against the rioters. The search for 'fundamental causes' allows for a separation of basic differences of approach on major political issues to be balanced by agreement on the need to deal firmly with the 'symptoms', such as arson, assault and looting. Thus the same speech by Hattersley accepts the government's call to support the police in 'restoring order', and argues that the people who commit criminal activities 'must be caught, prosecuted, convicted and punished and the police must be given whatever protective equipment is necessary for the proper and responsible discharge of their duties' (*Hansard*, vol. 8, 1981: col. 1405).

This duality explains why one of the main newspapers which explained both the 1981 and 1985 riots as the outcome of social deprivation carried an editorial on 8 July 1981 which labelled the Liverpool violence of the previous night 'A spree of naked greed' (*Daily Mirror*, 8 July 1981). This was a theme that was taken up later by Margaret Thatcher and that was to resonate through much of the coverage of the 1985 events.[19] But if one looks more closely at the editorial, what becomes clear is that it makes a distinction between the 'causes of the original troubles', namely housing, education and unemployment, and the actions of those who rode on the back of the socially deprived to accumulate consumer goods. The importance of the headline, however, is that it warns us against making too strict a separation between the themes of law and order, 'race', and social deprivation. In practice there were often components of all three of these themes mixed together, and influencing the inflection which was given to the link between the underlying causes and the symptoms of disorder.

In any case, the search for social causes for the riots did not necessarily involve a simple dichotomy between law and order and social discourses. During a tense intervention in Parliament, a number of Labour MPs sought to point out to the Prime Minister that unless she took measures to deal with unemployment among the young, particularly black youth, she would be allowing conditions to flourish that could bring about further riots. To this she responded

> It is because our young people are unemployed that we give priority to the youth opportunities programme . . . In the area where violence and rioting has occurred a good deal of it has been carried out by children of school age, some of them aged between 9 and 16. That has nothing whatever to do with the dole queue.
>
> (*Hansard*, vol. 8, 1981: col. 576)

This line of argument in effect succeeded in expressing concern for unemployment and at the same time asserting that, because of the age of some of those involved, that 'violence and rioting' was not necessarily related to the dole queue. From this Mrs Thatcher was able to conclude that the violence in the streets of areas such as Toxteth was 'totally inexcusable and totally unjustifiable'.

Precisely because the social deprivation model of the riots was related closely to the problem of the impact of government policies on the poor residents of the inner city areas and the young unemployed it was perhaps the most contested symbol. Even an ambiguous admission of a link between youth unemployment and the riots raised the question of whether violent protest was a legitimate weapon in the struggle to change the priorities of economic policy. In this sense the responses to the riots were linked to broad questions about political legitimacy.

(d) Political legitimacy and participation

The centrality of the question of political legitimacy in all debates about the riots was captured clearly by much of the popular media coverage, as well as the Scarman Report and parliamentary debates during this period.[20] During the same main parliamentary debate on the July riots, William Whitelaw made this point succinctly when he argued that the riots represented a danger to the whole moral order and the rule of law which must (a) be dealt with quickly by the police, and (b) be responded to by social and political measures which 'promote the conditions in which violence does not flourish but is rejected, so that a peaceful and harmonious society is a reality and seen to be a reality for all people' (*Hansard*, vol. 8, 1981: col. 1402). Recognising that the riots were a sign of failure on the part of society and its consensual framework, Whitelaw called for a concerted strategy to promote the integration of all groups within the institutions of the political system, thus making sure that 'violence cannot flourish'.

The threat to political legitimacy which the riots represented was perceived somewhat differently by Ronald Butt, who saw them as a sign of the imposition of large-scale immigration against the wishes of 'ordinary people', with the consequent challenge this represented to 'their own sense of identity' (*The Times*, 9 July 1981). From this perspective the fault was not with the society, but with the politicians who let immigration happen and with the black migrants and their descendants.[21]

Whichever of these two perspectives was adopted, however, the challenge to political legitimacy was clear enough to see during 1981, and through 1982, and the various attempts by the government to respond to the fears that the political stability of society as a whole was under threat. While the riots of 1980–1 may not have been a full-blown 'legitimation crisis' of the Habermas model,[22] they certainly succeeded in pushing onto the public policy agenda a debate which had been going on at various levels of the state about the future of political order and legitimacy within British society. At an embryonic level, elements of this debate about the future of 'order' and 'disorder' in British society were evident from the 1960s onwards, certainly in relation to violent protest and partly in relation to 'race' (Hall *et al.*, 1978; Dearlove and Saunders, 1984). As I have argued elsewhere:

> The image of forces beyond the control of ordinary 'British people' is a recurrent theme in neo-conservative racist 'theory', particularly since it fits in with the common sense notion that enemies within – subversive moles – are undermining the

structures of society. It connects with common sense ideas about why racial 'problems' arise by identifying 'racial violence' as an illegitimate alien presence.

(Solomos *et al.*, 1982: 29)

Within this framework the threat to 'legitimacy', whether real or not, was not caused by one factor alone since it was the whole social fabric that was at stake.

This was made even more clear by the official reaction to the 1980–1 riots which saw the 'rule of law' as being under threat from street violence and disorder in a way which had not been experienced in 'living memory'. The sinister nature of this threat was given added meaning by the linking of the riots to wider political agitation and extremist politics. While the media portrayed the actions as largely 'mindless violence' and a 'spree of hooliganism' there were also constant references to 'outside agitators', 'masked men' and 'riot organisers' throughout the period from April to July 1981 and afterwards.[23] Sometimes this imagery was directly related to 'race' by labelling the outsiders as 'black militants' or by linking them to specific black organisations and individuals. At a more banal level, however, the violence was seen as the natural outcome of the 'tinder-box' environment which had been developing in inner city areas for decades, particularly in those that were defined as 'multi-racial'. As we shall see this was a theme that became even more central in ideological and policy responses during and after the 1985 riots.

1985: Here we go again

During the period from early 1982 to the outbreak of violence in Handsworth over 9–10 September 1985 there was much debate around the theme of 'Where did the riots go?' Various explanations were offered as to why the serious outbreaks of 1981 were not repeated during 1982, 1983 or 1984, ranging from changing police tactics, the impact of social policy measures, the cathartic effect of 1980–1 and the changing forms of black political participation.[24] Any complacency that had developed, however, was shattered by Handsworth exploding on a scale which had been forecast many times, but had never actually occurred. After all this was the area which was seen as a model of police–community relations, where police tactics during 1981 had been praised by Lord Scarman, and where on 7–8 September 1985 a 'successful' Handsworth Festival had been reported in the local press (*Birmingham Evening Mail*, 9 September 1985).

The 'shock' and 'surprise' of the police in the area may have been somewhat contrived but the impact of Handsworth locally and nationally was clear enough to see in press coverage.[25] The local Birmingham press and the national papers noted that Handsworth had been singled out in 1981 by Lord Scarman as an area where the use of community policing and other strategies by the police, along with help from black leaders and the local authority, had helped to defuse a politically explosive situation (Scarman, 1981: appendix B). *The Guardian* editorial on September 11 was headed 'Suddenly it all goes wrong again' and resonated with comparisons with 1981, and expressions of concern about why a place like Handsworth could explode so suddenly. Questioning whether either explanation based on the role of the police or on social deprivation was adequate the editorial argued:

> Handsworth, in the immediate aftermath, is an event for signal dismay simply because, amid the rubble, there is no neat overwhelmingly evident root of the rampage. At Brixton one could identify things that went wrong. Here, almost as the last of the local carnival drums fell silent, everything went wrong for no apparent reason.
>
> (*The Guardian*, 11 September 1985)

Immediate responses to the Handsworth riot highlight such phrases as the 'riot that blew out of nothing', 'carnival to carnage', 'nightmare of 1981 returns', 'a long anticipated explosion', along with images of war such as 'the blitz of Handsworth'. To see the riots in this light helped to perpetuate the image that had developed between 1981 and 1985 that the responses to the 1980–1 riots had helped to bring about relative peace. It also focused attention on Handsworth as an area with a reputation for crime, drugs and general lawlessness.[26]

Whatever the impact of the Handsworth events, however, it was nothing compared to the public and official response to the subsequent events in Brixton 9–10 September, Toxteth during 1 October, and Tottenham during 5–6 October. The sequence of events is summarised in table 6.2.

The extent of these events once again helped crystallise a set of symbolic political and ideological responses which attempted to explain the events and suggest possible solutions. Many of the themes that were evident in 1980–1 recurred again in 1985, particularly in relation to the question of black youth. But precisely because 1985 was seen as a recurrence, albeit on a new scale, of earlier events the symbolic language used to explain and describe both what happened and the necessary solutions took on somewhat new forms. These centred particularly around the following four core issues: (a) the vicious cycle of inner city

Table 6.2. *Major street disorders during September–October 1985*

Date	Description of event
7–8 September	Handsworth Festival takes place, and police and the local press report it to be a great success.
9–10 September	Confrontations between police and groups of youth and other residents in the Handsworth area of Birmingham.
28 September	Mrs Cherry Groce is hit by a police bullet during a search of her house in Brixton; major confrontations occur between crowds of youth and the police.
29 September	Brixton disorders continue in the evening and late into the night.
1 October	Tension rises in Toxteth, Broadwater Farm Estate in Tottenham, and Peckham in South London
5 October	Mrs Cynthia Jarrett collapses and dies during a search of her house on Broadwater Farm Estate by police; tension rises in the area as news of her death spreads.
6 October	Confrontations between police and local residents take place at Broadwater Farm Estate in Tottenham; during confrontations a policeman, PC Keith Blakelock, is killed.

Source: Newspaper coverage during September–October 1985.

deprivation; (b) the social condition of young blacks and youth in general; (c) policing the 'enemy within'; and (d) the 'riot-torn society'. In analysing the language and symbols used to construct these explanations the comparison with 1980–1 will be kept to the forefront. This will then tie in with the impact of both periods on the political agenda about the position of young black people in British society, an issue discussed in the concluding section of this chapter.

(a)   The vicious cycle of inner-city deprivation

The references above to the immediate responses to the Handsworth riot show how the question of the specific nature of the localities in which the disorders took place figured largely in debates during September–October 1985, and in the subsequent debates which developed during the various inquiries into the riots. But the symbolic meanings attached to the notion of inner city deprivation took on a somewhat different form in 1985 as compared to 1981.[27] These were over-determined by the interventions of the Home Secretary, Douglas Hurd, the West Midlands Chief Constable, Geoffrey Dear, and the local Labour MP for the area in which the Handsworth riot took place, Jeff Rooker. During the week after the Handsworth riot all three made public statements which attempted to construct an explanation of the events, and particularly to explain what, if any, relation there was between the violence and inner city deprivation.

All three were clear that although there were social problems in the area, the immediate cause of the riot was not this background of deprivation but the growth of crime and drug dealing in the area and the consequent vicious cycle of deprivation–crime–police response. Geoffrey Dear, for example, stated the day after the first disorders that after years of good community relations the only way to see the events was as 'pure naked vandalism and outrageous violence and theft' (*Daily Mail*, 10 September 1985). The idea that drugs and criminal activity were a causal factor was corroborated by Rooker, and by another Labour MP, Robin Corbett, who saw the riot as 'more drug and crime-related than anything else' (*Birmingham Evening Mail*, 10 September 1985). Despite the intervention of other Labour politicians, including Neil Kinnock, to warn against too easy a dismissal of unemployment, heavy policing and social deprivation as causal factors, the notion that crime was a mainspring of the events took hold. The resonant themes were not the 'social evils' which had figured so prominently in 1981 but images of 'a lust for blood', an 'orgy of thieving' and 'pure naked hooliganism', a 'cry for loot and not a cry for help'. Such images were no longer seen necessarily as symptoms of urban deprivation but part of a 'vicious spiral of hate' which was threatening the very existence of civilisation and democracy.[28] These were themes that were taken up in the press, in Parliament and in related official statements on the riots in Brixton and Tottenham as well. As Home Secretary, Douglas Hurd, took the lead in developing such arguments and using them to portray a model of what should be done to 'ride the storm'. In a series of press and parliamentary statements he articulated a version of the riots which saw them as 'unjustifiable' and a 'criminal activity'.[29] In a widely reported speech to police chiefs he was reported as saying:

> Handsworth needs more jobs and better housing. But riots only destroy. They create nothing except a climate in which necessary development is even more difficult.
>
> Poor housing and other social ills provide no kind of reason for riot, arson and killing.
>
> One interviewer asked me whether the riot was not a cry for help by the rioters. The sound which law-abiding people heard at Handsworth was not a cry for help but a cry for loot.
>
> That is why the first priority, once public order is secure, must

be a thorough and relentless investigation into the crimes which were committed.

(*The Daily Telegraph*, 13 September 1985)

What is even more interesting is that this argument was used by Hurd as support for his decision to set up a police inquiry into the events rather than a Scarman-type investigation.[30] What was needed he argued was not a review of general social issues or questions about youth unemployment but a clear, factual account of the crimes committed. The logic of this position was that the riots were not a sign of the failure to carry out the concerted social policy reforms recommended in 1981 by Lord Scarman and others, but a sign that a spiralling wave of crime in inner city areas had produced the need for a firmer police line against criminal activities.

Even though the spread of the violence to Brixton, Tottenham and other areas by early October raised doubts about the relevance of the 'crime' factor in all areas, it was this mythology of the 'crime-ridden inner city ghettoes' that acted as a linking theme in both media and political responses to the riots.[31] The Broadwater Farm events were explained in much of the press by references to the nature of the estate and the people who lived there. Thus the black people who lived there were pathologised once by their 'black culture' and again by their association with the cultures of poverty of the inner city areas. *The Daily Telegraph* compared the area with an infamous area of Belfast when it described Broadwater Farm as 'Like the Divis Flats with reggae' (8 October 1985) and *The Observer* described it as a 'Fortress on a knife-edge of violence' (13 October 1985).

The pathology of inner city, particularly largely black, localities was used to explain why the riots occurred even by those who were critical of the more simplistic explanations based on crime and drugs. Within the Labour party Gerald Kaufman acted as the main critic of the government and police explanations, by stressing the issues of social deprivation, unemployment and racial disadvantage. Disagreeing with Labour colleagues such as Jeff Rooker, he asked the Home Secretary why, if the riots were 'not a social phenomenon but crimes', 'the crimes were committed in Handsworth and not in the Home Secretary's constituency of Witney?' (*Hansard*, vol. 84, 1985: col. 349). Lending support to Lord Scarman's argument that certain social conditions created a predisposition towards violence, he pointed out that Birmingham, Brixton and Broadwater Farm were among the most deprived areas in the United Kingdom and suffered very high rates of unemployment. From this he concluded that the basic reasons for the riots lay in social deprivation,

racial discrimination, bad housing and unemployment, and not in crime
and drugs. He saw such social conditions as producing a situation of
'inner despair', and a cycle of growing urban violence and policing
responses which bred more violence and disorderly protest.[32]

Other more ambiguous uses of social deprivation and inner city
pathology arguments were evident in responses to the 1985 riots. A good
example is represented by the construction by sections of the press, some
politicians and a number of writers on 'race', of the Handsworth riot as
an example of growing internecine warfare between the West Indian and
Asian communities in the area.[33] Such explanations took on-board the
notion that a culture of poverty was a common feature of many of the
depressed inner city areas, but gave this argument a markedly different
twist from the arguments outlined above. Rather than seeing such areas
as breeding grounds for generalised violence and anti-police sentiments,
the 'West Indians vs Asians'-type explanations saw them as leading to
increasing ethnic competition between the economically successful and
unsuccessful components of the local minority population. Although
such notions were criticised by both the local West Indian and Asian
Handsworth communities, and later by other commentators, in the first
days of debate about the causes of the riots they played an important role
in the articulation of the notion that in the context of the inner city
localities violence was a normal aspect of relations between black groups
as well as in relations between such groups, the wider society, and the
police.[34]

The 'cities in the frontline' were constructed through such arguments
into places where a combination of factors had created dangerous classes
of people, particularly young blacks, who were in a sense outside of the
norms of society as a whole. Among these dangerous classes it was the
young, and particularly young blacks, who were seen as representing the
main danger to order and political stability.

(b) The social condition of young blacks and youth in general

The second important theme in responses to the 1985 riots centred
around the specific question of the social conditions of young blacks in
inner city areas, and the position of the young unemployed more
generally. This was an important issue during 1980–1 as well, and indeed
played a central role in Lord Scarman's model of the social causes of
violent protest.[35] By 1985, however, youth unemployment generally,
and black youth unemployment in particular, had become much more
politicised and was widely debated by the media, in Parliament, and in
numerous official and quasi-official bodies (Solomos, 1985; Moon and
Richardson, 1985). This increased politicisation was reflected in the ways

in which the interconnections between the 1985 riots and the social conditions of young blacks and inner city youth in general was constructed.

Taking the issue of young blacks first, as argued above the responses to the whole phenomenon of urban violence were in many ways structured by the question of 'black youth' and the various meanings attached to this social category. These meanings were by no means unchanging, and there certainly seems to have been a major change between 1981 and 1985. In 1981 the debate about black youth and the riots was organised around the question of unemployment. In 1985, however, references to youth unemployment tended to form part of a wider package of issues about youth and the socio-political position in Britain in the 1980s. Public debate on the riots resonates with references to the interplay between the growing social dislocation of youth in a society of mass unemployment, the special position of young blacks in a society which rejected them, and the impact of urban decay on the propensity of black and white youth to engage in acts of violent disorder. But even when questions relating to the social position of all young people were raised, the presence of 'black youth' in the social construction of the riots was not necessarily displaced.[36]

Again the Handsworth riot and the press coverage which it received provides a good example of this interplay between 'race' and 'youth' in the explanation of the riots. On 11 September most of the tabloid papers carried a picture of a petrol bomber in action on the streets of Handsworth. The youth in the picture was variously described as 'the menacing face of Handsworth', 'a black thug', and as having a 'petrol bomb flaming in his hand and hate burning in his heart'. Even when the press did not label the youth in question as black the very form of the picture carried the image that the 'fear' which stalked Handsworth was that of young blacks 'on the rampage' and what *The Sun* called 'race terror'.[37]

The image of the riots as the work of rootless young blacks engaging in an orgy of violence was given further credibility by the attempt in the police report on the Handsworth riot to construct it as the work of a small group of young blacks who were unrepresentative of the black community as a whole. This construction has strong similarities with the arguments developed by John Brown in 1977 about young blacks in Handsworth (Brown, 1977), arguments already analysed in chapter 3. While the report contained scattered references to the social context of the riots, the effects of discrimination and unemployment on young blacks, and other 'social ills', its basic argument was that violent disorder that broke the 'consensus values of society' was essentially the work of a criminal minority:

The majority of rioters who took part in these unhappy events were young, black and of Afro-Caribbean origin. Let there be no doubt, these young criminals are not in any way representative of the vast majority of the Afro-Caribbean community whose presence has contributed to the life and culture of the West Midlands over many years and whose hopes and aspirations are at one with those of every other law abiding citizen. We share a common sorrow. It is the duty of us all to ensure that an entire cultural group is not tainted by the actions of a criminal minority.

(Dear, 1985: 69)

The aim of this formulation is to link the actions of the 'criminal minority' to the wider social context, but in doing so dismisses the relevance of such 'criminal' actions to the legitimate interests of the 'vast majority'. Additionally, however, it serves to create an explanation which rationalises the tough actions of the police and the call for more police resources and equipment in defence of the values of the majority against a desocialised minority. As Fogelson (1971) has shown, in relation to the 1960s riots in America, such a formulation of the riots sees them as outside of the mainstream of society, as the work of 'riff-raff' who have no attachment to existing cultural and political values.

This formulation, as argued above, was also a central theme in the government response to the riots, which essentially saw them as a 'criminal enterprise' and a celebration of hooliganism and thuggery. Here too the social condition of youth played a central role, but it was youth in general that was seen as the problem. The young people living in 'cities of despair' were seen as providing a reservoir of discontent that could explode violently at any time and lead, not only to violent confrontations with the police, but to a crisis of political authority and legitimacy. The 'tinderbox towns', argued Paul Wilkinson, a scholar of urban violence and terrorism, were the product of something deeper than social and economic deprivation, since whether they were employed or not young people were becoming alienated from the values of 'responsible citizenship' (*Daily Mail*, 11 September 1985).

Compared to 1981 therefore, when youth unemployment was a central symbol used to refer to the reason why young people were engaging in violent disorder, responses to the 1985 riots were dominated by a deeper fear: namely, that the young, whether employed or not, were becoming caught up in a vicious spiral of alienation and violence which would be very difficult to reverse.[38]

(c) Policing the 'enemy within'

Despite the rejection of Powell's calls for repatriation by all the main-stream sections of the three major parties, there seems little doubt that the 1985 riots helped to strengthen the imagery of blacks, and young blacks in particular, as an 'enemy within the very heart of British society'. Such images are not in themselves specific to British society, and various accounts of the 1960s riots in the United States point to the persistent use of metaphors which see the rioters as a danger to society 'from within' (Edelman, 1971; Lipsky and Olson, 1977). But in the British context the interlinking of such images with the wider issues of policing, urban decay, and 'immigration' have rendered new meanings to such metaphors.

It is worth recalling here the nature of Powell's intervention in the debate about the 1985 riots. Just as in 1981 his role was not just limited to Parliament, since he made use of the press and public speeches to express his call for repatriation.[39] In addition his call for 'serious' debate about the 'race problem' received support or limited endorsement from a number of press commentators.[40] But his main intervention during the debate in Parliament on 20 October 1985 provides an interesting example of the way in which he attempted to displace the blame for the riots from both the police and the underlying social conditions. He situated the riots within the context of his projection that 'in the foreseeable future not less than one third of the population of inner London will be New Common-wealth and Pakistan ethnic', and from this he drew the conclusion that

> What we have seen so far in terms of the transformation of the population, like what we have seen so far in terms of urban violence, is nothing to what we know is to come. This know-ledge, which is not hidden from ordinary people who live in those places, overshadows those cities and inner London.
>
> (*Hansard*, vol. 84, 1985: col. 376)

Using language reminiscent of the 1981 statements which Powell had used in the *Daily Mail*, a number of Tory MPs and the Monday Club all joined in calls for the question of 'race' as a cause of the riots to be taken seriously.[41] Yet others argued that a 'silence over race' represented a danger to society as a whole, since by failing to discuss this issue seriously mainstream politicians were failing to allow the fears of ordinary British people about the future of 'their' society a fair hearing.[42]

The 'danger from within', however, was not seen as coming simply from the 'race' issue in isolation. In 1985 Britain the 'enemy within' could take on different forms and was represented as such. Apart from the 'hooligans' and 'black thugs' on the streets, there were the other enemies who were often inside the political institutions which the government represented as under threat.

It is clear, for example, that the treatment of Bernie Grant, the Labour leader of Haringey Council, after the Broadwater Farm riot represents a particular example of 'enemy within' type arguments at work. From a rather obscure local political reputation he achieved a national notoriety in just a few days.[43] In the aftermath of the death of PC Blakelock on the Broadwater Farm estate Grant was quoted as attacking the police and expressing support for the actions of the young rioters. His failure, unlike other Labour spokespersons, to condemn the rioters or even the death of a policeman was taken as a sign of his support for violence and disorder against the forces of order, and this support was seen as undermining the role of the police and of established authority. His stance was in turn taken as symbolising a wider malaise of the left, whose actions were seen as a threat to the police, and there were numerous press stories which accused the GLC, ILEA and other Labour-controlled authorities of indulging in propaganda which amounted to 'hate on the rates'.[44]

A similar point can be made about the use of symbols such as 'agitators', 'red butchers', 'the men behind the riots', and 'merchants of hate' to situate the individuals or organisations who were blamed by the press and even by government spokespersons for causing the riots.[45] Throughout September and October 1985 the 'outside agitators' were regularly blamed for all three major riots, and in some cases with specific acts, such as the death of PC Blakelock.

(d) Towards a 'riot-torn society'

During the course of September–October 1985 a recurrent theme in public debate was the question: is Britain becoming a riot-torn society? The resonance of this theme was indicated by the images constructed in the media, in the parliamentary debates and in the pronouncements of politicians and government ministers. It was a particular concern of the Home Secretary, Douglas Hurd, who, as shown above, played a leading role in orchestrating the government response to the riots. A clear expression of this theme is the following statement by the Home Secretary during the parliamentary debate on the riots on 23 October, in which he was responding to Gerald Kaufman:

> I ask the House to be wary of the argument underlying what (Gerald Kaufman) said – that more spending equals fewer riots. That is too simple by half. It leaves out many factors all too obviously present in the particular incidents we are discussing. It leaves out the excitement of forming and belonging to a mob, the

> evident excitement of violence leading to the fearsome crimes
> that we have seen reported and the greed that leads to looting –
> not the looting of food shops, but looting that leads to the theft
> of television sets, video recorders and other things that can be
> disposed of quickly. To explain all those things in terms of
> deprivation and suffering is to ignore some basic and ugly facts
> about human nature.
>
> (*Hansard*, vol. 84, 1985: col. 356).

These arguments in terms of 'basic and ugly facts of human nature'
explain why Hurd was a vehement opponent of any Scarman-type
inquiry and why his definition of the riots as 'a cry for loot and not a cry
for help' resonated through the statements of government politicians and
press commentators. After all, asked one famous newspaper columnist,
what kind of democratic society could afford to give in to the 'rule of the
mob' and still maintain its cultural and political integrity (Worsthorne,
1985).

The fear which seems to underly such images is that without firm
control over the move towards violence certain inner city areas could
become 'badlands' where the police could not exercise their authority
and where in effect what counted was 'mob rule' or the 'rule of the thug'.
The pathology of the 'inner city' and the violence associated with areas of
multiple deprivation was particularly clear in the coverage of the
Broadwater Farm riot, since the estate was seen as a symbolic representation of the fundamental reasons why certain localities become 'no-go
areas' for the police. The day after the riot broke out the descriptions of
the estate ranged from images of it as 'a fortress' to the more emotive
'terror estate'.[46] A feature article in *The Mirror*, went as far as to
describe the estate as a 'living hell', and went on to describe what it sees
as the feelings of the people living there:

> If you don't live in desolate apartments where no one seems to
> care – and even the police have declared a no-go area, you have
> no idea how awful your daily life can be.
>
> (8 October 1985)

When combined with no jobs, inadequate facilities, and no real help
from government, *The Mirror* went on, such areas can become 'another
world', a world where disillusion and violence are every day facts of life.

The prospect of inner cities becoming no-go areas was linked to a
broader fear that violence would thus become in Lord Scarman's words a
'disease endemic to our society'. As shown in chapter 3, this fear has a
long history in debates about the future of 'race relations' from the 1960s

onwards. Quite apart from this history, however, the riots of 1980–1 and 1985 shook the foundations of the mythology that violent disorder was somehow foreign to the body politic in contemporary Britain. By so doing they opened up the whole issue of whether anything could be done to stop riots from recurring, and the question of what kinds of reforms were possible.

Implications for the future: social policy and the promise of reform

The central argument of this chapter has been that, given the nature of the official discourses on the 1980–1 and 1985 riots, the reform aspects of responses to the violent protests since 1980 have been inherently limited, contradictory and can be seen as successful only at a symbolic level. This failure can be understood at two levels. First, as the outcome of the political languages used to make sense of the riots, which seemed to marginalise issues such as racism and arouse fears based on stereotypes of the causal factors. Second, it can be seen as the outcome of the wider socio-economic context within which government and other agencies have had to respond to the riots. Certainly the wider realities of economic change and restructuring, increasing emphasis on the free market and law and order, reduction in state expenditure and social welfare, have given little room for a successful strategy to tackle the roots of urban unrest: namely racism, the economic and social decline of many urban areas, unemployment, heavy policing of these localities and political marginalisation. If anything the conditions of urban existence which prevailed in 1980–1 have become worse today, as indicated by the 1985 outbursts. But political decisions and non-decisions have contributed to the current malaise.

Perhaps one of the most prescient warnings about the course of development since 1979 was published in 1980 by Keith Middlemas, a leading conservative academic. He warned at the time of widespread social and political unrest if unemployment and social inequalities grew and then asked the following question:

> What will Britain look like after even three years of 2 million unemployed? Divisions which for half a century governments have tried to abolish will show nakedly between the two geographical Englands, with Scotland, Wales and Northern Ireland on the periphery, like the Italian Mezzogiorno; between those in work and the unemployed; between the mature and young, between white and black. They already exist. If they are

heightened by the sort of political conflict allied to a capital/ labour antithesis which nearly every Conservative leader since Baldwin has tried to prevent, or by an unthinking and indiscriminate assault on trade unionism which confuses structural backwardness with moral turpitude, or by an intolerant repudiation of the post-war consensus rather than a reasoned attempt to find out what went wrong, then it will recall the old tag: 'ubi solitudinem faciunt, pacem appellant' – where they make a desert they call it peace.

(Middlemas, 1981: 151)

Since the time when this warning was written most of the issues that Middlemas mentions have forced themselves onto the political agenda. But the ways in which they have been added to the political agenda have themselves helped to curtail the possibilities for effective action to deal with the root grievances that underly the riots. The divisions and contradictions which gave rise to the violent outbursts in 1980–1 and 1985 have, as I have shown above, been interpreted in a number of divergent ways, but largely in ways in which did not touch on structural problems. Each of these interpretations contains an implicit or explicit set of policy proposals for preventing future outbreaks or for ameliorating their impact on the wider society. But what the experience of the period since 1980 has shown is that there is a clear gap between promises of reform and their implementation.

Perhaps one way of concretising this generalisation is by reference to the policy agenda which has been articulated by the government in the post-1985 period. There have been a number of 'initiatives' or 'statements' by ministers since the 1985 protests, ranging from promises to review inner city policy, reshape employment policies to help young blacks, take more positive action on racial discrimination, to measures to help specific localities cope with their problems.[47] Yet is it also clear that the issue of the restoration of order was central to the concerns of the government. As the Home Secretary, Douglas Hurd, argued: 'It is not a case history for sociologists to pore over, but a case for the police' (*The Guardian*, 23 September 1985). This statement reflects one of the central problems which faced the government after the riots: namely, the need to distance the outbreaks of violence from the 'social problems' (such as unemployment and inner city decay) which were popularly seen as partly the outcome of government policies. The construction of the events as a matter for the police, and ultimately the Home Office, provided a link in this chain of analysis. It was a constant theme in official statements through September–November 1985, much as it had been during 1982 in the aftermath of the 1980–1 events.

Precisely because 'social issues' are located within an explanatory framework that priotises policing problems the official discourse about the riots externalises them and locates them as outside of the 'British way of life'. As Jeremy Seabrook argues:

> By outlawing social causes, they (the government) leave a vast blank, leaving the public to draw its own conclusions to interpret what is meant by 'criminal element' and 'outsiders'.
>
> (*The Guardian*, 14 October 1985)

If unemployment, poverty, and repressive policing of urban localities are constructed as minor issues which do not explain violent disturbances, the policy conclusion seems to be that it is only through strong support for the police and the reassertion of authority that a sound basis can be laid for more long-term social policy reforms.

This is a scenario which has influenced policy-makers both in 1980–1 and in 1985. The promise of reform has been used as a symbolic political gesture to indicate official concern for the problems of the poor, youth unemployment, the racially disadvantaged or those living in depressed inner city areas. At the same time the strengthening of the police, both in terms of resources and powers, has been pushed through apace on the premise that a strong stance on law and order will create conditions in which violent disturbances are less likely to occur.

In 1980–1 this double-edged strategy took the form of (a) a series of economic and social initiatives which were intended to prevent the recurrence of riots in the future, and (b) measures to restore and maintain order on the streets through improving police tactics and equipment necessary for the handling of civil disorder. This is a scenario which looks like being repeated in the aftermath of 1985, though the actual form of the initiatives has changed somewhat in-between.

Take the example of economic and 'social' measures proposed to deal with the roots of urban unrest. In the aftermath of 1980–1 the Department of the Environment took the lead in making promises that it would adopt a more active stance to help regenerate inner city areas and reverse the decline of employment and the spread of urban decay. At the same time the Home Office responded to the riots by attempting to make sure that the police were better equipped and trained to respond to and contain riot situations. In addition it made some tentative efforts to encourage the police authorities to adopt some of Lord Scarman's suggestions relating to police–community relations. In 1985 it was the Home Office, through Douglas Hurd, that took the lead in responding to the riots through his parliamentary and public pronouncements on the riots. This shift from a 'social' department to a law and order department signified the ambiguity with which the government viewed the social aspects of the Scarman Report, a fact made clear by the government's resistance to another Scarman-type inquiry. No longer did the government feel the need to link its law and order tactics to a wider social programme, since it sought to explain violence and disorderly protest as the outcome of 'criminal greed' and 'pure evil', rather than social disadvantage and inequality.

This is not to say that no 'social' measures have been proposed in the aftermath of the 1985 riots. Rather, the government has sought to pursue such measures without linking them directly to the riots, by seeing them as part of a more long-term programme of action to regenerate inner city areas and increase the effectiveness of its social and economic restructuring project. Thus, for example, there have been promises of measures to help create 'real jobs' for inner city areas, encourage local enterprise and ethnic business, and improve housing and other social conditions for young people. Special measures to help young black people have also been hinted at.

Bearing these promises in mind, it is perhaps worth recalling that a recurrent theme during the 1985 street disorders and their aftermath was: whatever happened to Scarman? This was a question posed by the media, in Parliament, by black groups, the CRE, and to a limited extent by Lord Scarman himself. Gerald Kaufman called for a promise by the government to implement the social-policy reforms which were called for by Lord Scarman, and for a new Scarman-type inquiry into the 1985 riots (*The Guardian*, 8 October 1985). John Clare, Community Affairs Correspondent of the BBC, wrote an eloquent appeal calling for a new look at the social policy aspect of the Scarman Report (Clare, 1985). What then was the substance of the reform programme outlined in the Scarman proposals of 1981?

In substance the Scarman Report was more to do with policing than social policy, a feature determined by the nature of its brief. It was therefore much more narrow in focus than the Kerner Report in the USA, with which it is often compared.[48] But the Report produced by Lord Scarman did have a strong emphasis on the need to link issues of policing within a wider social policy framework.

In Part IV of the Scarman Report, on 'The disorders and social policy', a framework was outlined for linking a strategy aimed at improving the effectiveness of policing to a wider social policy for dealing with the problems of the inner city and of racial disadvantage. As throughout the Report, the question of the social position of young blacks was a central, if not the major, aspect of this social policy framework (Scarman, 1981: paras. 6.10 to 6.42). Arguing that various forms of racial disadvantage and discrimination create a 'potent factor for unrest', Lord Scarman linked the reform of the police to a wider social programme on 'race':

> The attack on racial disadvantage must be more direct than it has been. It must be co-ordinated by central government, who with local authorities must ensure that funds made available are directed to specific areas of racial disadvantage. I have in mind particularly education and employment. A policy of direct co-ordinated attack on racial disadvantage inevitably means that the ethnic minorities will enjoy for a time a positive discrimination in their favour. But it is a price worth paying if it accelerates the elimination of the unsettling factor of racial disadvantage from the social fabric of the United Kingdom. I believe this task to be even more urgent than the task of establishing on a permanent basis good relations between the ethnic minorities and the police. Good policing will be of no avail, unless we also tackle and eliminate basic flaws in our society. And, if we succeed in eliminating racial prejudice from our society, it will not be difficult to achieve good policing.
>
> (Scarman, 1981: para. 9.4)

In the months after the Report was published numerous feature stories in the press looked at the process by which it could be implemented, and saw it as a crucial element of any strategy which aimed to prevent riots from recurring. In addition Lord Scarman himself wrote a number of papers and made a number of speeches during the period 1982–5 which argued for the implementation of all of his Report rather than just the more narrow policing recommendations.

Yet, despite much publicity and debate in the intervening period, Gerald Kaufman was perhaps close to the mark when he commented that in relation to unemployment and deprivation the situation in 1985 was worse than when the Scarman Report was published in November 1981 (*Hansard*, vol. 84, 1985: col. 352). The promise of reform evident both in 1981 and 1985 has therefore had, at best, an ambiguous impact on the actual social conditions which are faced in the areas where the riots occurred.

In relation to policing, however, the trend already evident after 1981 towards a greater emphasis on riot-control equipment and more effective riot tactics had taken shape by 1985. The emphasis by the present government on seeing the riots as 'not a social phenomenon but crimes' has strengthened the move towards the role of the police as central to the management of riot situations and their aftermath. During the 1985 riots police organisations were not slow to follow the lead of the government and call for stronger measures to handle riot situations and more expenditure on police manpower and riot-control equipment. A theme that resonated through the press coverage was that the riots showed the need to combine community-based policing tactics with strong-arm measures to control rising violence and suppress violent protest.

Lord Scarman's call for the 'elimination of prejudice in our society' has been formally acknowledged by the government both in 1981 and in 1985. But the problem remains, however, that measures to tackle this issue have been marginal and tokenistic since no attempt has been made to strengthen legal provisions or increase the political clout of anti-discrimination bodies such as the CRE. It is worth noting, for example, that although in the immediate aftermath of the 1985 riots the government has promised to take more positive action on racial discrimination and black youth unemployment, it has steadfastly refused to strengthen the 1976 Race Relations Act or even to fill in some of the most obvious loopholes. The Commission for Racial Equality submitted to the government in 1983 rather modest proposals for reform, but as yet it has received no positive answer or even an indication of support (CRE, 1983c and 1985a).

Given this background symbolic statements by the government to the effect that it wants to 'speed up inner city jobs drive', 'review inner city aid', or 'review action on racial disadvantage' need to be read as part of the need felt at the time of the 1985 riots to be seen to be changing priorities on some of the most contested issues. Whether such statements lead to substantive changes in practice over the longer term will depend not only on the agencies set up to implement programmes of reform but on a wider set of political actions. The example of the inner city job creation task forces set up after the 1985 riots is a case in point. From one perspective such 'task forces' are evidence of government intentions to solve and ameliorate the problems of youth unemployment and racial disadvantage. But from another perspective, they can be seen as an exercise in symbolic reassurance since the actions they propose cannot tackle the roots of the problems they are supposed to solve. The limited changes achieved since 1981 would seem to indicate that even when social policy reforms are proposed and agencies set up to implement them, they do not necessarily succeed in transforming the types of economic, social and political inequalities which form part of the wider structures of inequality.

Conclusion

In an earlier paper, written in 1984, I argued that ameliorative reforms and symbolic gestures (along with stronger law and order tactics) may have produced short-term stability but that

> Given the lack of fit between the promises for change and the everyday experiences of young blacks it is unlikely that we are now witnessing anything more than a temporary truce, and one which is unlikely to last unless there is a noticeable closing of the gap between the promises on which policies have been made and their actual outcomes.
>
> (Solomos, 1984: 25)

The prospects after the riots in Handsworth, Brixton, Tottenham and elsewhere do not look any brighter. To be sure there have been promises of more radical actions to tackle problems such as youth unemployment, police–community relations, racial discrimination and the decline of the inner cities. But are such promises going to lead to the fundamental structural changes which are necessary to tackle the lack of employment, urban decline and rampant racism?

There seem to be a number of basic reasons why promises of more 'positive action' are not likely to produce the fundamental changes called for. First, the tendency over the last few years has been to use symbolic promises of reform in the future as a mechanism for defusing the outbreak of violent protests. Such promises fit into a broader context of policies which attempt to manage 'insoluble social problems' through public pronouncements which show that the government is actually doing something: such symbolic actions succeed in constructing a short-term truce even if they do not bring about any long-term changes in practice, precisely because they bridge the gap between political language and 'reality'. Second, the gap between the resources allocated to 'help' inner city areas and the massive outflow of resources away from such areas (a phenomenon discussed in chapter 5) shows no sign of being closed. After both 1981 and 1985 there has been much talk about the resources which are going into declining areas and the 'special help' being given to disadvantaged groups, such as young blacks. But this emphasis tends to obscure the outflow of jobs and economic resources which results from wider political and economic processes. Third, the preoccupation with keeping the young unemployed 'off the streets' has deflected attention away from the fundamental question of how to tackle the underlying causes of high levels of unemployment among the young, particularly among those from ethnic minority backgrounds.

Perhaps even more damaging to the prospects of reform is the evidence that despite the reforms implemented since the Scarman Report in 1981 the day-to-day reality of police–black contact is structured around both symbolic and real confrontations, and examples of systematic harassment and confrontations with young blacks (Reiner, 1985; Benyon, 1986b). A black-led review of the grievances of the local black communities in the Handsworth area concluded that the police issue is in many ways the 'front line', and that promises of reform retain little or no validity when young blacks are systematically singled out for 'special treatment' (Ouseley *et al.*, 1986). A similar finding emerges from the inquiry led by Lord Gifford into the events at Broadwater Farm (Gifford *et al.*, 1986). No amount of symbolic political language will hide this 'reality' forever, and this means that what we can safely say is that violent collective protests remain on the agenda. The 'symbolic reassurance' of inner city task forces, official reports, the reform of police training, and greater expenditure on the environment of areas such as Brixton, Handsworth, Tottenham and Toxteth can be seen as a success in the immediate political conjuncture. But a continuing failure to tackle the economic, social and ideological aspects of racial inequality will ensure that issues such as violent collective action by young blacks and whites, black youth unemployment and the policing of inner city areas will remain high on the social policy agenda for some time to come. As we shall see in the next chapter, this is partly due to broader developments in the politics of racism and the continuing transformation of racist ideologies, but also results from a failure to learn any lessons from the experiences of 1980–1 and 1985.

7

'The enemy within': black youth and urban disorder in 1980s Britain

Introduction

The previous chapter analysed in some detail the role of urban unrest and disorder in producing shifts in the ideology of 'black youth'. This chapter will expand this analysis by examining the consequences of urban unrest for the continued racialisation of key decisions about youth policy, law and order and social policy.

The expansion of state intervention in relation to young blacks has become inextricably linked to the overall ideological debate about urban disorder and racism in late 1980s Britain. It is important, therefore, to explore the links that have developed between the various agencies which have helped to construct policy and practice in relation to the 'black youth question'. In this chapter this will be done through an explication of the ways in which the development of urban unrest has influenced debates about (a) the future of policies towards young blacks and (b) transformed common sense images of the 'problems' which young blacks are seen as having in relation to employment, the police and other social institutions.

Within the current political environment such an analysis can only be tentative. The whole issue of social policy and 'race relations' is in turmoil, a fact which has been recognised at both a national and local level.[1] Much soul-searching is going on within and outside the major political institutions about the future of the 1976 Race Relations Act, the role of local and central government in promoting equal opportunities, the high levels of unemployment in the black communities and the expression of feelings of injustice by black politicians and activists (Layton-Henry, 1984; Jenkins and Solomos, 1987). Additionally, broader economic and social restructuring is clearly having an impact on the main issues which have been discussed in this book. A good example

is the issue of employment and unemployment and the growing importance of 'race' in political debates about this question. Another is the
transformation of many of the inner city localities in which black
communities live, through the de-industrialisation and relocation processes discussed in chapter 5.

All of these changes are important in their own right, and it is
impossible to discuss them in detail here. But it is crucial to examine the
dynamics of the current situation, even if only to provide a tentative
framework for making sense of the post-riot discourses about young
blacks. A useful starting point for this analysis is the interaction between
racism, politics and ideology which we are currently witnessing.

Racism, politics and ideology in the 1980s

During the 1970s the transformation of political ideologies about 'race',
and black youth as a specific racialised category, focused on two main
issues. First, there emerged a new morphology of racism which conver-
ged around the notion that specific groups of the black population
represented a 'threat' to British society and its social and political
cohesion. Within this morphology various meanings were attributed to
'race' and its role in the broader crisis faced by society. Second, a major
expansion took place of political interventions which were meant to
control the anti-social and disruptive consequences of racialised politics.
Political practices around the issues of employment, housing, welfare
and youth have all been deeply racialised, and this has been reflected in a
massive growth in the bureaucracies which are designated to manage the
'race' question nationally and locally.

Perhaps the most important influence on both these strands of intervention is the notion, articulated in various ways, that the core of the
'race problem' is comprised of the communal and psychological characteristics of the black communities themselves.[2] This links up with the
notion which had been forcefully articulated by Powell and others from
the late sixties onwards that the 'problem' was external to the structure of
British society as such, since it had been imposed from the 'outside'
(Powell, 1969; Smithies and Fiddick, 1969; Berkeley, 1977). But it also
resulted from a much broader ideological construction of black communities as 'pathological', as the bearers of discrete cultural and social
relations which were fixed and historically invariable.

By the 1980s, however, there had been a noticeable transformation in
the dominant ideological framework used to interpret the social position
of young blacks, and of the black communities as a whole. This had been
brought about by two major events. First, the establishment in popular

and official discourses of an image of young blacks as involved in an on-going confrontation with the police and other institutions of law and order. Second, the identification of the 1980–1 riots as largely the work of young blacks who had become criminalised and alienated from the mainstream of British society helped to transform ideologies about 'race'. These events allowed a re-interpretation of the 'black youth' question around the themes of urban unrest and violent disorder.[3] But they also highlighted the way in which the debates in the 1960s and 1970s about black youth as a 'social time bomb' had moved on by the 1980s to the overarching concern of how to prevent young blacks' anger from exploding again. This, despite the fact that major outbreaks of unrest occurred in 1980, 1981, 1985, 1986 and 1987 has been perhaps the dominant theme in policy debates.

The overriding concern of the government after both the 1980–1 and 1985 explosions of urban unrest was how to develop measures at both a national and local level which could (a) provide buffers that may prevent further unrest on the same scale, and (b) remedy some of the grievances expressed by young blacks and other young people through the riots. But as we saw in chapter 6, the government could not seriously tackle the second issue without admitting to some degree that the riots were an expression or a symptom of genuine grievances.

The pronouncements of government ministers and politicians after the 1985 riots reflect this dilemma, and amplify the nature of official concerns about the future of urban unrest in the late 1980s.[4] In statement after statement during late 1985 and 1986 government ministers sought both to de-contextualise the riots from the wider socio-economic changes taking place and to promise to alleviate some of the grievances which popular debate linked to the riots. Douglas Hurd, the Home Secretary, announced a number of times during 1985–7 that although the riots were not a 'cry for help' that he was determined to ensure that young blacks should be helped to achieve greater participation at all levels of British society.[5] In January 1987, for example, he announced: 'My vision of Britain is one in which young people from the black community can climb ladders across the range of opportunities, throughout British society' (*The Weekly World*, 31 January 1987). The political dilemma facing the government was how to placate the demands emerging from the black community without damaging its claims to legitimacy. Achieving this objective required that it adopt a two-pronged strategy aimed at: reducing the threat to law and order which street violence signalled and reassuring public opinion that it was not purposely ignoring real concerns about social inequality and the anger and discontent to which this gave rise within the black communities.

The riots did, however, challenge the notion which successive governments had articulated since the 1960s, that 'good race relations' could be produced through interventions by the state in the form of immigration controls and race relations legislation. They highlighted the changing context of official thinking about 'race' and the volatile nature of black anger and frustration within the political climate of the 1980s. Perhaps the single most important consequence of the riots was the fact that they shattered the notion that ameliorative measures of reform and symbolic promises of 'equal opportunity' could keep the lid on the growing force of resistance and protest that was emerging from within the black communities. But the riots are also an important factor in understanding the transformation of neo-right ideologies about 'race' and 'nation'.[6] As I showed in chapter 6 the participation of young blacks in the riots, and in other confrontations with the police, provided the basis for a wide-ranging public debate about the interplay between 'race' and 'violent unrest'. Politicians, newspaper commentators, social policy professionals and the police used the riots as a rationale for rethinking the question of black youth in contemporary Britain, and the future of 'race relations' in the coming decades.

This has become even more evident in the aftermath of the 1985 riots, but it is in fact a process which has its origins in the responses to the 1980–1 riots. It is perhaps during this period that the language of 'enemies within' was fully marshalled in relation to young blacks. In both press and parliamentary debates 'enemy' themes were used to define the dangers which lay beneath the surface of the riots: the 'outside agitators', 'alien cultures', 'political activists' and 'criminalised young blacks' were used symbolically to mobilise opinion and to deflect attention from issues such as racism, socio-economic disadvantage and urban decline. According to this line of argument the riots were thus not an unconventional means of voicing political opinion and taking action to achieve specific objectives, but were a symbol of a deeper and more pervasive threat to British society 'from within'. This 'threat' represented a challenge to the generation of legitimacy and order in British society as a whole, and particularly in multi-racial localities.[7]

By rioting, therefore, young blacks were seen as not only breaking the rules of conventional politics, but as engaging in activities which were somehow 'alien' and outside the culturally sanctioned norms of British society. But what is new in the 1980s is not so much the symbolic political language about 'enemies within', since this can be traced back to the 1960s; the real novelty is the way this symbol was combined with images of 'race' and 'urban unrest' in the aftermath of the riots so as to make every black person *a priori* a suspect, a potential criminal, a potential agitator. It is to this issue that I now turn.

Disorderly protest, black youth and urban change

Chapter 6 provided a detailed analysis of the impact of the 1980–1 and 1985 riots on the social construction of policies towards young blacks. But even in the short period since 1985 it has become clear that the question of disorderly protest remains an active constituent element of the political agenda. More disorders took place during 1986, and skirmishes between the police and young people have been regularly reported since then.[8] In early 1987, for example, a minor confrontation took place in Wolverhampton as a result of the death of a young black man while he was being arrested by the police on suspicion of using a stolen credit card.[9] A number of statements by the police seem to indicate that they see such events as an integral feature of many inner city areas within the current context of economic and social restructuring.[10] The long-term consequences of these disorderly protests remain to be seen. But as chapter 6 has already indicated their impact on the perception of the black youth question has been profound. Apart from their impact on other areas of state intervention, including inner city and employment policies, their role in transforming police ideologies about 'black youth' has proved to be important.

I have already referred to Geoffrey Dear's account of the Handsworth riots, and his attempt to link the events to a specific group of young blacks in the area (Dear, 1985: 69–71; see also Gaffney, 1987). But Dear's account of Handsworth is by no means the only policy response to urban unrest which provides an insight into police ideologies about young blacks. Sir Kenneth Newman, Chief Constable of the Metropolitan Police until 1987, has produced a number of papers which attempt to draw some lessons for the police from both the 1980–1 and 1985 riots.[11] During the period from 1982–7 Newman has made a number of influential speeches on two themes:

(a) the specific problems faced in policing multi-ethnic areas; and
(b) the growth of violence and disorder in Britain during the 1970s and 1980s.

In a speech to an international conference on policing, held in Cambridge in August 1983, he outlined in summary form a programme of action for police forces in the aftermath of the 1980–1 riots, and in the process highlighted the importance of the disorders in reshaping ideologies among the police about young blacks. Arguing that policing works best where there is a homogeneous community and a shared consensus about norms and values, he contrasted this abstract ideal to the reality of enforcing law and order in inner city areas:

> In many multi-ethnic areas police encounter not merely apathy and unhelpfulness when making enquiries or engaging in order maintenance, but outright hostility and obstruction. It is commonplace in some multi-ethnic areas for a policeman making a legitimate arrest or intervention to be surrounded by a hostile crowd bent on 'rescuing' the prisoner or interviewee. This can occur even when the victim is black. This brand of obstruction and hostility is at its height in certain parts of ethnic areas which have become a focal point for congregation and association by black youths. In these locations confrontations with the police are often deliberately engineered either to make a political point or to create a diversion to facilitate organised crime in relation to drugs or stolen property.
>
> (*Police*, September 1983: 28)

For Newman this process was the key to understanding why policing of certain areas of major cities was volatile, and how it could become even more so in the future:

> If allowed to continue, locations with these characteristics assume symbolic importance, a negative symbolism of the inability of the police to maintain order. They encourage law-breaking in other areas, affecting public perception of police effectiveness, heighten fear of crime and reinforce the phenomenon of urban decay.
>
> (*Ibid.* 28)

This analysis was written in the aftermath of the 1980–1 riots and was influenced by police ideologies which constructed certain areas of black settlement as 'problem areas'.[12] The events of 1985, particularly the killing of PC Blakelock on the Broadwater Farm Estate in Tottenham, have helped to give further credence and support to ideologies about black youth as an 'enemy within', and to reinforce the following two arguments. First, the events in Tottenham seemed to support the categorisation of some housing estates and even whole localities as areas where the police are unable fully to maintain order on the streets or to achieve the consent of the local population for their actions. Second, the fact that such areas were generally 'multi-ethnic' was interpreted as an important reason as to why riots occurred in some areas rather than others. Here again the outbreak of violence on 'England's streets' helped to intensify the politicisation of racial questions and to link them with broader fears about lawlessness, disorder and political legitimacy.

The Dear report on Handsworth (Dear, 1985) and the Metropolitan

Police's review of *Civil Disturbances 1981–1985* (Metropolitan Police, 1986) can best be understood as responses to this broader set of issues and not just as immediate reactions to the riots as such. The Metropolitan Police review of the disturbances is the most enlightening in this regard. Although it warned that the maintenance of law and order meant that 'no go' areas were out of the question, it also stated that the police had to take into account:

(a)   the frustrations which 'difficult social conditions' give rise to;
(b)   the problems faced by the younger generation in areas with a lack of 'community identity'; and
(c)   the reasons which lead sections of the local population to distrust the police and their tactics (Metropolitan Police, 1986: 15–17).

Indeed the review contains in many ways a model of policing which goes beyond the narrow issue of police tactics and weapons, and looks at the broader social and political conditions necessary for effective social control. Since 1985 it is this theme which has been returned to continuously in public policy debates.

In an important speech made after the 1985 riots, the Metropolitan Police's Chief Constable re-interpreted the events as an outcome of a number of interlinked, and fundamental, transformations in British politics and society. Pointing out that the last time a policeman was killed in a riot was in 1833, he linked the breakdown in consent to political authority and police powers to four issues: acquisitiveness, changing personal standards, unemployment and drug abuse (Newman, 1986: 1–2). All of these issues were linked together by a 'devastating spiral of violence and crime' which resulted in the constant undermining of the role of the police and authority structures, and in extreme circumstances in outbreaks of violent public disorder. The fundamental factor which the police and governments had to face, according to this analysis, was the lack of cohesion in society as a whole:

> In a stable society, one where people are born, grow up, spend most of their working lives, and die in one community, the permanent nature of the contact with neighbours, with a whole network of other members of the community and relatives, provides a constant reinforcement of the knowledge that crime is not normal, that most people do not commit it. But for many of us, our membership of a neighbourhood is transient; we do not have time to put down roots and to develop relationships which daily reassure us of the normality of being law-abiding.
>
> (Newman, 1986: 5)

Such transience and lack of roots in the local community was accen-

tuated by ethnic diversity, although not caused by it, and the transformations brought about by social and economic restructuring. In
Newman's terms, therefore, the policing of multi-racial localities necess-
itated a 'multi-agency' approach (involving the police, central government departments, local authorities, and agencies such as the Manpower Services Commission), aimed at reconstituting the 'social
contract' between the police and the local population (Newman, 1983:
30–2).

Such an approach to policing has been put on the political agenda by
the riots, but the long-term issue which underlies the whole question is
the position of young blacks and the likelihood of them engaging in
violent forms of protest in the future. In this sense what we may be witnessing at the present time are the first stages of a shift in the policies
pursued towards young blacks over the last two decades. As argued in
chapters 2 and 3 the underlying assumption of state policies towards
young blacks was the need to integrate them into the mainstream of
British society and to allow them equal access to jobs and services. Once
the 'social time bomb' had exploded, however, the logic of this
approach came under fire from a number of perspectives.

On the one hand, the failure of policies pursued prior to the 1980s was
interpreted as a sign of the need for new initiatives to ameliorate the
anger and frustrations of young blacks. On the other hand, the 1980s
have seen a re-working of the 'enemy' themes which I referred to earlier
around the questions of black youth and disorderly forms of protest.
Additionally, a sharp debate has developed around the whole issue of
'race' and 'nation' in 1980s Britain. A brief analysis of each of these dimensions follows.

The re-making of an 'enemy within'

As argued above the resonance of images of crime and disorder within
official ideologies about young blacks is most clear in the development
of official thinking on this issue over the last few years. The polarity
between young blacks and the rest of the society has been constructed in
a variety of ways by various state institutions, and there is no space here
to deal with all of them. But the central polarity is captured by the following statement by Tony Judge, who at the time was both a Labour
member of the Greater London Council and Director of Public Relations for the Police Federation:

> There are two conflicting demands. One is to stop harassing
> young blacks in the inner cities. The other is to stop young

blacks harassing other people in the inner cities. Which demand
do you respond to? It has to be the second.

(*The Guardian*, 20 November 1982)

If the logic of Judge's approach is accepted, the role of the police in
relation to young blacks assumes the form of a repressive institution; a
role legitimised on the grounds of stopping them from 'harassing other
people in the inner cities'. If the costs involve, to some extent, the
harassment of young blacks themselves, this is presumably a legitimate
price to pay.[13]

Arguments such as these are important. They encapsulate an emerging
polarity in official thinking, which has had quite drastic policy consequences, and will in all likelihood produce even more fundamental
transformations in relation to young blacks in the future. But official
ideologies are not the only arena within which common sense notions
about young blacks have been re-articulated. Within political institutions
similar, if contradictory, processes have also taken place.

Powell's re-articulation of the repatriation issue in the aftermath of the
riots is a good example of this process. For over a decade he had
articulated a racialised interpretation of the basic issues facing British
society, and had on a number of occasions called for repatriation as 'the
only solution'.[14] The unemployment crisis, growing urban violence, and
the decline of inner city areas had all been used by him to construct
ideologically the need for repatriation. In 1981 and 1985 he was able to
re-articulate all these themes around the question of the inevitability of
violence: according to Powell as the black population grew they did not
become part of the British society but remained an alien presence which
made violence and disorder the order of the day. For Powell there were
two 'facts' behind the riots:

(a) the growth of the black population, particularly the younger
     generation; and
(b) the prospect that over the next generation this population was
     likely to double, or even treble (*Hansard*, vol. 8, 1981: cols.
     1411–12).

The consequence of this situation in Powell's eyes, was one of inner cities
'becoming ungovernable' or 'violence which could only be effectually
described as civil war' (*ibid.* 1412). The 'solution' which Powell suggested
involved 'measures whereby that inevitable increase, that inevitable
doubling, will not take place' (*ibid.* 1414). He counterposed this to the
government's emphasis on policing and law and order, and the Labour
party's emphasis on measures to tackle poverty, unemployment and
deprivation.

From the late sixties onwards the discourse of Powellism had situated 'race' as a social problem which had been imposed on the British 'people from the outside'. By the eighties, however, Powell's language emphasised not just the imposition of unwanted immigration but the transformation of the social make-up of inner city localities. During the same parliamentary debate referred to above, he used a favourite debating technique of his to make this point, by quoting at length from a letter sent to him by a correspondent, who explained to Powell that

> What the riots in England are all about basically is that the immigrant areas are not static pools . . . but expanding entities. Therefore it follows that as they expand house by house, street by street, area by area, so the indigenous population must retreat house by house etc. at the same rate . . . As they continue to multiply and as we can't retreat further there must be conflict.
> (*Hansard*, vol. 8, 1981: col. 1412)

Powell went on to add that many other correspondents had expressed to him 'their sense of relief that they are too old to live to see what they know lies ahead' (*Hansard*, vol. 8, 1981: col. 1416). Powell's only hope was that when people saw the 'reality and the magnitude of its peril and the choice which it faces, this nation will rise to its danger' (*ibid*.: col. 1417). The 'nation' would then impose what, for Powell, was the only possible solution: namely the exclusion of black people from the national boundaries so as to reduce the dangers of further conflict from within the body politic, particularly in multi-racial inner city localities.[15]

What this shows clearly is that the riots have changed the terrain of public debate about race, and pushed the issue of disorder and violence onto the forefront of political debate about 'race' in new and complex ways. While Powell and other politicians had been warning that 'race riots' were the logical outcome of the growth of the black population, the post-Bristol riots gave the repatriation lobby a more dynamic symbol: the 'threat' of violence had been replaced by the question 'Where will riots occur next?'

Once the 'social time bomb' had exploded it became a question not of debating what to do to prevent an 'American-type' situation from developing on the streets of Britain, but of how to manage and control those elements that were popularly seen as the leading forces behind the outbreaks of violence. Edelman in his study of the 1960s riots in America, notes that a central focus of policy and popular debates was the identification of the 'enemies' who were behind the events: 'The alien, the stranger, or the subhuman are the themes struck repeatedly' (Edelman, 1971: 115). In a similar fashion the disorders analysed in chapter 6 helped to construct a political language which identified the 'enemy' against which the body politic had to be defended, and engendered contradictory beliefs about the prospects of future conflict along 'racial' lines in British society.

This returns us to a theme which I have emphasised throughout this study. This is the point that the racialisation of policies and programmes involves the engendering of contradictory, and incompatible, definitions of what the 'problems' to be confronted are. This phenomenon has been made even more clear by the responses to the riots since 1980. While in the media and in the rationalisations of governmental policies the riots have been perceived as the actions of a small minority, others have seen them as the only viable form of politics for people denied influence through conventional means. Attempts by sections of the black communities to counter the 'enemies within' arguments by labelling the riots as 'rebellions' against injustice and inequality form part of this on-going struggle to define and re-define the meaning of urban protest within contemporary Britian.[16] By questioning the dominant governmental and political rationalisations of the riots black and radical commentators have sought to place on the political agenda an alternative model of action in response to urban disorder. Rather than attempting to identify the riots with specific groups they have suggested that the outbreak of violence is an expression of the anger and frustration which has resulted (a) from historical patterns of incorporation and exclusion of black workers and (b) from the policies (or non-policies) pursued by successive administrations and their failure to tackle the roots of racial inequality. This alternative explanation of the riots links them to the broader transformations of the economic and social landscape of contemporary Britain, and this in turn questions the assumption that they are largely the result of 'mindless hooliganism' or 'subversive' action by 'aliens' and 'outsiders'.[17]

Thus, while the dominant themes in political debates about the riots were those that saw them as the work of a small minority, the outbreak of violence on the streets of British cities also engendered public concern about the socio-economic position of black communities, and particularly young blacks. Even within the mainstream of government thinking on this question there are those who question the 'solutions' advocated by the law and order lobbyists and neo-right ideologues. A Tory Reform Group pamphlet, produced in the aftermath of the 1981 riots, argued that if the ethnic minorities were not to become 'permanent under-privileged under-class' citizens there was a need for positive government action to tackle past and present discrimination and disadvantage. Pointing out the divisive aspects of social disadvantages and discrimination against blacks, the pamphlet pointed out that

> For a Conservative this is an intolerable state of affairs since a prime tenet of Conservatism is the belief in One Nation which is rejection of all unnecessary divisions within society such as those between rich and poor, north and south, and black and white. A Conservative believes in equality of opportunity for all and thus must support all positive action to enable specially disadvantaged groups in society to have the chance to compete relatively equally with their neighbour.
>
> (Tory Reform Group, 1982: 2)

In introducing this report, Peter Walker, a notable member of the 'wet' section of the parliamentary Conservative party, stressed that

> For two decades the position has declined and not improved. It is vital that the decline ends and the improvement begins; for to tackle this problem is not just in the interests of the young blacks but it is in the interest of the total cohesion of our society.
>
> (*Ibid.* Foreword)

Whilst written from a Conservative perspective, statements such as these are a clear indication of the ways in which the riots raised important questions about political cohesion and the future stability of political institutions. They also highlight the degree of uncertainty about the future which the riots had produced, and the fear that the plight of young blacks could cause problems for society as a whole.

Which one of the main political options is adopted remains to some extent an open question. The regularity with which urban unrest has forced itself onto the political agenda since 1980, and to a more limited extent from 1976, suggests that it would be unwise to analyse the current situation from the perspective of a static analytic framework. It would also be unwise to suggest that a uniform and linear course of action will be followed by the current Conservative administration or by future governments. The position is too unstable to enable us to make any such predictions, but it is possible to make a few tentative remarks in the direction of suggesting at least what options will be placed on the political agenda.

The first point to make is that despite the calls by groups such as the Tory Reform Group and by individuals such as Lord Scarman for positive action to help transform the position of young blacks, there has been no significant sign that a national programme of action to tackle discrimination and disadvantage against them is forthcoming.[18] Rather, there have been symbolic promises of action which have not led to fundamental changes on the ground. Second, the period since 1980–1 has witnessed a strengthening of ideologies which construct young blacks, and blacks in general, as an 'enemy within' and as a danger to the social fabric of the society.[19] Indeed, what is particularly striking is that while official expressions of concern about the extent of racial discrimination have been common they have not been matched by efforts to question the assumptions of immigration control policies and race relations policies. Third, the development of disorderly protest has led to a politicisation of the whole question of law and order and policing in specific localities, particularly ones which official ideologies define as 'problem areas'.

The articulation of these three developments has produced a situation which is likely to result in a further racialisation of important aspects of policies about such issues as unemployment, policing, youth policy, welfare policy and local government policy. The eventual outcome of this racialisation will be determined by a complex totality of economic, social and political factors, some of which will be analysed in the concluding chapter.

An important determinant, however, will be the success or failure of neo-right ideologists in reconstructing the place of 'race' and 'nation' in contemporary political ideologies.

'Race' and 'nation' in neo-right ideology

One of the most important developments over the last decade in the politics of racism has been the articulation of a neo-right analysis of the role of 'race' and 'nation' in contemporary British society. The writings of a group of authors connected with *The Salisbury Review* have been much discussed.[20] Without exaggerating the importance of this debate it is important to look at it in some detail since it is likely to help influence the course of political debate about black youth in the future, particularly under a sympathetic administration. The neo-right is particularly concerned with the position of young blacks in the current period, and their analysis of the interplay between 'race' and 'nation' therefore needs to be critically analysed.

There has been much debate about whether these neo-right writings can be said to constitute a 'new' racism (Barker, 1982; CCCS Race and Politics Group, 1982; Seidel, 1986a; Gordon and Klug, 1986; Miles, 1987). Without getting caught up in a terminological dispute, there are a number of elements of neo-right ideology on 'race' and 'nation' which can be said to signal new developments in the politics of racism as it has been constituted and re-formed since the 1960s. There are four which I shall discuss here, although a number of writers have identified more.

These are: (a) the location of 'race' and 'nation' as historical invariables; (b) a definition of national identity around powerful images of culture, way of life and the family; (c) a perception of blacks as an 'alien wedge' within the polity; and (d) the perception of 'race' as a major factor in explaining the growth of violence in British society. I shall highlight the most salient features of all these elements before returning to the question of their impact on ideologies and practices in relation to young blacks within the context of mounting urban disorder.

(a) 'Race' and 'nation'

The centrality of notions about 'race' and 'nation' in the writings of the neo-right has been clear for some time (Seidel, 1986b: 107–31; Gordon and Klug, 1986: 24–42; Parekh, 1987). Indeed Powell's speeches during the period from 1968–80 were in many ways organised around the idea that the main 'threat' was represented not by immigration *per se* but the impact of the 'growing number' of black workers and their descendents on the 'national character' and on the character of the areas in which they lived. But the 1980s have witnessed an important shift in public debates about this issue which have resulted from the outbreak of violent protest in areas such as Bristol, Brixton, Liverpool and other localities. The riots and related events resonate through much of the neo-right writings on 'race' issues, and provide the point of reference for the construction of 'enemy' themes. Writing at the time of the 1985 riots the *Daily Mail* made the following diagnosis about the contradictions between 'race' and 'nation':

> Either they obey the laws of this land where they have taken up residence and accepted both the full rights and responsibilities of citizenship, or they must expect the fascist street agitators to call ever more boldly and with ever louder approval for them to 'go back from whence they come'.
>
> (*Daily Mail*, 5 October 1985)

In this context the term 'they' referred to the black youth who were disobeying the 'laws of the land' as well as the communities of which they formed a part. Without directly calling for repatriation as such, arguments such as this served to establish the distinction between 'race' and 'nation' in popular discourses, and to marginalise debate about the material basis of urban unrest.[21]

As I showed in chapter 1, during the 1960s and 1970s there was a noticeable shift in public debate and policies away from a preoccupation with immigration issues as such and towards a new-found concern with the black communities settled in the United Kingdom. But in the present political climate we are witnessing a more fundamental and worrying shift in ideology. The issue which has come to the forefront in public policy debate in the aftermath of urban unrest and disorder is the basic problem of whether Britain could become a multi-racial 'nation' – indeed whether it should aim to become one, and at what cost to 'British nationhood'.

(b) Definitions of 'national identity'

A recent study of the meaning of 'Englishness' notes that it is a term whose meaning has constantly changed: 'Englishness has had to be made and re-made in and through history, within available practices and relationships, and existing symbols and ideas' (Colls and Dodd, 1986: i). Within the context of contemporary Britain the racialisation of political debate does not involve merely the question of 'race' but a re-definition of the notions of 'Englishness', 'national culture' and the 'British way of life'.[22] The position of black minority communities within the constantly changing inner city localities may be the immediate point of reference, but at a broader level the question raised by current debates relates to the nature of the majority culture and the transformations which it is undergoing.

Perhaps a clear example of this point is the debate that ensued in the press after both the 1980–1 and 1985 riots about the meaning of 'Englishness' and the wider concept of the 'British nation'. Media coverage of these events, as shown in chapter 6, was partly organised around the question of 'race', and particularly the participation of young blacks in most of the major riots. But the construction of young blacks as an 'alien' element within the polity also involved a reassertion of what the attributes of the national identity of the majority population – ranging from shared language, customs, religion, family ties, sport etc. Such culturally sanctioned attributes were constructed in such a way as culturally to exclude from the category of 'British' those who were of a different culture, religion, lifestyle. A notable press commentator on 'race' and other social issues, Peregrine Worsthorne, questioned the logic of 'multi-racialism' by arguing that the integration of black people within a 'British identity' was especially difficult because (a) their allegiances lay with 'enemies of the west' and (b) their cultures were significantly different and less developed than the dominant white culture. Pointing out that 'ethnic minorities seem to be integrating less and less' with the white majority, Worsthorne concluded that 'a large number of them don't want to stop hating this country, let alone start loving it' (Worsthorne, 1985).

Arguments such as this served to rationalise a conception of an embattled white majority culture defending itself against the threats posed by new minority cultural values and identities – by 'alien' cultures. In practice this helped to popularise a conception of 'British culture' which was monolithic and stereotypical. But the strength of the appeal to naturalistic definitions of the culture of the dominant section of British society can be traced in the debates in Parliament about the riots and wider 'race' questions during the 1980s (see Solomos, forthcoming). Since the 1981 riots there have been a number of debates in Parliament about immigration, urban disorder and specific political issues which have involved concerted attempts to define and give meanings to the whole question of national identity, and they have all involved either directly or indirectly some reference to racial symbols and ideas.[23] At the same time more specific debates about education and race, local authority policies on racism and on the 'loony left' have involved wideranging discussions about the implications of the politicisation of 'race' for the white majority culture and way of life.[24]

(c)   From immigrants to an 'Alien Wedge'

In chapter 2 I outlined the shifting ideologies and practices which led to the transition from the politics of immigration *per se* to the politics of the second generation 'black British'. What we are perhaps witnessing today is a transformation of popular images about 'race' around the idea of a threatening black presence – which is not 'British' and which is maturing within the national boundaries. Such a reworking of the concepts of 'nation' and 'citizen' not only denies the possibility that black people can share the native population's attachment to the national culture – it rationalises the exclusion of black people from equal participation in social institutions and reproduces tensions between those excluded and those included within the definition of citizenship.

I have tried to show in this chapter some of the reasons why the riots have resulted in new ideologies about the interplay between 'race', youth and violence in contemporary Britain. But I am not arguing that these ideologies will necessarily prove to be functional for the smooth running of society as a whole. As Stuart Hall points out, the failure to tackle the roots of racism and the construction of 'race' as a problem can produce only limited social cohesion:

> Unless a society operates towards its citizens as if there is some minimal sense in which they are intrinsically a part of that society, central to it, with a right to belong to it, with certain established formal and informal economic, political and cultural rights; and unless the society recognises, even in a general sense,

an overall responsibility towards the preservation of life and the guarantee of a decent standard and style of life for the people as a whole – as a fundamental fact of their entering into the social contract at all – the society cannot call on the population to feel loyalty and a sense of belonging.

(Hall, 1987: 50)

It is important to note therefore that the social construction of young blacks, or other groups of black people, as an 'alien' group can also help to delegitimise the actions of the polity and of authority institutions in relation to this group. Once such a process is set in train it becomes difficult to reconstruct relations of participation between 'alienated' groups and conventional political institutions. Such a process seems to be in progress at the present time, and its long-term consequence may be the development of new forms of violent protest by those who are excluded from the construction of 'citizenship' established by the political debates surrounding the riots during the 1980s.

(d) 'Race', youth and violence

I have already noted that the policies and ideologies about black youth in the 1980s have been dominated by the experience of the post-1980 riots and the imagery of violence on the streets, particularly in so-called 'multi-ethnic' areas. It is this imagery that will determine the development of future policies towards young blacks, but the experience of the post-1980 period suggests that within the present political climate it is unlikely that we shall witness fundamental changes in the social and economic position of young blacks merely as a result of the riots. The likelihood is that 'race' will continue to be linked closely to the whole question of 'violence' – whether in the form of riots, various forms of street crime or subversive actions.

If this proves to be the case there are clearly dangers in store for black communities already under attack and being labelled as 'alien' and undesirable. It is already clear that right-wing political groups are using the riots, and images of young blacks as 'violent hooligans', to mobilise support for their programmes of repatriation and exclusion of black people (Seidel, 1986a; Gordon and Klug, 1986). At the same time a number of politicians, newspaper columnists and commentators are advocating what amounts to a challenge to the whole principle of anti-racism by questioning the very meaning of 'racism' (see, for example, Palmer, 1986; and various issues of *The Salisbury Review*). Within the present political climate the government has not attempted to question the construction of neo-right ideologies about 'race' but has sought to use questions about race and immigration for its own political ends at particular conjunctures. Recent examples include the re-drafting of immigration rules and attacks on the work of left-wing local authorities on equal opportunities and racism (*Hansard*, vol. 83, 1985: cols. 965–89; vol. 112, 1987: cols. 705–85).

This is not to say, of course, that the black communities are likely to accept such a situation without expressing their anger and frustration. Indeed it is quite likely that as long as the fundamental conditions remain the same that disorderly protest by blacks and other excluded groups will remain on the political agenda. Hall's poignant statement summarises the dilemma that we currently face:

> When an indentifiable group in the society is so alienated from the processes of political, social and cultural incorporation that it feels itself to be the outsiders – 'the alien wedge' – they are open to the expression of anger, to the expression of a lack of commitment to social norms and goals which at one point or another will produce a violent form of unrest.
>
> (Hall, 1987: 50)

Given this context and the reality of inaction on positive measures against racism and racial inequality the racialisation of protest and disorder will continue and take on new forms in the late 1980s and 1990s.

Conclusion

In this chapter on the emergence and articulation of images of young blacks as an 'enemy within', I have concentrated on the dimension of urban disorder and racialised political action and in this way I have complemented the emphasis in earlier chapters on the development of policies and programmes within the institutions of the state. It has been argued that the weight of recent developments has favoured the popularisation of images of young blacks as (a) a violent and disorderly element within the very heart of the inner city areas, and (b) a group which needed to be controlled through a combination of policing tactics and ameliorative social policy measures to remedy some of their grievances. The contradictory balance between these images has helped to reshape the dominant concerns about the 'future of young blacks' around the question of urban unrest. The questions that are being asked are: What can be done to prevent young blacks from drifting away from the mainstream of society? How can they be stopped from engaging in violent confrontations with the police? Can the unemployed young blacks be prevented from becoming a destabilising force in society as a whole?

The political urgency of these questions has been highlighted because since 1980 violent unrest in inner city areas has become established on the political agenda. Serious outbreaks of urban unrest occured in 1980, 1981, 1985, 1986 and 1987 (Benyon and Solomos, 1987). There seems to be both a likelihood and an expectation that more disorders are on the way and will occur during the late 1980s and 1990s. But what is also clear is that there has been a lack of any serious effort to tackle the root causes of the grievances and feelings of injustice which are felt by young blacks. The response of the government and the police to the riots of 1985, for example, was to blame the events of hooliganism, drugs, outside agitators and greed. Such responses can only help to give support to ideologies which see young blacks as a kind of 'alien wedge' within the heart of Britain's cities – which has to be controlled and perhaps expelled from the body politic.

The options for the future remain open, but only to a limited extent. There is a clear danger that the emergence and articulation of racial ideologies which construct black communities, and particularly young blacks, as an 'enemy within' can become a way of making more politically acceptable strategies of repression and repatriation which have been marginal to the political agendas of the major political parties. The danger signals are there. The task of challenging and undermining the arguments on which such political agenda are based is therefore of immediate importance within the current political economic and social environment. There is no room to waver in tackling the racism which young blacks face; their situation represents a test case for any serious commitment to an anti-racist political agenda.

Conclusions

This book has been concerned with the genesis, development and contradictions of ideologies and policies in relation to the question of the position of 'black youth' in British society. In the process of developing this analysis, I have been concerned particularly with two issues. The first of these, which was the starting point of parts one and two of the book, was the importance linking the question of 'black youth' to the wider set of contradictions which have shaped the politics of racism in contemporary Britain. The second was the importance of evaluating the interplay between ideological constructions of the 'problem' of 'black youth' and the policy outcomes which we have witnessed in relation to policing, social policy and unemployment. Both these issues have been analysed extensively in the preceding chapters and there is no need to repeat the arguments here. Nevertheless there are number of points which emerge from the above analysis which need to be mentioned briefly in bringing this book to a close.

Black youth, racism and the reproduction of inequality

In the introduction I explored the question of how racial inequality has been reproduced in British society over the last four decades, and the importance of analysing the role of the complex totality of economic, social and political processes which can help explain the institutionalisation of racism. The immediate reference point of this book has, however, been the specific question of how the category 'black youth' was put on the political agenda, the ideologies and practices which were evolved to manage this issue, and the articulation of policies towards young blacks with other 'race relations' policies. As we saw in chapter 6, however, the pursuit of specific ameliorative policies towards young blacks has been far from a non-contradictory process. It has been characterised by tensions and conflicts over the very definition of what the 'problem' to be tackled actually is. For example, is the 'problem' the result of the ways in which black minorities are incorporated and excluded from British society, or does it result from the characteristics attributed to these communities? Are the personal and psychological problems of young blacks the source of the problem? Or is the fundamental issue the way in which a 'complex of disabilities' emerges in inner city localities, particularly those with a high proportion of ethnic minorities?

It cannot be said that government policies or the actions of voluntary agencies have been wholly influenced by one definition in isolation from the others, since in practice the kind of policies pursued have been based on a variety of 'sometimes contradictory' objectives. But, as I have shown, particularly in chapters 2 to 5, the constituent elements of official ideologies about young blacks were organised around notions about 'special problems' and 'special needs' which were biased towards the notion that racism was merely one element of a complex of disabilities from which young blacks suffered – ranging from language, family, environmental, cultural and psychological issues. The exact emphasis given to these variables varied from policy to policy, but there were certain continuities nevertheless from the 1960s to the 1980s. The most important of these were:

(a) an emphasis on policies to meet the 'special needs' of young blacks;

(b) the assumption that young blacks position 'between two cultures' was a problem;

(c) the notion that racism was merely one variable in a broader complex of disabilities; and

(d) the assumption that 'equality of opportunity' could be achieved through ameliorative measures rather than structural reforms.

It is assumptions such as these which have given rise to the contemporary situation where young blacks find themselves in a position which shows little sign of any fundamental change, despite promises of action for over two decades. The failure to tackle racism as it affects young blacks through a concerted programme of political action has resulted in the kind of dismal employment situation which I described in chapters 4 and 5, and the persistent failure of numerous initiatives to produce any noticeable impact.

In the face of all this, my basic argument in this book has attempted to bring out two main points. The first is that the history of state interventions in relation to young blacks cannot be analysed as a unified set of logical responses to rational policy debates. This is not to endorse the view that policies developed in an *ad hoc* and incremental manner, or the view that the policies of the state can be reduced to a conspiratorial policy objective of 'oppressing' or 'criminalising' young blacks. But it is to recognise that there is no necessary logic to all the policies pursued by the state on racial or other social policy issues. As we saw in chapters 2 and 3 the genesis and development of ideologies and policies about young blacks during the 1960s and 1970s did not come about as a result of a static and linear course of racialisation. Rather it can be said that there were various dimensions to the policies pursued, and indeed that some of these dimensions contradicted each other.

The second point is that there is no necessary tie-up between policy objectives and outcomes. A good example is the issue I have discussed in a number of chapters – namely, the 'social time bomb' argument. In chapter 2 I showed how a key determinant of early thinking and policies about young blacks was the fear that they could become a class of permanent second-class citizens, alienated and angry, who could drift towards crime or violent political action. The importance of this theme was also discussed in chapters 3 and 4. The stated policy response of successive governments to this fear has been to promise to take decisive action to prevent the condition of young blacks from reaching the stage where they would be prepared to engage in violent protest. Such policies have, however, not necessarily resulted in the implementation of policies which tackled the roots of urban unrest. Quite often the promises of decisive action have been made in such a way that they implied that change would come about incrementally. The paradox, however, is that the speed of change has been such that the conditions which successive governments have argued must not be allowed to develop are actually part of the everyday reality of inner city areas. This is the theme I explored in chapter 6, when I analysed the interplay between urban protest, youth unemployment and social policy.

Urban conflicts, crisis management and social policy

My discussion of different areas of state intervention in relation to black youth has served to highlight the complex determinants of policies in this field. This complexity has become even more clear in the aftermath of the 1980–1 and 1985 riots. During this period the linkage of 'race' to the question of urban unrest has become established in both policy and popular debates. Although the fixing of 'causes' to the riots involved 'race' as one variable among others (including social, economic and local issues), in common sense accounts of why the riots took place in certain areas 'race' has come to play a central role. What are the prospects for the effective pursuit of social policies in relation to 'race' in this new context? How have the riots changed ideologies and policies about 'race relations' and the role of state institutions in managing them?

Chapters 6 and 7 of this book have shown the importance of the riots which have taken place since 1980 in determining the morphology of state intervention in relation to young blacks today. In almost every area of social policy the riots have had an important impact on both the way 'problems' are perceived and on the policies which are proposed in order to tackle them. In much of the discussion since 1980 it is generally agreed that five key characteristics are manifest in areas where the riots occurred: high unemployment, widespread deprivation, manifest racial discrimination and disadvantage, political exclusion and powerlessness and common mistrust of and hostility to the police. But it is equally clear that such conditions are not necessarily translated into disorder and violent notions. An analysis of the post-1980 situation which merely looked at social conditions will only grasp one dimension of the root causes of unrest since, as I argue in chapter 5, the main trend since the 1970s has been a rising feeling of injustice by young blacks suffering from racism, deprivation and police activity. Evidence discussed in a number of the substantive chapters of this book, particularly chapters 2 to 5, suggested that racism has systematically excluded young blacks from equal participation in British society and defined them as a 'problem'. The political, social and economic environments have increasingly put all black communities, and particularly the young, under pressure, and in such a context the lack of remedies through mainstream institutions makes outbursts of violent protest and anger likely.

Lord Scarman's Report on *The Brixton Disorders* contained the argument that:

> Where deprivation and frustration exist on the scale to be found among the young people of Brixton, the probability of disorder must, therefore, be strong.
>
> (Scarman, 1981: para. 2.38)

But what also needs to be stressed, and this a point argued at length in chapter 6, is that attempts to explain the riots merely by reference to the identity of the rioters run the risk of stereotyping a whole grouping while doing little to explain why they feel moved to engage in violent action. Any discussion of young blacks and violent protest must, therefore, be contextualised against the background of the history of systematic exclusion of young blacks, and the increasing gap between the everyday experiences they have (in employment, in relation to the police, and in society generally) and their expectations of justice and equal participation.

The argument in chapter 7 is that whatever the promises of reform which have been made since 1980 have actually achieved in practice, the increasing pressures on young blacks (as an 'enemy within') are likely to result in discontent and anger. The long-term consequences of this are hard to gauge, but a likely result, bearing in mind American evidence, may be a reduction in the identity of young blacks with the polity, their perception of the legitimacy of its rules and agents, and their voluntary consent to its actions. A Home Office study of the 1981 riots concluded that:

> Where any social group perceives government institutions as being indifferent to its needs, the authority and legitimacy of social controls ultimately promulgated by those same institutions will be increasingly questioned. In such circumstances a riot may occur in which individuals will participate for a great mixture of motives, and some will undoubtedly have no more than material gain in mind. At the root of it will be the failure of the relevant authorities to retain the support of the community.
>
> (Field, 1982: 33)

The question which underlies this kind of analysis is also central to the core arguments of this book: *Why should people who are systematically excluded identify with the system which is excluding them?*

The lack of effectiveness of government policies which promise to tackle racial disadvantages, unemployment and inner city decline cannot be said to support any move towards increasing the legitimacy of authority. But additionally the lack of authority norms cannot be overcome simply by repression, as long as the legitimacy of political institutions is built around notions of participation and consent. This is the dilemma which the post-1980 riots have put firmly on the political agenda and which shows little sign of being overcome by the contradictory response of state institutions.

The deep-seated nature of the problem is shown by the fact that the information we have shows that both black and white inner city youngsters took part in the riots. The sense of frustration and anger which white youngsters feel may not have been expressed in exactly the same way as black youngsters, but the collapse of consent to the forces of law and order incorporated groups of both whites and blacks who felt excluded from the institutions and values of contemporary Britain.

What I have attempted to show in this book is that the roots of the present situation have a history in the experiences and stresses faced by young blacks over the last four decades. Unless we analyse this background, understand the stresses that it has created, and its relation to the material realities of racism we have to expect that the basis for further unrest and disorderly protest remains.

Equal opportunity and the limits of reform

Throughout this book I have emphasised that the development of genuinely anti-racist policies and initiatives requires that we contextualise the pursuit of 'equal opportunity' within the larger reality of economic inequality, social deprivation and political exclusion which determine the position of racialised minorities in British society. Without this larger totality the promises which underlie many government initiatives in this, and related policy fields, are likely to remain symbolic and tokenistic if they do not tackle the roots of racism and other discriminatory practices.

The previous discussion may seem a somewhat over-pessimistic assessment, though there are a number of reasons why such a dismal course of development can be predicted. Apart from the notable failure of the existing social policies to have any major impact on levels of youth unemployment generally, there are several reasons for doubting the effects of initiatives aimed at providing young blacks with 'equality of opportunity'. The most important of these relate to the weakness of enforcement measures, the ambiguous nature of the concept of 'equality of opportunity', and the contradictory links between this concept and measures aimed essentially at preserving social stability and order. The last factor has gained particular importance in the aftermath of the 1980–1 riots, and has effectively pushed government responses since then further along the road of seeing the black youth question as essentially one of social control.

The climate of opinion represents an important blockage in the way of effective action against institutionalised racialism as it affects young blacks. Although a whole array of measures are being undertaken or proposed in relation to issues such as 'equal opportunity', 'community policing' and 'urban renewal', the objectives underlying them usually remain vague or contain conflicting elements. In the aftermath of the Scarman Report in 1981 there was some hope that the content of policies on race relations would become more explicit and that more effective mechanisms for bringing about greater equality in access to basic services and employment would be established. Hope was aroused among a large section of the black communities that more fundamental changes in their conditions were on the way. The available evidence on the implementation of policies is inconclusive, but the levels of black unemployment have remained high and there is little evidence to show that the youth training schemes are helping young blacks overcome the racism which prevails in the labour market. Moreover, there is at least some plausibility to the argument that the success of programmes such as YOP and YTS in 'helping' black youngsters has been seen largely in quantitative rather than qualitative terms.

In sum, the weakness of existing definitions and assumptions which have helped shape policy intervention in this area is that they have taken for granted a number of images of black youth which have tended to ignore the issue of racism and emphasised instead personal or communal handicaps. Far from being based on 'objective' analysis, the various stages of response discussed in this book would seem to indicate the importance of common sense fears about 'race' in the construction of policies towards young blacks. The symbolic evocation of the danger represented by young blacks has at best produced a series of contradictory responses and counter-responses, and at worst helped popularise images of young blacks which are negative. It shows though little sign of bringing about the kind of social reform necessary to improve the material conditions of young blacks.

This is partly because, as a number of authors have pointed out, there are severe limits on the impact of political intervention on structurally based patterns of inequality. Furthermore, these limits result from the previous inability of successive governments to mount a concerted offensive against institutional discrimination, given their underlying assumptions concerning the 'problems' faced by young blacks. At most, agencies such as the MSC and CRE have been able to promise to take account of the 'special needs' of the black unemployed, but they have been able to do little to mount a concerted challenge against the causes of racial inequality in employment. The promise held out by the setting up of the Scarman Inquiry in 1981 of a national effort to bring about more 'equality of opportunity' for young blacks has thus fizzled out to such an extent that the riots of 1985 and their aftermath have brought into question the government's willingness to pursue an aggressive strategy against racial inequalities (Benyon and Solomos, 1987). As the CRE argued in 1982:

> So far the response (to the Scarman report) by the Government and others has been disappointingly inadequate. It lacks the sense of urgency that runs through Lord Scarman's report in particular. Of course, it is more difficult in a time of recession, when unemployment is high and resources are scarce, for a

massively expensive effort to be made. But it is precisely at such a time that the vulnerable sections of society suffer most, and even steps that require only a comparatively modest outlay are not being taken by the Government.

(CRE, *Annual Report*, 1981: 3)

This pattern of low-level response has been criticised repeatedly by bodies such as the CRE and at a more political level by the Labour party. Moreover there seems little recognition of the complex ways in which more general policies pursued by the present government, e.g. on industry, urban redevelopment, employment and trade, may be acting to the disadvantage of groups which are already in a weak position.

From the standpoint of the late eighties, it appears that promises concerning equal opportunity and 'special needs' have done very little to alter the social standing of young blacks. In the labour market the idea of 'training for jobs' has little real meaning in inner city areas where over half of young blacks are unemployed, with little or no likelihood of finding future employment. The failure to achieve reform and the emergence of political conflicts around the issue of racism reveal policy options that are severely limited and inherently contradictory.

Part of this contradiction is exemplified by the former Home Secretary, William Whitelaw, who argued that 'it is a deplorable reflection on our society that in all too many instances young people from the ethnic minorities find it harder to get work than their white colleagues with the same background and experience'. He nevertheless still felt inclined to emphasise the importance of a 'strong economy' in holding out hope for the future:

> People in the ethnic minorities stand to benefit particularly greatly from a strong economy. I believe that the best single thing we as a government can do for ethnic minorities in this country is to control inflation and create a climate where real jobs flourish and unemployment falls.
>
> (Whitelaw, 1980: 3)

Looked at in this way, any measures to provide 'special help' are likely to be subordinated to the overall objective of creating the conditions for a 'strong economy' and 'real jobs'.

The chances too that the government will pursue what Lord Scarman has called 'an effective co-ordinated approach to tackling inner city problems' remain slim. This will not necessarily mean a recurrence of the events of 1980–1 and 1985 during the late eighties or nineties, but the pursuit of a policy on training which means training for unemployment and a strengthening of the police as a mechanism of social control will not solve the problems faced by young blacks in employment or other areas. At best such measures may 'keep the streets clear and the young people quiet'. The tensions and the political dilemmas will remain.

The wholesale restructuring and 'de-regulation' of the labour market which the Conservative administration has pursued since 1979 also has important negative implications for equal opportunity. It has become a commonplace to argue that training initiatives such as YTS will help the pursuit of racial equality in the youth labour market. This is argued at two levels. The first is that 'special measures' on such schemes can help unemployed black young people overcome the specific problems they face in entering the labour market. Second, it is argued that the creation of a robust economy with 'jobs for the future' will enhance the chances of young workers securing permanent jobs once they have been trained to meet the needs of a fast-changing economy. But despite such assertions initiatives which aim to enhance the ability of young blacks to compete equally for jobs are severely constrained by the established patterns of racial inequality in employment and by the pressures on employers to compete and maximise their profitability in order to survive.

The pursuit of 'equality of opportunity' within this context will remain at best a contradictory process, and at worst a symbolic gesture with little impact on the everyday realities of racism and racial inequality. It produces an unstable truce, and the same problems remain or new ones emerge.

Prospects for the future

It is a customary practice, though a necessarily hazardous one, in books of this kind to make some reasoned assessments about future prospects. The very volatility of this area makes this a particularly hazardous task, particularly since during the 1980s we have witnessed a sharp politicisation of questions about young blacks as a result of urban unrest in 1980, 1981, 1985, 1986 and 1987. This book has put forward a historical and contemporary analysis of the position of young blacks in British society which has argued that the transformations in ideologies and policies over the past two decades have done little to challenge existing and new patterns of inequality which affect them as a group and as individuals. It is on the basis of this analysis that I would dispute assumptions that the pursuit of 'equality of opportunity' and acknowledgement of the 'special needs' of young blacks can lead to a fundamental change in their current position. The options for most young blacks are, if anything, becoming more narrow as a result of the social and economic restructuring of the major urban conurbations. Hence the promise that more opportunities for employment and self-achievement lie ahead will do little to change current realities unless it is linked to a programme of action at national and local levels; a programme involving black youngsters and their communities in deciding on their futures.

The paradox, however, is that as black youngsters become the personification in neo-right ideologies of a dangerous 'enemy within' such policies are becoming less and less likely. Political agencies and institutions seem only to become interested in doing something about the social conditions faced by young blacks at times of crisis and disorder. As we saw in 1981 and 1985 promises of positive action are made after riots, only for the government to carry out a very limited programme of reform in practice. Without fundamental social, economic and political changes, however, young blacks face the bleak prospect of remaining on the margins of British society and a target for attack. No number of promises will remedy the deep-seated inequalities which have been created over the past four decades. As early as 1967 Stuart Hall argued that politicians and decision-makers should not place the label of 'problem' on young blacks without 'understanding what it is like for them' (Hall, 1967: 14). In 1986 a young black resident of Broadwater Farm made a similar point somewhat differently: 'Unless you understand what being black in Britain really means, you will never understand why people are prepared to stand up and fight the officers of the law' (Stafford Scott, *The Guardian*, 17 January 1986). As we edge closer to the 1990s it is important to begin any initiatives aimed at improving the position of young blacks from this perspective, for policies over the past twenty years have clearly failed to understand young blacks feeling of injustice. The fruits of that failure await to be reaped unless radical reforms are implemented urgently.

Notes

Introduction

1 The impact of the post-1980 riots on the question of black youth and race-related issues generally is analysed in detail in Solomos, 1986, and in chapter 6 of this volume. The origins of this politicisation can be traced to a number of important symbolic events, e.g. the Notting Hill Carnival of 1976, but it will be argued throughout this book that the riots represent an important watershed in the history of 'race' in contemporary Britain.

2 The origins and common sense usage of all these terms need to be located against the background of the changing political language about 'race' in post-war British society, and more concretely in relation to specific policy problems as defined by political debate and practice. This is a point that is analysed more fully in my study of the politics of racism; see Solomos, forthcoming.

3 The question of the distinctiveness of the experience of Afro-Caribbean and Asian youth is taken up in chapter 2.

4 Studies of the position of young blacks in the labour market during the seventies are usefully summarised in Brooks, 1983 and Solomos, 1985. Black youth unemployment became a central area of academic and policy concern from the mid-1970s onwards, and the Department of Employment and the Manpower Services Commission were instrumental in commissioning a number of research studies of this question.

5 Chapter 1 attempts to outline briefly some of the central aspects of the political context of 'race relations' in contemporary Britain; for a number of different perspectives on the inter-relationship of race and politics see Layton-Henry and Rich, 1986.

6 See Benyon, 1984 for a detailed account of the immediate impact of the Scarman Report on political and ideological debates. For a reassessment of the situation in the aftermath of the 1985 riots, see Benyon and Solomos, 1987.

7 This realisation of the importance of racialisation in the analysis of British politics is rooted in the political and intellectual debates that took place during the 1970s. This phenomenon will be analysed fully in Solomos, forthcoming.

8 For some discussion of the political debates that took place in these journals see Hall *et al.*, 1978: chapter 10; Gilroy, 1987.

9 This debate is analysed more fully than is possible in this chapter in a number of texts published during the early 1980s, including CCCS Race and Politics Group, 1982 and Miles, 1982. It is also an issue that will be analysed more fully in chapter 7 in relation to the current debates about racial ideology.

10 In particular a constant theme that runs throughout this volume is the question of symbolic political language, and the work of Murray Edelman has proved particularly helpful in this regard.

11 A useful and critical review of the terms of this complex debate can be found in Jessop, 1982.

12 See Skocpol, 1980; Skocpol and Ikenberry, 1983; Orloff and Skocpol, 1984.

1 The politics of racism and state intervention

1 A full discussion of these various explanations of the changing context of political intervention during the post-war period is beyond the scope of this study. But a useful review of alternative models can be found if one looks at: Deakin, 1968; Rose *et al.*, 1969; Freeman, 1979; Sivanandan, 1982; Layton-Henry, 1984; Miles and Phizacklea, 1984.

2 The most important of these studies are Ben-Tovim *et al.*, 1986; Gilroy, 1987; and Carter, Harris and Joshi, 1987.

3 But see Solomos, forthcoming, chapters 1, 2, and 5.

4 The history of this period is being written by Clive Harris at the Centre for Research in Ethnic Relations, who is analysing in detail official documents available at the Public Records Office.

5 This is a subject that deserves wider attention than it has achieved so far. Very little work has been done on the coverage of 'immigration' and 'race' issues in the press during this period, despite the fact that it is likely to prove a valuable resource in the construction of the politics of the post-war period. Additionally, we need to know more about the role of 'race' and related issues in national and local political debates.

6 The best introductions to the complex history of these debates can be found in Freeman, 1979, and Layton-Henry, 1984; but useful evidence about the dynamics of this process of political racialisation can also be found in Rose *et al.*, 1969, which contains a detailed account of the formulation and evolution of official ideologies about these issues.

7 Preliminary analysis of these documents has served to question common assumptions about the period from 1948 to 1962 as one of *laissez-faire* in relation to immigration and race issues. Brief reviews of some of the main aspects of these documents can be found in Carter and Joshi, 1984; and Carter, Harris and Joshi, 1987. There is clearly a need, however, for a more detailed analysis of (a) the internal state dynamics of policy formulation, and (b) of the reasons for the delay in passing restrictive legislation until 1962.

8 A limited account of the political impact of the riots can be found in Layton-Henry, 1984 and Miles, 1984. A more detailed and critical analysis of the context, nature and consequences of the 1958 events is attempted in Harris and Solomos, forthcoming.

9 The mobilisation of political opinion during 1958–62 in favour of controls has been analysed in some detail, e.g. in Deakin, 1968; Deakin, 1972; and Miles and Phizacklea, 1984. What is also clear is that the racialisation of

political debate was also proceeding apace in the broader context of local and national politics as well. See Solomos, forthcoming, chapter 4.

10 The debates in Parliament exemplify the changing nature of political opinion during this period: 'Immigration control', *Hansard*, vol. 596, 1958: cols. 1552–97; 'Immigration from the commonwealth', *Hansard*, vol. 613, 1959: cols. 1121–30; 'Control of immigration', *Hansard*, vol. 634, 1961: cols. 1929–2024; 'Immigration', *Hansard*, vol. 645, 1961: cols. 1319–31.

11 See the critical analysis of this literature, in the light of historical and contemporary evidence, in Solomos, forthcoming, chapters 3, 4 and 5.

12 This argument should not be taken to imply that the evolution of state policies on immigration and 'race' issues was uniform and monolithic. There were important contradictions within the various government departments and between officials and politicians about how to react to the construction of immigration as a political issue. See Ben-Tovim *et al.*, 1986, for an explication of this point.

13 The ideological and political impact of this White Paper, particularly in the light of the Labour party's history on the immigration issue, can be gauged from the discussion in Rose, *et al.*, 1969 and Freeman, 1979.

14 The formulation and implementation of these twin objectives is an issue which takes us beyond the limits of this book. But see the collection of papers in Abbott, 1971, for an analysis of some of the most important features of this two-pronged formulation of the objectives of government policies.

15 Perhaps the most important threat to the legitimacy of government policies on race over the last two decades emanates from the growing disillusion of the black communities with the achievements of the various anti-discrimination measures. This is a theme which I shall develop later in chapters 6 and 7.

16 Examples of parliamentary debates which hinge on this issue include the debates on changes to the Immigration Rules and related issues. See for example: 'Immigration rules', *Hansard,* vol. 980, 1980: cols. 1010–1106; 'Immigration', *Hansard*, vol. 31, 1982: cols. 692–761; 'Immigration', *Hansard*, vol. 83, 1985: cols. 893–964.

17 The articulation between neo-right political ideologies and questions about 'race' has become a consistent theme throughout the last decade. For partial but valuable accounts of this development see: Barker, 1982; Seidel, 1986a and 1986b; and Gordon and Klug, 1986.

18 The criticism of Powell's views by most sections of parliamentary opinion and the press seemed to marginalise political debate about the question of repatriation. But this marginalisation should not be taken to imply that his interventions had no influence on the trajectory of political debate during this period. Indeed, sections of political opinion were clearly, if only partially, influenced by his analysis of the 'root cause' of urban unrest and violence.

2 From assimilation to special needs: ideologies and policies

1 The emergence of the younger generation of black and 'half-caste' children as an issue of social concern became particularly clear during the 1930s, leading to representations by local voluntary agencies to central government departments and the setting up of enquiries into the social and cultural conditions in the main port settlements. On this point the best accounts are Rich, 1986 and Harris, 1987.

2 See e.g. *News Chronicle*, 3 November 1952, 'Colour-bar road asks for help'; *Sunday Graphic*, 26 October 1952, 'From Tiger Bay'.

3 This is not to argue that the contemporary situation can be equated to that of the 1930s; merely that there are continuities between the official ideologies and discursive languages used in relation to the 'half-caste' issue and the question of black youth today.

4 On this specific point see the analysis in Drake, 1954 and Little, 1947, for an account of the immediate impact of the war period and post-war black migration in Britain.

5 See e.g. CO876/17 (1942–3) 'Welfare of colonial people in the UK'; CO537/ 1124 (1946) 'Colour discrimination in the UK'; CO876/196 (1950) 'Colour prejudice in the UK'.

6 A measure of this shift can be found in the recently released documents from the Public Records Office which document the shift during 1945 to 1955 from the issues specific to the established black settlements to the newly arrived black migrant communities, and the changing official ideologies about this latter group.

7 Examples of this debate can be found in the parliamentary debates during this period and in the coverage of papers such as *The Times*, which began to discuss the question of black migration to Britain on a regular basis during this time.

8 See e.g. the coverage of the aftermath of the Notting Hill and Nottingham riots in *The Times* and the *Manchester Guardian* during 1958 and 1959.

9 A more detailed account of the period after the 1958 riots can be found in Harris and Solomos, forthcoming, where we show that this process of racialisation was closely linked to common sense images of black immigrants as a source of 'social problems', particularly in relation to housing, law and order and employment.

10 Miles, 1984, outlines some of the main components of this policy response. But see also Rose *et al.*, 1969.

11 Patterson, 1969: 158–86, provides an outline of the emergence of this issue during this period. But see also the coverage of the issue in the *IRR Newsletter*, and the increasing focus of this publication on the development of domestic race relations during this period.

12 See e.g. S. Patterson (ed.) (1964), *Immigrants in London: report of a study group set up by the London Council of Social Service*, London: National Council of Social Service; London Council of Social Service (1967), *Commonwealth Children in Britain*, London: National Council of Social Service.

13 See e.g.: National Committee for Commonwealth Immigrants, *The Second Generation: report of a conference at St Edmund Hall, Oxford, 18–20 March 1966*; and National Committee for Commonwealth Immigrants, *Are These Teenagers Different?*, conference organised with the Friends Race Relations Committee, Friends House, London, 8 November 1968.

14 This is not to say, of course, that these were the only concerns which fed into the official construction of this issue. There were a number of other problems which came to occupy a central role in policy debates about this question, and I shall touch on these later on in this chapter.

15 The consequences of this approach to policies on 'race relations' and racial discrimination are discussed more fully in Solomos, forthcoming.

16 The situation in the United States was often cited as an example of the

political dangers of creating a group of 'second-class' citizens outside the main institutions of society. This was a theme that was to become even more prevalent from the late sixties onwards, as we shall see later in this chapter.

17 See the account of notions of 'integration', and their changing meanings in Patterson, 1969: 108–130; Rose *et al.*, 1969; Abbott, 1971; Jenkins and Solomos, 1987: 30–53.

18 Other similar conferences were organised during this period, and they were intended both for welfare professionals and for policy-makers. The underlying theme of such conferences seemed to be that the 'integration' of young blacks could be brought about through greater education and discussion of the problems that they faced.

19 The membership of the Committee was: Lord Hunt, J. Cheetham, S. Hall, J. Klein, F. W. Milson and P. Stephenson.

20 See the discussion of the impact of the Hunt report in the *IRR Newsletter*, June–July 1967 and January 1969.

21 This is a point that will be discussed more fully, particularly in relation to law and order issues, in chapter 3.

22 The notion of cultural conflict between the 'first' and 'second' generations was linked to wider concerns in British society about the 'youth problem' as a whole; but through the 1970s the preoccupation with 'black youth' became more pronounced. On this point see Hall *et al.*, 1978.

23 For a discussion of some of the most common concerns about the future of young blacks in Britain see 'Second generation blues', *IRR Newsletter*, March 1967.

24 'Jobs or strife warning on coloured youth', *The Times*, 26 September 1969; 'Teenage racialism grows in Brixton', *The Observer*, 12 January 1969; 'Schools and police are blamed for migrant discontent', *The Guardian*, 16 November 1970.

25 The pamphlet, entitled 'The Young Englanders', was originally published in June 1967, but it was republished three times during the late 1960s. It was referred to widely, both in academic discussions and by the 1969 Select Committee report. Hall was also a member of the Committee that produced the 1967 Report on 'Immigrants and the youth service'.

26 Even during the relatively 'full employment' climate period of the 1960s there was evidence that black workers, young and old, were discriminated against in the labour market and were disproportionately affected by unemployment. The full implications of these processes only became apparent, however, during the late 1960s and 1970s.

27 See DES, 1967: 114–15, 149 and 230.

28 It should be said that the controversy relates less to the substance of Beetham's research than to his use of terms such as 'unrealistic aspirations'. The mythologisation of this term and its influence on practitioners does not necessarily result from Beetham's research, but the relative paucity of other accounts of black youth employment helped to concentrate attention on his study.

29 Heginbotham, 1967, argued, for example, that 'many immigrants have job aspirations based upon the value structures of their home territories' and that it was therefore necessary to advise them to pursue 'more realistic' aspirations.

30 See e.g. 'The picture of prejudice', *The Guardian*, 10 July 1969; 'Radical new

deal urged for coloured citizens', *The Times*, 10 July 1969; 'Colour myths and dangers', *The Daily Telegraph*, 10 July 1969.

31 The influence of this report on official ideologies about the 'second generation' and young blacks more generally has been traced in more detail in Solomos, 1983b, and Solomos, 1985.

32 It is worth noting in this regard that the evidence submitted to the Select Committee included submissions from government departments, voluntary bodies, black community groups and academic researchers on a 'race' issue which had not been fully analysed before. In this sense the Report and the minutes of evidence are a major landmark in the history of this question.

33 The language of 'complex disabilities' is something to which I shall return in subsequent chapters; I shall in particular explore the changing meanings attached to this notion and the consequences of these changes for policy and practice.

34 This study will not include a detailed account of the development of policies on 'race and education'. This is a field of study which has witnessed a massive number of studies over the years and it needs to be analysed in its own autonomy. But I do agree with Troyna and Williams, 1986, that one cannot fully understand the racialisation of youth questions without some reference to developments in the field of education.

35 The question of the involvement of young blacks in the American 1960s riots is analysed in some detail in Fogelson, 1971: 26–49.

36 The resonance of such images became even more evident during the late 1970s and in the aftermath of the 1980–1 and 1985 riots. This is a point to which I shall return in chapter 6.

37 The emergence of this issue as an area of concern for the police as a front line institution is being explored in the PhD Thesis of Suganya Ranganathan on 'Race relations, law and order and policing', Aston University, in preparation.

38 The articulation of such fears also relied on the image that certain areas were, or were in the process of becoming, localities in which crime and disorder could thrive. Areas such as Brixton and Handsworth were some of the earliest to be identified in this manner.

3 Black youth, crime and the ghetto: common sense images and law and order

1 The early twentieth-century anti-immigrant political mobilisation was resonant with references to the link between crime and immigration. See for example the account of this theme in Gainer, 1972: 51–3, 203–6. This is not to argue that the images applied to the largely Jewish immigrants of that time were the same as those applied to the black migrants of the post-1945 period. But the continuities are ones which do warrant some closer examination; see Miles and Solomos, 1987.

2 See Harris and Solomos, forthcoming; for a more general review of this question, but one which does not analyse the historical issues in any detail, see Gilroy, 1987.

3 The 1969 report on *Colour and Citizenship* by Rose *et al.*, contained numerous examples of how the questions of law and order and policing were beginning to surface as important areas of concern for the black communities and for the official institutions themselves.

4 The circular was linked to an overall rethinking of government policy on race and policing, which evolved along the lines that there was a need for 'special measures' to foster good relations between the police and black communities. See Lambert, 1970: 177–87.

5 Examples of this trend are the following: *IRR Newsletter*, 'Immigrants and the police', September 1967; H. Rose, 'The police and the coloured communities', *IRR Newsletter*, October 1968; D. Nandy, 'Immigrants and the police', *Race and Immigration*, October 1970.

6 For a general overview of the history of the debate about 'race and policing' see Gordon, 1985. On the specific period of the late 1960s and early 1970s see: *Race Today*, June 1969; September 1970; June 1972; November 1972; and December 1973.

7 The assumption seems to be that one can treat the issue of policing as almost synonymous with the 'youth' question. But this has meant that the particular reasons for the confrontations between the police and young blacks, as opposed to the black communities as a whole, have remained unexplored.

8 This theme has been explored in some detail in Solomos, 1985, where I show how the construction of the 'alienation' issue depended on the policy concerns of both central and local government institutions. See also Gaskell and Smith, 1981.

9 An exploratory analysis of the dynamics of black political mobilisation and state responses can be found in Mullard, 1982. Few attempts have been made to analyse the complex processes which led to the formation of a 'black political consciousness'. But for a descriptive account see Ramdin, 1987.

10 A review of other reports and studies of this period can be found in Gordon, 1985.

11 See Suganya Ranganathan, 'Race relations, law and order and policing', PhD. Thesis, Aston University, in preparation.

12 One measure of this concern is the increasing coverage given to this issue in journals such as *Race Today* and in papers such as *The Times* and *The Guardian*. See also the regular coverage of this question in the Runnymede Trust's *Race and Immigration* during 1969–73.

13 *Race Today*, October 1970 and November 1971.

14 *The Observer*, 15 November 1970, 'It's hell to be young (and black) in Handsworth'; *The Sunday Times*, 4 January 1970, 'Must Harlem come to Birmingham?'

15 For a general review of this history see Benyon, 1986b; but in particular see: Humphry, 1972; Banton, 1973; Pulle, 1973; Demuth, 1978. See also the theoretical and analytical arguments in Jefferson and Clarke, 1973, and Hall *et al.*, 1978.

16 See the discussion of the language and interpretation of this report in Clarke *et al.*, 1974, for an explication of its role in articulating political ideologies about the police–community relations dynamic.

17 This is not to deny the pertinence of analysing the origins of official ideologies about this issue before this report, and this is something that clearly needs to be done. But the purposes of this study are best served by analysing the genesis and impact of this report in some detail. For the analytical problems posed by the analysis of official texts and discursive frameworks see Burton and Carlen, 1979.

18 This public debate is itself closely reflected in the evidence submitted to the

Select Committee, but also in the coverage of 'race and policing' issues in the national and local press. The language used to describe this process was resonant with categorisations of young blacks as a danger to social order and stability.

19 For the social history of the political debate about mugging see Jefferson and Clarke, 1973; Hall *et al.*, 1978.

20 Demuth, 1978, provides a detailed analysis of the legal and policing practices that characterised this shift, particularly in relation to the use of the 'sus' legislation as a mechanism for the social control of young blacks.

21 On the intermingling of political concerns about the 'inner city' with popular concerns about 'race' see Edwards and Batley, 1978; Higgins *et al.*, 1983; Edwards, 1987.

22 This imagery of a 'small minority' working to undermine society from within is something to which I shall return in chapters 6 and 7.

23 *The Times*, 13 October 1971, 'Police responsibility in race harmony'; *The Sunday Times*, 28 November 1971, 'The life and needless death of the man society spurned'; *The Guardian*, 1 November 1973, 'Police deny catalogue of brutality to immigrants'; *The Sunday Times*, 3 July 1973, 'The disturbing truth behind a mythical "race" riot'.

24 *The Guardian*, 6 February 1970, 'Alabama Staffs'; *The Sunday Times*, 23 July 1973, 'The growing danger of the jobless young blacks'; *The Sunday Times*, 5 January 1975, 'Danger signals from the streets of Lambeth'.

25 P. Harrison, 'Black and white', *New Society*, 21 June 1973.

26 These 'everyday confrontations' have received surprisingly little attention, though they are clearly of great importance to any rounded understanding of the subsequent history of urban unrest and disorder. It is beyond the scope of this study to discuss them in any detail, though it would clearly be of value to see more detailed case studies of the social history of black communities during this time.

27 See various issues of *Race Today* during 1970–6. Also see *Black Liberator*, vol. 2, nos. 1, 2 and 4.

28 See, for example, the reporting of such an incident in *The Sunday Times*, 3 July 1973. Such events were also described in the Select Committee's reports on *Police/Immigrant Relations* (1972) and *The West Indian Community* (1977).

29 *Race Today*, November 1971, 385; A. X. Cambridge, 'On the Metro Saga', *Black Liberator*, 1 (4), 1973, 155–68; P. Medlicot, 'The Brixton scene', *New Society*, 12 April 1973, 64–6.

30 An overall chronology of some of these events can be found in Sivanandan, 1982 and Gilroy, 1987.

31 See the detailed content analysis of these sources in Suganya Ranganathan's 'Race relations, law and order and policing', PhD Thesis, Aston University, in preparation.

32 The linkages between growing official concern about violence and disorder and racialised political discourses are explored in Solomos *et al.*, 1982; Benyon, 1986b; and Gilroy, 1987.

33 *The Times*, 2 November 1973, 'Problems of full employment: immigrants no longer arriving to fill urban jobs'.

34 Such views were criticised widely from within the Conservative party, even though they were supported by a group of MPs belonging to the fringes of the

party. But they were widely reported in the press and widely circulated in popular debates about 'race' and immigration issues.

35 This may perhaps be seen as a somewhat exaggerated statement for the period I am discussing here. Yet what the recent riots have made clear is that the expectation of violent confrontations with young blacks is by no means a 1980s phenomenon. See e.g. Newman, 1986.

36 See e.g. J. Shirley, 'Mugging: statistics of an "unacceptable crime"', *The Times*, 14 March 1982; R. Butt, 'Mugging: facing the hard facts', *The Times*, 18 March 1982; R. Butt, 'Who pays for the blues in the night?', *The Times*, 1 April 1982; P. Worsthorne, 'Cant about colour and crime', *The Sunday Telegraph*, 27 March 1983.

37 *The Sunday Times*, 5 January 1975, 'Danger signals from the streets of Lambeth'. But see also Select Committee, 1977, *The West Indian Community*, vol. 2, 'Memorandum by the Community Relations Commission'.

38 *Birmingham Post*, 12 April 1976 and 13 April 1976.

39 Select Committee, 1977, *The West Indian Community*, vol. 2; 'Memorandum by the Metropolitan Police'; 'Memorandum by the Community Relations Commission'; 'Additional Memorandum by the Metropolitan Police'.

40 *The Guardian*, 1 September 1976; *Birmingham Post*, 1 September 1976; *The Guardian*, 31 August 1977; *Birmingham Post*, 31 August 1977; *The Economist*, 4 September 1976, 'London's black carnival'; *The Economist*, 20 August 1977, 'England's hot summer'.

41 *The Sunday Times*, 8 June 1976, 'Killing stokes new fears of race violence'; *Birmingham Post*, 9 June 1976, 'Jenkins in surprise visit to Southall'.

42 *The Observer*, 21 August 1977; *The Sunday Times*, 21 August 1977.

43 *Birmingham Post*, 23 March 1976, 'The wild bunch'; *Birmingham Post*, 25 March 1976; *The Economist*, 17 April 1976, 'Not black and white'.

44 *Birmingham Evening Mail*, 11–13 May 1976, 'The angry suburb'; see also readers' responses in the 20 May edition.

45 See references in n. 43.

46 On the social and political context of community policing in Handsworth see Rex and Tomlinson, 1979; Gilroy, 1982; Brown, 1982.

47 *Birmingham Post*, 30 November 1977; *Birmingham Evening Mail*, 8 December 1977; see also the correspondence in the *Birmingham Post* on 6 December 1977.

48 *The Guardian*, 24 March 1983; *The Times*, 24 March 1983; see also *New Society*, 31 March 1983.

4 The social construction of black youth unemployment and state policies

1 The genesis of this shift in official concern about young blacks can be traced, as I have already shown, to the period of the mid-1960s. But the point I am trying to make here is that there was during the late 1970s a significant shift in the priorities of state institutions. A more detailed explanation of the historical origins of this transformation can be found in Solomos, 1985.

2 See the contrasting accounts of the politics of unemployment in Moon and Richardson, 1985; Jackson, 1985; and Ashton, 1986, for a critical analysis of the policy networks of what is increasingly referred to as the 'unemployment industry'.

3 This delay in responding to demands for greater racial equality was not

limited merely to the question of black youth unemployment. At a broader
level the lack of a sustained political programme to tackle racial inequality
reflected inequalities in access to power, which resulted in black communities
having a minimal impact on the political agenda.

4 For a more detailed account of the politics of black youth unemployment
   during this period see the analysis in Solomos, 1983.

5 A review of processes leading up the 1976 Race Relations Act can be found in
   Solomos, 1987: 35–40. Some of the wider issues surrounding race relations
   legislation are critically explored in Lustgarten, 1980; Feuchtwang, 1981;
   McCrudden, 1982; and Mullard, 1982.

6 *The Observer*, 9 June 1974, 'Our lost black generation'; *The Times*, 10 June
   1974, 'Discrimination leads young black people into trouble with law'.

7 This process of amplification was eventually to lead by the late 1970s to the
   focusing of official concern around the phenomenon of public disorder and
   urban violence, particularly in the aftermath of the outbreak of violence
   during the Notting Hill Carnivals of 1976 and 1977. But during the period I am
   analysing here the issue was one of the involvement of young blacks in street
   crime rather than their participation in collective forms of protest.

8 A measure of this can be found in the increasing importance of young blacks
   as a central source of concern for the race relations agencies set up by the
   state. Increasingly during 1972–6 the Community Relations Commission had
   become concerned with young blacks as a particular 'social problem'. This
   concern was to be even more central in the work of the Commission for Racial
   Equality from 1977 onwards.

9 The voluminous evidence to the Select Committee from state agencies, black
   community groups, voluntary agencies and researchers attests to the widespread nature of concern about the problems confronting young blacks. At
   the same time David Smith's survey of racial disadvantage in Britain (Smith,
   1977) reported the question of young second-generation blacks as a central
   area of concern.

10 A detailed account of the MSC's response to black youth unemployment can
   be found in chapter 5. In this chapter I want to concentrate more specifically
   on the wider political context of this question from the mid-1970s onwards.

11 This notion of 'integration' was to a large extent distinct from the more liberal
   principles pursued by Roy Jenkins while Home Secretary during the mid-
   1960s. Rather it was a notion of state intervention to bring about 'integration'
   on the terms which were defined as 'good for society as a whole'.

12 The trajectory of the MSC's development from the mid-1970s onwards is not
   within the scope of this book. Nevertheless, a number of useful accounts of its
   history and development can be found. An account of its early history is to be
   found in Howells, 1980. For its subsequent expansion and the development of
   its various programmes see: Gleeson, 1983; Bates *et al.*, 1984; Moon and
   Richardson, 1985; Finn, 1987.

13 The pursuit of this objective of controlling the wider consequences of high
   levels of black youth unemployment need not imply that a mechanical 'social
   control' framework can be applied to this area of state intervention. But it
   does mean that where the concern with controlling social instability is shown
   to be important empirically that one cannot ignore its impact.

14 The dynamics of this increased public concern cannot be understood fully
   without reference to the processes of political response to the 'crisis' of black

youth more generally which have been analysed in chapter 3. But see John, 1981, for one account of the ways in which this increased public concern was reflected in policy change during this period.

15 On the ideology of 'special needs' and its implications for the kind of policies pursued by the CRE and the MSC during this period see Solomos, 1985.

16 The widespread pertinence of this concern can be gauged from the concern with the consequences of excluding young blacks from employment for their social 'integration' and their relations with the police. See *The Observer*, 5 September 1976, 'Young, bitter and black'.

17 See the arguments, for example, in MSC 1980a and 1980c. On the broader framework of labour market policy during this period see the account in Fairley and Grahl, 1983.

18 This is not to say that all the people involved, or arrested during, the riots were unemployed young blacks and whites. The evidence on this point is not so direct. But it does seem clear, as I shall discuss later, that there was a preponderance of young people among riot participants.

19 *Hansard*, vol. 8, 1981: cols. 1397–1502; vol. 13, 1981: cols. 1009–956; *The Guardian*, 6 July 1981, 'Editorial: a detritus that won't wash away'.

20 *Daily Mirror*, 6 July 1981, 'Jobless, hopeless, lawless'; *The Times*, 7 July 1981, 'Liverpool: why the clue to violence is economic, not racial' (Philip Waller); *The Times*, 6 June 1982, 'Riots linked with jobless' (Peter Evans).

21 Apart from the Select Committee Reports cited already see the evidence submitted to the Home Affairs Committee during 1980–1 on the issue of *Racial Disadvantage*.

22 See for example: *Race Today*, March 1975: 65–6; *Race Today*, April 1975: 80–2; *Race Today*, August 1974, 'No Jesterin': 171; *Race Today*, July–August 1976: 149–50; *Race Today*, February–March 1982: 52–3.

23 The most important contributions in this regard are John, 1981 and Fisher and Joshua, 1982.

24 Crick, 1980; Tarling, 1982; Gilroy, 1982 and 1987; Lea and Young, 1984; Benyon, 1986b.

5 The politics of youth training and equal opportunity: from 'special needs' to the Youth Training Scheme

1 For a concise analytical discussion of how social policies can work against the interests of the groups that they are supposed to help see Edelman, 1977. Edelman's account of social policies and political language represents one strand of influence on the approach of this and the previous chapter.

2 The MSC has, particularly since 1981, produced a number of advisory documents on equal opportunity issues: MSC, 1982d, 1982f, 1983b, 1984a; see also the MSC's *Annual Reports* during this period. For the general framework of government policy see the evidence by the Department of Employment and the Manpower Services Commission to the House of Commons Employment Committee (1986–7).

3 The most clear examples of racialised political processes over the last two decades are policies which have aimed at bringing about greater equality of opportunity in relation to employment, housing and areas of welfare delivery. Although I cannot discuss the details of the various policy initiatives under these headings a detailed account of them can be found in Solomos,

forthcoming, particularly chapters 4 and 5. But see also the analysis in Benyon, 1984.

4 On the processes through which issues enter the political arena and are integrated into the policy agenda see the useful discussions in Edelman 1977, Kingdon 1984, and Katznelson 1986. Their frameworks have influenced the operationalisation of my research approach in this project.

5 On the notion of a 'complex of racial disadvantage' see the usage of this notion in the Select Committee's 1969 report on *The Problems of Coloured School Leavers* and the Home Affairs 1981 report on *Racial Disadvantage*. For a critical review of the conceptual problems involved see Morris, 1986 and Edwards, 1987.

6 The notion that the position of young blacks could be equated with other 'disadvantaged' and 'handicapped' groups is in itself not new. But the advent of mass unemployment has ensured that it has gained currency along new lines, particularly in the context of the politicisation of the whole youth unemployment question and the urgent need to legitimate the high levels of unemployment among certain groups of the population.

7 On these research projects see Stares, Imberg and McRobie, 1982; Cross, Edmonds, Sargeant, 1983; Fenton *et al.*, 1984.

8 Benyon, 1984; Benyon and Solomos, 1987; Gilroy 1987.

9 See also the references in n. 2, above.

10 On the implications of this point in relation to gender issues see: Wickham, 1986; Cockburn, 1987.

11 A notable influence on the course of this debate about young blacks, unemployment and public disorder was the report by Lord Scarman on the Brixton riots of April 1981. He highlighted the socio-economic position of young blacks as an underlying cause of the riots, and this argument elicited both criticism and support.

12 The directions and consequences of this influence will be discussed in more detail in chapter 6. Here I am merely concerned with the broad contours of the transformations taking place during this period.

13 The period from July 1981 to early 1982 is resplendent with promises from government politicians and officials that the fight against youth unemployment was central to the government's overall objective of creating a strong economy. But the course of the state's response to this question also reflected its wider preoccupation with distancing itself from any 'blame' for high unemployment.

14 On the specific context of MSC policies on equal opportunities and 'race' see Troyna and Smith, 1983; Cross and Smith, 1987. On the wider background to the policies pursued by the MSC in managing the social contradictions of youth unemployment see Bates *et al.*, 1987; Finn, 1987; Cockburn, 1987.

15 See for example DES, 1983 and 1985; DE and DES, 1984 and 1985. But see more specifically Fenton and Burton, 1987; Cross, 1987.

16 The research of Malcolm Cross, who has analysed the educational background of black and white participants on the Youth Training Scheme, questions the validity of such assumptions. See Cross, 1987; Cross, Wrench and Barnett, 1987.

17 Edelman, 1977: 18–19, notes that government policies and official pronouncements necessarily involve the categorisation of 'problems' in terms of individual and institutional causes. The definition of 'problems' as an

outcome of social and economic processes is resisted because it may well call into question the legitimacy of the overall political process. He notes that 'What events mean for policy formation depends on whether they are defined as exceptional or, alternatively, as one set of incidents in a world that is constantly in crisis' (43).

18 For a systematic treatment of this question see Braham and Rhodes, 1981 and 1987.

19 The origins and development of this approach to the labour market are analysed in Finn, 1983 and 1987; and Fairley and Grahl, 1983. For the wider context of economic policy changes since 1979 see: Gamble, 1981; Krieger, 1986; Thompson, 1986.

20 The dynamics and contradictions of this approach are analysed in detail in Thompson, 1986: chapter 4.

21 See House of Commons, Employment Committee, 1985–6.

22 Krieger, 1986: chapter 3.

23 In this sense these policies can be seen as a success only in a very limited way. They help to manage the immediate crisis of unemployment and to deflect criticism but they do not resolve the underlying contradictions caused by high levels of unemployment and the reproduction of social inequality. It is thus possible to see the whole issue of black youth unemployment as an example of what Edelman, 1977, calls intractable social problems, that defy resolution within the limits of an essentially inegalitarian economic and social structure.

6 The 'social time-bomb' explodes: urban protest, youth unemployment and social policy

1 The wider context of policies and practice in the field of 'race' and 'race-related' political issues is analysed in Solomos, forthcoming. There the question of what are the implications of this racialisation for the British political system is explored in some detail, particularly in chapters 8 to 10.

2 This preoccupation with the US experience has been evident in Britain since the 1960s, particularly with the emergence of 'race' onto the national political agenda. Some of the complexities of the comparison are emphasised in Benyon and Solomos, 1987. This volume brings together the proceedings of a conference on urban unrest, which included speakers from both the US and UK.

3 This is a theme which is discussed in some detail in relation to the US by Edelman, 1971.

4 For a discussion of aspects of this history see Joshua and Wallace, 1983. Some of these historical connections will also be discussed in my joint work with Clive Harris on the 1958 riots, Harris and Solomos, forthcoming.

5 See Hall *et al.*, 1978, and Solomos *et al.*, 1982 for a discussion of this history.

6 An historical account of these fears about 'law and order', and one which links contemporary changes to the question of 'race', can be found in Freeman, 1984, and Reiner, 1985.

7 A useful discussion of the language of the 'inner city' and its link with images of disorderly protest can be found in Burgess, 1985.

8 A useful critique of some of the dominant explanatory models can be found in Benyon, 1986a.

9 See Reiner, 1985, and Benyon, 1986b, for an overview of this issue.

10 *Sunday Mirror*, 'The lost children', 12 July 1981; *Daily Mail*, 'Don't their parents care?', 8 July 1981; *The Sun*, 'Parents will be fined, warns Willie', 10 July 1981; *The Times*, 'Why so many children take to the streets', 11 July 1981.

11 The changing nature of political language during 1981 and 1985 was most evident in relation to the question of 'race'. During both periods a number of commentators challenged the adequacy of the term 'race riot', but the complex linkage established between 'race' and 'disorder' remained a heavily contested issue, e.g. in parliamentary debates. Miles, 1984, makes a similar point in relation to the responses called forth by the 1958 riots.

12 A review of the experience of the Scarman Inquiry and the subsequent (non)impact of the Report is central to any account of the events discussed in this paper. See Benyon and Solomos, 1987, for divergent perspectives on this issue.

13 Apart from his interventions in Parliament, which received wide-spread coverage, Powell wrote the following articles during July 1981 which give a flavour of his viewpoint: 'Well, well! look who's talking about lackeys and loyalty', *Sunday Express*, 12 July 1981; 'Why I see hope in the riots', *The Sun*, 13 July 1981.

14 R. Butt, 'Race and the mischief makers', *The Times*, 9 July 1981 (also published in the *Daily Mail*, 10 July 1981); other discussions of issues raised by Powell abound in the coverage of *The Daily Telegraph*, *Daily Express*, *The Sun* and *Sunday Express* during this period.

15 This theme was to recur even more centrally during the 1985 events. An interesting account of how official political language attempts to distance the 'decent majority' from the actions of the 'small minority' or 'riffraff' can be found in Fogelson, 1971.

16 An example of the specific impact of such fears on both Conservative and Labour opinion during 1981 can be found in my analysis of the politics of black youth unemployment during this phase, where I show the increasing importance of law and order in symbolic political language. See Solomos, 1984 and 1986b.

17 Although Lord Scarman's Report was carefully worded and avoided any attempt to blame the riots on the social conditions of inner city areas as such, it did attach some weight to the need for action against social disadvantage and racial inequality if the underlying conditions which precipitated riot behaviour were to be tackled and further riots prevented.

18 During the parliamentary debates on the riots and the parliamentary debate on the Scarman Report the Labour speakers followed a basically 'social' explanation of the events, though they were also keen to express their support of the police and opposition to disorderly violence. The tension and ambiguity in their calls for greater social equality on the one hand and the prevention of social disorder on the other was to become even more clear in the course of the debates about the 1985 riots.

19 The *Daily Mirror*'s coverage of the 1981 events and common sense usage of images of urban decay and the ghetto is usefully analysed by Hansen, 1982 and Burgess, 1985. See also Murdock, 1984, for an overview of the role of the media.

20 The issue of political legitimacy and the influence of minority politics on the white power structure was a central theme in the 1960s riots in America as

well. See Edelman, 1971, and Fogelson, 1971, for a discussion of this point, and the papers in Benyon and Solomos, 1987, for contrasting views on the British situation.

21 This is a point which has been made consistently by Enoch Powell since the 1960s, and has been a constant theme in the writings of neo-right commentators on race. See Solomos *et al.*, 1982 for a discussion of this point.

22 See Habermas, 1976, for a discussion of the concept of 'legitimation crisis'.

23 *Daily Mail*, 'Search for the masked men', July 1981; *Daily Mail*, 'Extremists master plan for chaos', 10 July 1981; *The Sun*, 'Walkie-talkie warfare', 10 July 1981; *Daily Express*, 'Hidden face of protest', 16 July 1981.

24 For an overview of these arguments see M. Kettle, 'Will 1982 see more riots?', *New Society*, 18 February 1981, and 'Where did the riots go?', *New Society*, 9 September 1981.

25 See for example: *The Economist*, 'Now Handsworth burns', 14 September 1985; *Financial Times*, 'Law and disorder in Handsworth', 16 September 1985.

26 This is a point that is made with some force in the report of the review panel chaired by Herman Ouseley, which looked into the grievances of the black communities in Handsworth. See Ouseley *et al.*, 1986.

27 For the 1981 context see Burgess, 1985.

28 See for example *Daily Express*, 'Not the England that we should live in', 8 October 1985; P. Worsthorne, 'Tories v mob rule', *The Sunday Telegraph*, 13 October 1985.

29 For a review of the evidence and arguments about crime and disorder in Handsworth see *The Observer*, 15 September 1985, where the arguments of the local police and the Home Secretary are analysed.

30 *The Daily Telegraph*, 'Riots a cry for loot, says Hurd', 13 September 1985; *The Guardian*, 'Cabinet opts for police report on Handsworth riot', 13 September 1985.

31 The interplay of common sense images of crime and disorderly protest was most evident in the Dear report on Handsworth, but it also played a role in the Richards report on Tottenham and in Kenneth Newman's report on the disturbances in London generally. See in particular Newman, 1986.

32 This approach to the riots was later to gain a wider currency through the independent reports on the Handsworth and Broadwater Farm events. See Ouseley *et al.*, 1986; Silverman *et al.*, 1986; and Gifford *et al.*, 1986. See also Gaffney, 1987.

33 See e.g. R. Kerridge, 'Why the West Indians hate Asians', *The Sun*, 12 September 1985. For a review of how this theme was used in the press generally see D. Rose, 'I was there in Fleet Street's tribal bloodbath', *The Guardian*, 16 September 1985.

34 The Asian vs West Indian explanation of the events in Handsworth was yet another example of the processes through which the media and politicians attempted to construct the events as an internecine war of attrition in inner city areas which lacked a community spirit and social cohesion. Yet it is interesting to note that in a survey of young people in Handsworth the inter-communal rivalry argument was overwhelmingly rejected as a main cause for the riots. See unpublished 'Attitude survey of young people in Handsworth', West Midlands County Council, February 1986.

35 See Benyon, 1986a, for a more specific discussion of this point.

36 See Solomos, 1986a.
37 The use of news pictures to portray the events of 1981 and 1985 is beyond the scope of this paper. Some perceptive comments can be found in Hansen, 1982. But there is clearly a need to analyse this question more deeply, and to analyse the role of television in the representation of the events.
38 See for example Newman, 1986.
39 *Daily Express*, 'Powell in race speech storm', 21 September 1985; *The Sun*, 'Enoch: pay blacks to quit Britain', 21 September 1985. The call for repatriation was also taken up by some Conservative MPs during this time, and repeated by them since.
40 P. Worsthorne, 'End this silence over race', *The Sunday Telegraph*, 25 September 1985; J. Vincent, 'Vincent's view', *The Sun*, 9 October 1985; M. Hastings, 'The curse of isolation', *The Sunday Times*, 15 September 1985.
41 See *The Daily Telegraph*, 8 October 1985, 'Monday Club's call for black immigration ban'.
42 This line of argument was forcefully expressed by Ronald Butt, who interpreted the race issue as an aspect of wider threats to British society. See 'Race: weapon in a class war', *The Times*, 17 October 1985.
43 The coverage of his reported remarks on the death of PC Blakelock on Broadwater Farm was the key variable here, and it is an issue which still arouses much interest in the media.
44 *The Daily Telegraph*, 'Agitators stirred Brixton riot', 1 October 1985; *The Star*, 'Red butchers', 8 October 1985; *The Daily Telegraph*, 'GLC leftists undermining the police', 9 October 1985.
45 Once again it needs to be emphasised that the 'outside agitator' theme was central to the interpretations of the American riots, particularly in relation to the growth of the Black Power movement.
46 See Gifford *et al.*, 1986.
47 *The Guardian*, 'Riots prompt review of inner city aid', 6 November 1985; *The Sunday Telegraph*, 'Task forces to find work for jobless', 2 February 1986.
48 This point is made forcefully by Gareth Pearce, a solicitor who acted for many of those arrested in 1981, in 'What Scarman might have learned from LBJ', *The Guardian*, 30 November 1981.

7 'The enemy within': black youth and urban disorder in 1980s Britain

1 The remarks in this chapter are necessarily tentative, but in their totality they are intended to draw together the fundamental arguments of the previous chapters, suggest issues for further exploration and pinpoint the dialectics of change within the current context of racialisation. For a broader, and historically located analysis see: Solomos, forthcoming, chapter 10.
2 The pervasiveness of such notions in the post-war history of 'race' in British society has been noted by a number of authors, in particular through studies such as *The Empire Strikes Back* produced in 1982 by the Centre for Contemporary Cultural Studies. Additionally see Valentine, 1968; Hall *et al.*, 1978; Barker, 1982; Gilroy, 1987.
3 An exploration of this theme from the perspective of changing political language can be found in Solomos 1986b.
4 A critical analysis of these pronouncements is beyond the scope of this book but there is clearly a need for a more detailed analysis of the content of official

and oppositional responses to the riots, their impact on policy formulation and practice, and their role in changing the basis of state policies. See, for example, the preliminary analysis in Burgess, 1985, and Gaffney, 1987.

5 See, for example: *The Daily Telegraph*, 13 September 1985, 'Riots a cry for loot, says Hurd'; *The Financial Times*, 16 September 1985, 'Law and disorder in Handsworth'; *The Daily Telegraph*, 2 October 1985, 'Hurd promises to root out racial bias'; *The Guardian*, 3 May 1986, 'After the riots, the waste land'.

6 Examples of neo-right approaches to this issue are usefully collected in Palmer, 1986. This collection includes papers by Anthony Flew, Ray Honeyford, Tom Hastie, David Dale, Roger Scruton and Roy Kerridge, who have all written widely on the subject. But see also, Casey, 1982, Flew, 1984, and a number of articles in the journal *The Salisbury Review*.

7 The 'threat from within' line of argument is exemplified in both the media and the official response to the riots, but it has not been seriously discussed in the subsequent debates about the causes and the consequences of the riots. An exploratory discussion can be found in Solomos, 1986b.

8 One major example was the confrontations in the St Paul's area of Bristol during September 1986, which resulted initially from a police raid into the area. See the report on the events in *The Guardian* on 13 September 1986. See also W. Hatchett and D. Buckett, 'The view from St Paul's', *New Society*, 19 September 1986.

9 *The Guardian*, 21 February 1987; *The Independent*, 23 February 1987.

10 An example of this during 1987, was the statement by the Metropolitan Police to the effect that policing tactics alone could not manage the problems arising from wider social and economic policies (*The Guardian*, 7 April 1987). See also *The Guardian*, 20 April 1987, 'Newman warns of "volatile vapour" of social discontent'.

11 Apart from Newman, 1983 and 1986 see the regular reporting of Newman's pronouncements in *Policing London* (published by the GLC) and the *Police–Media Research Project Bulletin* (published by the Institute of Race Relations).

12 The notion of 'problem areas' has, as we saw earlier, a long history. But in the context of growing urban unrest it has acquired a new pertinence, particularly in relation to localities and housing estates which have experienced violent confrontations between the police and local black communities.

13 This common sense notion is popularised in much of the media coverage of young blacks, and in the interplay between everyday notions about them and official definitions of the 'crisis' of black youth. See the exploration of this point in Fisher and Joshua, 1982.

14 It is beyond the scope of this book to discuss the history of Powellism and its political impact and contradictions. A detailed analysis of this phenomenon can be found in Solomos, forthcoming. For a somewhat different account of the context of Powellism see Gilroy, 1987.

15 Such a process of 'exclusion' is not always linked directly to repatriation as such, but it does rely on the deep-seated idea that through immigration an 'alien' culture (and the 'problems' that ensue) have been imported into the very heart of British society.

16 A similar process of struggle over political language took place in the USA during the 1960s. Edelman, 1971, notes that black radicals tended to question

the definition of urban violence as 'riots' and to use the term 'rebellions' (30–1).

17 For a discussion of these different explanations of the post-1980 riots see the various papers in Benyon and Solomos, 1987, particularly the introductory and concluding chapters by the editors.

18 This is not to say, of course, that there have been no promises that such a national initiative against discrimination and disadvantage is being considered by the government. But there is a major gap between promises of major interventions and the limited changes achieved. See, for example, the analysis of this issue in Parkinson and Duffy, 1984; Benyon and Solomos, 1987.

19 For substantive accounts of the ideological and political context of this approach see: Levitas, 1986; Gordon and Klug, 1986.

20 Neo-right writers have by no means limited their concerns to the issues I discuss in this chapter. Examples of the breadth of issues covered by neo-right writers are usefully collected in Palmer, 1986, which includes a wide variety of papers on 'race-related' issues.

21 By externalising the causes of the riots such accounts effectively ruled out of serious consideration such issues as policing, racism, unemployment, social inequality and poverty. Rather they focused attention on the 'racial' background of rioters and decontextualised the riots from the wider socio-economic environment.

22 An exploration of this issue is of relevance not just to the contemporary period but to the whole history of British 'race relations'. See the analysis of this process in Rich, 1986; Seidel, 1986a; Gilroy, 1987; and Solomos, forthcoming.

23 Apart from the debates on the British Nationality Bill during 1981, see, for example: *Hansard*, vol. 37, 1983, 'Immigration'; *Hansard*, vol. 83, 1985, 'Immigration'; *Hansard*, vol. 103, 1986, 'Immigration'.

24 *Hansard*, vol. 88, 1985: cols. 929–1007, 'Inner cities'; *Hansard*, vol. 106, 1986: cols. 1176–246, 'Local government'; *Hansard (House of Lords)*, vol. 484, 1987: cols. 13–122, 'Inner city problems'; *Hansard (House of Lords)*, vol. 484, 1987: cols. 205–301, 'Local authorities: policies'.

Bibliography

Abbott, S. (ed.) (1971), *Prevention of Racial Discrimination in Britain*, London: Oxford University Press

AFFOR, All Faiths For One Race (1978), *Talking Blues*, Birmingham: AFFOR

Alderson, J. and Stead, P. (1973), *The Police We Deserve*, London: Wolf

Alford, R. and Friedland, R. (1985), *Powers of Theory: Capitalism, the State and Democracy*, Cambridge: Cambridge University Press

Allen, S. (1969), 'School leavers: problems of method and explanation', *Race Today*, October: 235–7

  (1975), 'School leavers in the labour market', *London Educational Review*, 4 (2/3): 64–74

Allen, S. and Smith, C. R. (1975), 'Minority group experience of the transition from school to work', in P. Brannen (ed.), *Entering the World of Work: Some Sociological Perspectives*, London: HMSO

Amos, V. and Parmar, P. (1981), 'Resistances and responses: the experiences of black girls in Britain', in A. McRobbie and T. McCabe (eds.), *Feminism for Girls: An Adventure Story*, London: Routledge and Kegan Paul

Andersen, M. L. (1976), 'American race relations 1970–1975: a critical review of the literature', *Sage Race Relations Abstracts*, 2 (1): 1–34

Anwar, M. (1976), *Between Two Cultures: A Study of Relationships Between Generations in the Asian Community in Britain*, London: Commission for Racial Equality

  (1982), *Young People and the Job Market: A Survey*, London: Commission for Racial Equality

Arnot, M. (1986), *Race, Gender and Educational Policy-Making*, Module 4, E333 Policy-Making in Education, Milton Keynes: The Open University Press

Ashton, D. N. (1986), *Unemployment under Capitalism: The Sociology of British and American Labour Markets*, Brighton: Wheatsheaf

Ashton, D. N., Maguire, M. J., and Garland, V. (1982), *Youth in the Labour Market*, Research Paper no. 34, London: Department of Employment

Banton, M. (1955), *The Coloured Quarter: Negro Immigrants in an English City*, London: Jonathan Cape

  (1959), *White and Coloured*, London: Jonathan Cape

  (1973), *Police–Community Relations*, London: Collins

  (1985), *Promoting Racial Harmony*, Cambridge: Cambridge University Press

Barber, A. (1980), 'Ethnic origin and the labour force', *Employment Gazette*, August: 841–8

(1981), *Labour Force Information from the National Dwelling and Housing Survey*, Research Paper no. 17, London: Department of Employment

Barker, M. (1982), *The New Racism*, London: Junction Books

Bates, I., Clarke, J., Cohen, P., Finn, D., Moore, R. and Willis, P. (1984), *Schooling for the Dole?*, London: Macmillan

Beetham, D. (1967), *Immigrant School Leavers and the Youth Unemployment Services in Birmingham*, London: Institute of Race Relations

(1969), 'A comment on the problems of coloured school leavers', *Race Today*, October: 166–9

Ben-Tovim, G. and Gabriel, J. (1979) 'The politics of race in Britain: a review of the major trends and of the recent literature', *Sage Race Relations Abstracts*, 4 (4): 1–56

Ben-Tovim, G., Gabriel, J., Law, I., and Stredder, K. (1986), *The Local Politics of Race*, London: Macmillan

Benyon, J. (1986a), 'Turmoil in the cities', *Social Studies Review*, 1 (3): 3–8

(1986b), *A Tale of Failure: Race and Policing*, Policy Papers in Ethnic Relations no. 3, University of Warwick, Centre for Research in Ethnic Relations

Benyon, J. (ed.) (1984), *Scarman and After*, Oxford: Pergamon Press

Benyon, J. and Solomos, J. (eds.) (1987), *The Roots of Urban Unrest*, Oxford: Pergamon Press

Berger, A. S., and Simon, W. (1974), 'Black families and the Moynihan Report: a research evaluation', *Social Problems*, 22 (2): 145–61

Bergesen, A. (1980), 'Official violence during the Watts, Newark and Detroit race riots of the 1960s', in P. Lauderdale (ed.), *A Political Analysis of Deviance*, Minneapolis: University of Minnesota Press

(1982), 'Race riots of 1967: an analysis of police violence in Detroit and New York', *Journal of Black Studies*, 12 (3): 261–74

Berkeley, H. (1977), *The Odyssey of Enoch*, London: Hamish Hamilton

Bernstein, B. (1971), 'Education cannot compensate for society', in B. Bernstein, *Class, Codes and Control*, London: Paladin

Billingsley, A. (1970), 'Black families and white social science', *Journal of Social Issues*, 26 (3): 127–42

(1973), 'Black families and white social science', in J. A. Ladner (ed.), *The Death of White Sociology*, New York: Vintage Books

Blau, Z. S. (1981), *Black Children/White Children*, New York: Free Press

Blauner, R. (1972), *Racial Oppression in America*, New York: Harper and Row

Blauner, R. and Wellman, D. (1973), 'Toward the decolonisation of social research', in J. A. Ladner (ed), *The Death of White Sociology*, New York: Vintage Books

Bourne, J. (1980), 'Cheerleaders and ombudsmen: the sociology of race relations in Britain', *Race and Class*, 21 (4): 331–52

Brah, A. and Deem, R. (1986), 'Towards an anti-sexist and anti-racist schooling', *Critical Social Policy*, 16: 66–79

Braham, P., Rhodes, E., and Pearn, M. (eds.), *Discrimination and Disadvantage in Employment: The Experience of Black Workers*, London: Harper and Row

Bridges, L. (1973), 'Race relations research: from colonialism to neo-colonialism?', *Race*, XIV (3): 331–41

Brier, A. and Axford, B. (1975), 'The theme of race in British social science and political research', in I. Crewe (ed.), *The Politics of Race*, London: Croom Helm

Brooks, D. (1983), 'Young blacks and asians in the labour market – a critical overview', in B. Troyna and D. I. Smith, (eds.), *Racism, School and the Labour Market*, Leicester: National Youth Bureau

Brown, C. (1984), *Black and White Britain*, London: Heinemann

Brown, C. and Gay, P. (1985), *Racial Discrimination: 17 Years After the Act*, London: Policy Studies Institute

Brown, J. (1977), *Shades of Grey*, Cranfield: Cranfield Police Studies

Burgess, J. R. (1985), 'News from nowhere: the press, the riots and the myth of the inner city', in J. R. Burgess and J. R. Gold, (eds.), *Geography, the media and popular culture*, London: Croom Helm

Burton, F. and Carlen, P. (1979), *Official Discourse*, London: Routledge and Kegan Paul

CAB 128/17 (1950) 'Coloured people from British colonial territories', London: Public Records Office

CAB 128/19 (1951) 'Immigration of British subjects into the UK', London: Public Records Office

CAB 129/28 (1948) 'Arrival in the UK of Jamaican unemployed', Memorandum by Secretary of State for the Colonies, London: Public Records Office

CAB 129/40 (1950) 'Coloured people from British colonial territories', Memorandum by Secretary of State for the Colonies, London: Public Records Office

CAB 129/44 (1951) 'Immigration of British subjects into the UK', Note by the Home Secretary, London: Public Records Office

CAB 129/78 (1955) 'Colonial immigrants', Memorandum by the Secretary of State for the Home Department, London: Public Records Office

CAB 129/81 (1956) 'Colonial immigrants', Report of the Committee of Ministers, London: Public Records Office

CAB 134/1210 (1956) 'Cabinet committee on colonial immigrants', London: Public Records Office

Cain, M. (1973), *Society and the Policeman's Role*, London: Routledge and Kegan Paul

Carnoy, M. (1984), *The State and Political Theory*, Princeton: Princeton University Press

Carter, B. and Joshi, S. (1984), 'The role of Labour in the creation of a racist Britain', *Race and Class*, XXV (3): 53–70

Carter, B., Harris, C., Joshi, S. (1987), *The 1951–55 Conservative government and the racialisation of black immigration*, Policy Papers in Ethnic Relations, no. 11, University of Warwick, Centre for Research in Ethnic Relations

Casey, J., (1982), 'One nation: the politics of race', *The Salisbury Review*, Autumn: 23–8

Cashmore, E. (1979), *Rastaman*, London: George Allen and Unwin

Cashmore, E. and Troyna, B. (1981), 'Just for white boys? Elitism, racism and research', *Multiracial Education*, 10 (1): 43–8

    (1983), *Introduction to Race Relations*, London: Routledge and Kegan Paul

Cashmore, E. and Troyna, B. (eds.) (1982), *Black Youth in Crisis*, London: George Allen and Unwin

Castles, S. and Kosack, G. (1973), *Immigrant Workers and Class Structure in Western Europe*, London: Oxford University Press

Castles, S., with Booth, H. and Wallace, T. (1984), *Here for Good: Western Europe's New Ethnic Minorities*, London: Pluto Press

CCCS Race and Politics Group (1982), *The Empire Strikes Back: race and racism in 70s Britain*, London: Hutchinson

Clare, J. (1985), 'Time to dust off the Scarman report', *The Listener*, 3 October: 6–7

Clarke, C. F. O. (1970), *Police/Community Relations: Report of a Conference at Ditchley Park*, 29 May–1 June 1970, Enstone, Ditchley Foundation

Clarke, J., Critcher, C., Jefferson, T., and Lambert, J. (1974), 'The selection of evidence and the avoidance of racialism: a critique of the parliamentary select committee on race relations and immigration', *New Community*, III (3): 172–92

CO 876/39 (1944–5), 'Report of investigation into conditions of the coloured colonial men in the Stepney area' (by Phyllis Young), March 1944, London: Public Records Office

CO 1006/2 (1948), 'Working party on the employment of surplus colonial labour in the United Kingdom', London: Public Records Office

Cockburn, C. (1987), *Two-Track Training: Sex Inequalities and the YTS*, London: Macmillan

Cohen, G. (1983), 'Youth training: the search for a policy', in C. Jones and J. Stevenson (eds.), *The Yearbook of Social Policy in Britain*, London: Routledge and Kegan Paul

Cohen, P. (1984), 'Against the new vocationalism', in I. Bates, J. Clarke, P. Cohen, D. Finn, R. Moore and P. Willis (eds.), *Schooling for the Dole?*, London: Macmillan

Collins, S. (1957), *Coloured Minorities in Britain*, London: Lutterworth Press

Colls, R. and Dodd, P. (eds.), (1986), *Englishness: Politics and Culture 1880–1920*, London: Croom Helm

Commission for Racial Equality (CRE) (1977–87), *Annual Reports*, London: Commission for Racial Equality

(1978), *Looking for Work: Black and White School Leavers in Lewisham*, London: Commission for Racial Equality

(1980a), *Youth in Multi-Racial Society: The Urgent Need for New Policies*, London: Commission for Racial Equality

(1980b), *Half a Chance: A Report on Job Discrimination Against Young Blacks in Nottingham*, London: Commission for Racial Equality

(1980c), *Ethnic Minority Youth Unemployment*, London: Commission for Racial Equality

(1983a), *Equal Opportunity and the Youth Training Scheme*, London: Commission for Racial Equality

(1983b), *Equal Opportunity, Positive Action and Young People*, London: Commission for Racial Equality

(1983c), *The Race Relations Act 1976 – Time for a Change?*, London: Commission for Racial Equality

(1984), *Racial Equality and the Youth Training Scheme*, London: Commission for Racial Equality

(1985a), *Review of the Race Relations Act 1976: Proposals for Change*, London: Commission for Racial Equality

(1985b), *Positive Action and Equal Opportunity in Employment*, London: Commission for Racial Equality

Commonwealth Immigrants Advisory Council (CIAC) (1964a), *Second Report*, Cmnd 2266, London: HMSO

(1964b), *Third Report*, Cmnd 2428, London: HMSO

Community Relations Commission (CRC) (1968–76), *Annual Reports*, London: Community Relations Commission

(1974), *Unemployment and Homelessness: A Report*, London: Community Relations Commission

(1977), *Seen But Not Served: Black Youth and the Youth Service*, London: Community Relations Commission

Crick, B. (ed.) (1981), *Unemployment*, London: Methuen

Crick, T. (1980), 'Black youth, crime and related problems', *Youth in Society*, no. 40: 20–2

Croft, S. and Beresford, P. (1983), 'Power, politics and the youth training scheme', *Youth and Policy*, 2 (1); 1–4

Cross, M. (1987), *A Cause for Concern: Ethnic Minority Youth and Vocational Training Policy*, Policy Papers in Ethnic Relations no. 9, University of Warwick, Centre for Research in Ethnic Relations

Cross, M., Edmonds, J. and Sargeant, R. (1983), *Ethnic Minorities: Their Experience on YOP*, Special Programmes Occasional Paper no. 5, Sheffield: Manpower Services Commission

Cross, M., Wrench, J., Barnett, S. (1987), *Ethnic Minorities and the Careers Service*, London: Department of Employment

Cross, M. and Smith, D. I. (eds.), *Black Youth Futures*, Leicester: National Youth Bureau

Daniel, W. W. (1968), *Racial Discrimination in England*, Harmondsworth: Penguin

Davies, B. (1986), *Threatening Youth: Towards a National Youth Policy*, Milton Keynes: Open University Press

Deakin, N. (1968), 'The politics of the Commonwealth Immigrants Bill', *Political Quarterly*, 39 (1): 24–45

(1969) 'The politics of integration: policies and practice', Paper presented at IRR Fourth Annual Conference on Race Relations, University of Aston, 18–19 September

(1970), *Colour, Citizenship and British Society*, London: Panther

(1972), *The Immigration Issue in British Politics*, Unpublished PhD Thesis, University of Sussex

Dear, G. (1985), *Handsworth/Lozells, September 1985: Report of the Chief Constable, West Midlands Police*, Birmingham: West Midlands Police

Dearlove, J. and Saunders, P. (1984), *Introduction to British Politics*, Cambridge: Polity

Deedes, W. (1968), *Race Without Rancour*, London: Conservative Political Centre

Demuth, C. (1978), *'Sus': A Report on the Vagrancy Act*, London: Runnymede Trust

Department of Education and Science (DES) (1967), *Immigrants and the Youth Service*, London: Department of Education and Science

(1983), *Young People in the Eighties*, London: HMSO

(1985), *Education and Training for Young People*, Cmnd 9482, London: HMSO

Department of Employment (DE) (1977), 'Racial disadvantage in employment', Paper to Home Office Race Relations Research Advisory Committee, 18 November

Department of Employment and Department of Education and Science (1984), *Training for Jobs*, Cmnd 9135, London: HMSO

(1985), *Employment: The Challenge to the Nation*, Cmnd 9474, London: HMSO

Drake, St C (1954), *Value Systems, Social Structure, and Race Relations in the British Isles*, Unpublished PhD Thesis, University of Chicago

(1955), 'The "colour problem" in Britain: a study in social definitions', *Sociological Review*, 3 (2): 197–217

Dummett, M. and Dummett, A. (1982), 'The role of government in Britain's racial crisis', in C. Husband (ed.), *'Race' in Britain: Continuity and Change*, London: Hutchinson

Edelman, M. (1971), *Politics as Symbolic Action: Mass Arousal and Quiescence*, Chicago: Markham

(1977), *Political Language: Words that Succeed and Policies that Fail*, New York: Academic Press

(1985), 'Political language and political reality', *PS*, XVIII (1): 10–19

Edwards, J. (1987), *Positive Discrimination, Social Justice and Social Policy*, London: Tavistock

Edwards, J. and Batley, R. (1978), *The Politics of Positive Discrimination*, London: Tavistock

Eggleston, J., Anjali, M., Dunn, D., and Wright, C. (1986), *Education for Some: The Educational and Vocational Experiences of 15–18 Year Old Members of Minority Ethnic Groups*, Stoke: Trentham Books

Esping-Andersen, G. (1985), *Politics Against Markets*, Princeton: Princeton University Press

Evans, P., Rueschemeyer, D. and Skocpol, T. (eds.) (1985), *Bringing the State Back In*, Cambridge: Cambridge University Press

Fairley, J. and Grahl, J. (1983), 'Conservative training policy and the alternatives', *Socialist Economic Review 1983*, London: Merlin Press

Fay, B. (1975), *Social Theory and Political Practice*, London: George Allen and Unwin

Fenton, S. and Burton, P. (1987), 'YTS and equal opportunity policy', in M. Cross and D. I. Smith (eds.), *Black Youth Futures*, Leicester: National Youth Bureau

Fenton, S., Davies, T., Means, R., and Burton, P. (1984), *Ethnic Minorities and the Youth Training Scheme*, Sheffield: Manpower Services Commission

Feuchtwang, S. (1981), 'Collective action and English law against racial discrimination in employment', *Politics and Power*, 4: 99–127

(1982) 'Occupational ghettoes', *Economy and Society*, 11 (3): 251–91

Field, S. (1982), 'Urban disorders in Britain and America: a review of research', in S. Field, and P. Southgate, *Public Disorder*, Home Office Research Study no. 72, London: HMSO

(1984), *The Attitudes of Ethnic Minorities*, London: HMSO

Finn, D. (1983), 'The Youth Training Scheme: a new deal?', *Youth and Policy*, 1 (4): 16–24

(1987), *Training Without Jobs: New Deals and Broken Promises*, London: Macmillan

Fisher, G. and Joshua, H. (1982), 'Social policy and black youth', in E.

Cashmore and B. Troyna (eds.), *Black Youth in Crisis*, London: George Allen and Unwin

Fletcher, M. E. (1930), *Report on an Investigation into the Colour Problem in Liverpool and Other Ports*, Liverpool: Association for the Welfare of Half-Caste Children

Flew, A. (1984), *Education, Race and Revolution*, London: Centre for Policy Studies

Fogelson, R. M. (1971), *Violence as Protest*, Garden City, N.Y.: Anchor Books

Foot, P. (1965), *Immigration and Race in British Politics*, Harmondsworth: Penguin

Freeman, G. (1979), *Immigrant Labor and Racial Conflict in Industrial Societies*, Princeton: Princeton University Press

Freeman, M. D. A. (1984), 'Law and order in 1984', *Current Legal Problems*, 37: 175–231

Freeman, M. D. A. and Spencer, S. (1979), 'Immigration control, black workers and the economy', *British Journal of Law and Society*, 6 (1): 53–81

Fryer, P. (1984), *Staying Power: The History of Black People in Britain*, London: Pluto Press

Fuller, M. (1982), 'Young, female and black', in E. Cashmore and B. Troyna (eds.), *Black Youth in Crisis*, London: George Allen and Unwin

Gaffney, J. (1987), *Interpretations of Violence: The Handsworth Riots of 1985*, Policy Papers in Ethnic Relations no. 10. University of Warwick, Centre for Research in Ethnic relations

Gainer, B. (1972), *The Alien Invasion: the origins of the Aliens Act of 1905*, London: Heinemann

Gamble, A. (1981), *Britain in Decline*, London: Macmillan

Garrard, J. A. (1971), *The English and Immigration 1880–1910*, London: Oxford University Press

Gaskell, G. and Smith, P. (1981), *Race and 'Alienated Youth': A Conceptual and Empirical Enquiry*, London School of Economics: Department of Social Psychology

Geschwender, J. (1977), *Class, Race and Worker Insurgency*, Cambridge: Cambridge University Press

Giddens, A. (1979), *Central Problems in Social Theory*, London: Macmillan

Gifford, Lord, Chairman (1986), *The Broadwater Farm Inquiry*, London: Karia Press

Gilroy, P. (1980), 'Managing the "underclass": a further note on the sociology of race relations in Britain', *Race and Class*, XXII (1): 47–62

    (1982), 'Police and thieves', in CCCS Race and Politics Group, *The Empire Strikes Back: race and racism in 70s Britain*, London: Hutchinson

    (1987), *There Ain't No Black in the Union Jack*, London: Hutchinson

Glasgow, D. (1981), *The Black Underclass: Poverty, Unemployment and Entrapment of Ghetto Youth*, New York: Vintage Books

Gleeson, D. (ed.) (1983), *Youth Training and the Search for Work*, London: Routledge and Kegan Paul

Gordon, P. (1985), 'Police and black people in Britain: a bibliographic essay', *Sage Race Relations Abstracts*, 10 (2): 3–33

Gordon, P. and Klug, F. (1986), *New Right, New Racism*, London: Searchlight Publications

Griffith, J. A. G., Henderson, J., Usborne, M., and Wood, D. (1960), *Coloured Immigrants in Britain*, London: Oxford University Press

Gutzmore, C. (1983), 'Capital, "black youth" and crime', *Race and Class*, 25 (2): 13–30

Habermas, J. (1976), *Legitimation Crisis*, London: Heinemann

Hall, S. (1967), *The Young Englanders*, London: NCCI

(1980), 'Race, Articulation and Societies Structured in Dominance', in UNESCO (ed.), *Sociological Theories: Race and Colonialism*, Paris: UNESCO

(1987), 'Urban unrest in Britain', in J. Benyon and J. Solomos (eds.), *The Roots of Urban Unrest*, Oxford: Pergamon Press

Hall, S., Critcher, C., Jefferson, T., Clarke, J. and Roberts, B. (1978), *Policing the Crisis: Mugging, the State, and Law and Order*, London: Macmillan

Halsey, A. H. (1970), 'Race relations: the lines to think on', *New Society*, 19 March: 422–4

(1972), *Educational Priority: EPA Problems and Policies*, London: HMSO

Hansen, A. S. (1982), *Press Coverage of the Summer 1981 Riots*, Unpublished MA Thesis, Centre for Mass Communications Research, University of Leicester

Harris, C. (1987), 'Images of blacks in Britain 1930–1960', Unpublished paper, Centre for Research in Ethnic Relations, University of Warwick

Harris, C. and Solomos, J. (forthcoming) 'Rethinking the 1958 riots: immigration, "Race" and social change'

Harrison, P. (1973), 'Black and white', *New Society*, 21 June: 672–3

Hebdige, D. (1976), 'Reggae, rastas and rudies': style and the subversion of form', in S. Hall and T. Jefferson (eds.), *Resistance Through Rituals*, London: Hutchinson

Heginbotham, H. (1967), 'Young immigrants and work', *IRR Newsletter*, May: 215–17

Heineman, B. (1972), *The Politics of the Powerless: A Study of the Campaign Against Racial Discrimination*, London: Oxford University Press

Higgins, J., Deakin, N., Edwards, J. and Wicks, M. (1983), *Government and Urban Poverty*, Oxford: Basil Blackwell

Hiro, D. (1971), *Black British/White British*, New York: Monthly Review Books

HO 213/350 (1936), 'Treatment of coloured people in the UK', London: Public Records Office

HO 213/352 (1936), 'Welfare of coloured persons in the United Kingdom', London: Public Records Office

Holmes, C. (1978), *Immigrants and Minorities in British Society*, London: George Allen and Unwin

Home Affairs Committee (HAC), Sub-Committee on Race Relations and Immigration (1981a), *Racial Disadvantage*, London: HMSO

(1981b), *Commission for Racial Equality*, London: HMSO

Home Office (HO) (1970), *The Problems of Coloured School Leavers: Observations on the Report of the Select Committee on Race Relations and Immigration*, Cmnd 4268, London: HMSO

(1973), *Police/Immigrant Relations in England and Wales: Observations on the Report of the Select Committee on Race Relations and Immigration*, Cmnd 5438, London: HMSO

(1975), *Race Relations Research: A Report to the Home Secretary by the Advisory Committee on Race Relations Research*, London: HMSO

(1976), *The Organisation of Race Relations Administration: Observations on the Report of the Select Committee on Race Relations and Immigration*, Cmnd 6603, London: HMSO

(1977), 'Towards an attitude survey of ethnic minority young', Note to the Home Office Race Relations Research Advisory Committee

(1978), *The West Indian Community: Observations on the Report of the Select Committee on Race Relations and Immigration*, Cmnd 7186, London: HMSO

(1982a), *Racial Disadvantage: The Government Reply to the Fifth Report from the Home Affairs Committee*, Cmnd 8476, London: HMSO

(1982b), *The Commission for Racial Equality: The Government's Reply to the Home Affairs Committee*, London: HMSO

House of Commons, Employment Committee (1984–5), *The Role of the Minister Without Portfolio in Relation to Employment Matters: minutes of evidence from the Rt. Hon. Lord Young of Graffham*, London: HMSO

(1985–6), *The Work of the Department of Employment Group*, HMSO

(1986–7), *Discrimination in Employment*, London: HMSO

Howe, D. (1973), 'Fighting back: West Indian youth and the police in Notting Hill', *Race Today*, December: 333–6

Howells, D. (1980), 'The Manpower Services Commissions: The First Five Years', *Public Administration*, 58, 305–32.

Humphry, D. (1972), *Police Power and Black People*, London: Panther

Humphry, D. and John, G. (1971), *Because They're Black*, Harmondsworth: Penguin

Hunt, G. and Mellor, J. (1980), 'Afro-Caribbean youth: racism and unemployment', in M. Cole and B. Skelton (eds.), *Blind Alley*, Ormskirk: Hesketh

Hunte, J. (1966), *Nigger Hunting in England*, London: West Indian Standing Conference

Jackson, M. P. (1985), *Youth Unemployment*, London: Croom Helm

Jefferson, T. and Clarke, J. (1973), *Down These Mean Streets: The Meaning of Mugging*, Centre for Contemporary Cultural Studies, Stencilled Paper 17

Jenkins, R. (1985), 'Black workers in the labour market: the price of recession', in B. Roberts, R. Finnegan and D. Gallie (eds.), *New Approaches to Economic Life*, Manchester: Manchester University Press

(1986), *Racism and Recruitment: Managers, Organisations and Equal Opportunity in the Labour Market*, Cambridge: Cambridge University Press

Jenkins, R. and Solomos, J. (1987), *Racism and Equal Opportunity Policies in the 1980s*, Cambridge: Cambridge University Press

Jenkins, Robin (1971), 'The production of knowledge in the Institute of Race Relations', unpublished paper

Jenkins, Roy (1966), 'Speech to the National Committee for Commonwealth Immigrants', 23 May

(1967), 'Address by the Home Secretary to the Institute', *Race*, 8 (3): 215–21

Jessop, B. (1982), *The Capitalist State*, Oxford: Martin Robertson

(1985), *Nicos Poulantzas*, London: Macmillan

(1986), 'The prospects for the corporatisation of monetarism in Britain', in O. Jacobi, B. Jessop, H. Kastendick and M. Regini (eds.), *Economic Crisis, Trade Unions and the State*, London: Croom Helm

John, G. (1970), *Race in the Inner City: A Report from Handsworth, Birming-ham*, London: Runnymede Trust

(1981), *In the Service of Black Youth*, Leicester: National Association of Youth Clubs

Joshua, H. and Wallace, T. (1983), *To Ride the Storm: The 1980 Bristol 'Riot' and the State*, London: Heinemann

Katznelson, I. (1976), *Black Men, White Cities*, Chicago: University of Chicago Press

(1986), 'Rethinking the silences of social and economic policy', *Political Science Quarterly*, 101 (2): 307–25

Keane, J. (1984), *Public Life and Late Capitalism*, Cambridge: Cambridge University Press

Keat, R. (1981), *The Politics of Social Theory*, Oxford: Basil Blackwell

Kettle, M. (1982), 'Where did the riots go?', *New Society*, 9 September: 425

Kingdon, J. W. (1984), *Agendas, Alternatives, and Public Policies*, Boston: Little, Brown and Company

Knopf, T. A. (1975), *Rumors, Race and Riots*, New Brunswick, NJ: Transaction Books

Kochman, T. (1972), *Rappin' and Stylin' Out*, Urbana: University of Illinois Press

Krieger, J. (1986), *Reagan, Thatcher and the Politics of Decline*, Cambridge: Polity Press

Kushnick, L. (1971), 'British anti-discrimination legislation', in S. Abbott (ed.), *The Prevention of Discrimination in Britain*, London: Oxford University Press

Ladner, J. (ed.) (1973), *The Death of White Sociology*, New York: Vintage Books

Lambert, J. R. (1970), *Crime, Police and Race Relations: A Study in Birming-ham*, London: Oxford University Press

Lambert, J. R. and Filkin, C. (1971), 'Race relations research: some issues of approaches and application', *Race*, XII (3): 329–35

Lawrence, E. (1981), 'White sociology, black struggle', *Multiracial Education*, 9 (3): 3–17

(1982), 'In the abundance of water the fool is thirsty: sociology and black "pathology"', in CCCS Race and Politics Group, *The Empire Strikes Back: race and racism in 70s Britain*, London: Hutchinson

Layton-Henry, Z. (1984), *The Politics of Race in Britain*, London: George Allen and Unwin

Layton-Henry, Z. and Rich, P. (eds.) (1986), *Race, Government and Politics in Britain*, London: Macmillan

Lea, J. (1980), 'The contradictions of the sixties race relations legislation', in National Deviancy Conference (ed.), *Permissiveness and Control*, London: Macmillan

Lea, J. and Young, J. (1984), *What is to be done about Law and Order?*, Harmondsworth: Penguin

Lee, G. and Wrench, J. (1983), *Skill Seekers: Black Youth, Apprenticeships and Disadvantage*, Leicester: National Youth Bureau

Levitas, R. (ed.) (1986), *The Ideology of the New Right*, Cambridge: Polity

Leys, C. (1983), *Politics in Britain*, London: Heinemann

Lipsky, M. and Olson, D. (1977), *Commission Politics: The Processing of Racial Crisis in America*, New Brunswick, NJ: Transaction Books

Little, K. (1947), *Negroes in Britain: A Study of Racial Relations in English Society*, London: Routledge and Kegan Paul

    (1958), *Colour and Commonsense*, Fabian Tract no. 315, London: Fabian Society and Commonwealth Bureau

Lloyd, J. (1985), 'Government aims to win high ground in unemployment debate', *Financial Times*, 29 March

Lowry, R. P. (1974), *Social Problems: A Critical Analysis of Theories and Public Policy*, Lexington: D. C. Heath

Lunn, K. (1980), *Hosts, Immigrants and Minorities*, Folkestone: Dawson

Lustgarten, L. (1980), *Legal Control of Racial Discrimination*, London: Macmillan

McCowan, A. (1952), *Coloured Peoples in Britain*, London: Bow Group

McCrudden, C. (1982), 'Institutional discrimination', *Oxford Journal of Legal Studies*, 2: 303–67

McGlashan, C. (1972), 'The making of a mugger', *New Statesman*, 13 October: 496–7

Macdonald, I. (1983), *Immigration Law and Practice in the United Kingdom*, London: Butterworths

MacDonald, J. S. and MacDonald, L. (1978), 'The black family in the Americas: a review of the literature', *Sage Race Relations Abstracts*, 3 (1): 1–42

Mackenzie, N. (ed.) (1956), *The West Indian in Britain*, Fabian Research Series 179, London: Fabian Colonial Bureau

Manley, D., de Souza, I., and Hyndman, A. (1960), *The West Indian Comes to Britain*, London: Routledge and Kegan Paul

Manpower Services Commission (1974–87), *Annual Reports*, London and Sheffield: Manpower Services Commission

    (1976), *Towards a Comprehensive Manpower Policy*, London: Manpower Services Commission

    (1977), *Young People and Work – the Holland Report*, London: Manpower Services Commission

    (1978a), *MSC Review and Plan 1978*, London: Manpower Services Commission

    (1978b), *Young People and Work: Research Studies*, London: HMSO

    (1979a), *Attitudes to the Youth Opportunities Programme*, London: Manpower Services Commission

    (1979b), *Review of the First Year of the Special Programmes*, London: Manpower Services Commission

    (1980a), *Outlook on Training: Review of the Employment and Training Act 1973*, London: Manpower Services Commission

    (1980b), *Review of the Second Year of Special Programmes*, London: Manpower Services Commission

    (1980c), *MSC Manpower Review 1980*, London: Manpower Services Commission

    (1981a), *A New Training Initiative: A Consultative Document*, London: Manpower Services Commission

    (1981b), *A New Training Initiative: An Agenda for Action*, London: Manpower Services Commission

    (1981c), *Review of the Third Year of Special Programmes*, London: Manpower Services Commission

(1981d), *Review of Services for the Unemployed*, London: Manpower Services Commission

(1981e), *MSC Manpower Review 1981*, London: Manpower Services Commission

(1981f), *Corporate Plan 1981–85*, London: Manpower Services Commission

(1982a), *Corporate Plan 1982–86*, London: Manpower Services Commission

(1982b), *MSC Manpower Review 1982*, London: Manpower Services Commission

(1982c), *Review of Fourth Year of Special Programmes*, London: Manpower Services Commission

(1982d), *Memorandum on Special Client Groups*, Unpublished Paper, London: MSC Special Programmes Division

(1982e), *Youth Task Group Report*, London: Manpower Services Commission

(1982f), *YOP Trainees: Special Client Groups*, Manpower Services Commission, Special Programmes Division

(1983a), *Corporate Plan 1983–87*, Sheffield: Manpower Services Commission

(1983b), *Equal Opportunities for Ethnic Minorities*, Manpower Services Commission, Youth Training Board

(1984a), *Equal Opportunities in the Youth Training Scheme*, Manpower Services Commission, Youth Training Board

(1985) *Development of the Youth Training Scheme*, Sheffield, Manpower Services Commission

Manpower Services Commission and Commission for Racial Equality (1979), *Ethnic Minorities and the Special Programmes for the Unemployed: The Problems, the Needs and the Responses*, London: Manpower Services Commission

Marable, M. (1983), *How Capitalism Underdeveloped Black America*, London: Pluto Press

Mark, R. (1970), 'The Metropolitan Police: their role in the community', *Community*, July 1970: 3–5

Means, R., Burton, P., Davies, T., and Fenton, S. (1985), 'Implementation of social goals in labour market policy: the case of black youth, equal opportunities and the Youth Training Scheme', *Policy and Politics*, 13 (1): 72–83

Metropolitan Police (1986), *Public Order Review – Civil Disturbances 1981–1985*, London: Metropolitan Police

Middlemas, K. (1979), *Politics in Industrial Society*, London: Andre Deutsch
(1986), *Power, Competition and the State*, London: Macmillan

Miles, R. (1982), *Racism and Migrant Labour*, London: Routledge and Kegan Paul
(1984), 'The riots of 1958: notes on the ideological construction of "race relations" as a political issue in Britain', *Immigrants and Minorities*, 3 (3): 252–75
(1987), 'Recent Marxist theories of nationalism and the issue of racism', *British Journal of Sociology*, XXXVIII (1): 24–43

Miles, R. and Phizacklea, A. (1984), *White Man's Country*, London: Pluto Press

Miles, R. and Solomos, J. (1987), 'Migration and the state in Britain: a historical overview', in C. Husband (ed.), *'Race' in Britain*, 2nd edn, London: Hutchinson

Milson, F. (1961), *Operation Integration: an enquiry into the experiences of West*

Indians living in Birmingham with particular reference to children and young people, Birmingham: Westhill College

(1966), *Operation Integration Two: the coloured teenager in Birmingham*, Birmingham: Westhill College

Moon, J. and Richardson, J. (1985), *Unemployment in the UK*, Aldershot: Gower

Moore, R. (1975), *Racism and Black Resistance in Britain*, London: Pluto Press

Morris, P. (1986), 'Being discriminatory about discrimination', *Politics*, 6 (1): 23–30

Moynihan, D. P. (1965), *The Negro Family: The Case for National Action*, Washington, DC: US Department of Labor

Mullard, C. (1982), 'The state's response to racism: towards a relational explanation', in A. Ohri, B. Manning and P. Curno (eds.), *Community Work and Racism*, London: Routledge and Kegan Paul

(1985), *Race, Power and Resistance*, London: Routledge and Kegan Paul

Muncie, J. (1984), *'The trouble with kids today': youth and crime in post-war Britain*, London: Hutchinson

Mungham, G. (1982), 'Workless youth as a moral panic', in T. L. Rees and P. Atkinson (eds.), *Youth Unemployment and State Intervention*, London: Routledge and Kegan Paul

Murdock, G. (1984), 'Reporting the riots: images and impact', in J. Benyon (ed.), *Scarman and After*, Oxford: Pergamon Press

Murray, A. (1973), 'White norms, black deviation', in J. A. Ladner (ed.), *The Death of White Sociology*, New York: Vintage Books

Myrdal, G. (1969a), *Objectivity in Social Research*, London: Duckworth

(1969b), *The American Dilemma: The Negro Problem and Modern Democracy*, New York: Harper and Row

Nairn, T. (1981), *The Break-Up of Britain*, London: Verso

Nandy, D. (1969), 'Unrealistic aspirations', *Race Today*, May: 9–11

(1970), 'Immigrants and the police', *Runnymede Trust Bulletin*, October

National Committee for Commonwealth Immigrants (1966–8), *NCCI Information*, London: NCCI

(1967a), *Report for 1967*, London: NCCI

(1967b), *Towards a Multi-Racial Society*, London: NCCI

(1967c), *Racial Equality in Employment: A Report of a Conference*, London: NCCI

Newman, K. (1983), 'Fighting the fear of crime', *Police*, September: 26–30; October: 30–2

(1986), 'Police–public relations: the pace of change', Police Foundation Annual Lecture, 28 July

Newnham, A. (1986), *Employment, Unemployment and Black People*, London: Runnymede Trust

OECD (1986), 'United Kingdom', National Report for OECD Conference on the Future of Migration, Paris, February

Offe, C. (1984), *Contradictions of the Welfare State*, London: Hutchinson

(1985), *Disorganised Capitalism*, Cambridge: Polity

Orloff, A. and Skocpol, T. (1984), 'Why not equal protection? Explaining the politics of public social spending in Britain, 1900–1911, and the United States, 1880s–1920', *American Sociological Review*, 49: 726–50

Ouseley, H., Chairman (1986), *A Different Reality: An account of Black people's experiences and their grievances before and after the Handsworth Rebellions of September 1985*, Birmingham: West Midlands County Council

Palmer, F. (ed.), (1986), *Anti-Racism – An Assault on Education and Value*, London: The Sherwood Press

Parekh, B. (1987), 'The "new right" and the politics of nationhood', in Runnymede Trust, *The New Right: Image and Reality*, London: Runnymede Trust

Parkinson, M. and Duffy, J. (1984), 'Government's response to inner-city riots: the Minister for Merseyside and the Task Force', *Parliamentary Affairs*, 37 (1): 76–96

Parmar, P. (1981), 'Young Asian women: a critique of the pathological approach', *Multiracial Education*, 9 (3): 19–29

Patterson, S. (1969), *Immigration and Race Relations in Britain 1960–1967*, London: Oxford University Press

Pearson, G. (1983), *Hooligan: A History of Respectable Fears*, London: Macmillan

Phillips, M. (1983), 'Danger! astrologers at work: a critical note on the narrow orthodoxy of race relations research', *Community Development Journal*, 18 (3): 263–9

Pollert, A. (1985), *Unequal Opportunities: Racial Discrimination and the Youth Training Scheme*, Birmingham: Trade Union Resource Centre

Poulantzas, N. (1973), *Political Power and Social Classes*, London: New Left Books

(1978), *State, Power, Socialism*, London: New Left Books

Powell, E. (1969), *Still to Decide*, Kingswood: Elliot Right Way Books

Pryce, K. (1979), *Endless Pressure*, Harmondsworth: Penguin

Przeworski, A. (1985), *Capitalism and Social Democracy*, Cambridge: Cambridge University Press

Pulle, S. (1973), *Police/Immigrant Relations in Ealing*, London: Runnymede Trust

Rainwater, L. and Pittman, D. (1967), 'Ethical problems in studying a politically sensitive and deviant community', *Social Problems*, 14 (4): 357–73

Rainwater, L. and Yancey, W. (eds.), (1967), *The Moynihan Report and the Politics of Controversy*, Cambridge, Mass.: MIT Press

Ramdin, B. (1987), *The Making of the Black Working Class in Britain*, Aldershot: Gower

Reid, J. (1956), 'Employment of Negroes in Manchester', *Sociological Review*, 4 (2): 199–211

Reiner, R. (1985), *The Politics of the Police*, Brighton: Wheatsheaf Books

Report of the Commissioner of Police of the Metropolis, (1970–86) *Annual Reports*, London: HMSO

Rex, J. (1973a), 'The future of race relations research in Britain: sociological research and the politics of racial justice', *Race*, XIV (4): 481–8

(1973b), *Race, Colonialism and the City*, London: Routledge and Kegan Paul

(1981a), 'Errol Lawrence and the sociology of race relations: an open letter', *Multiracial Education*, 10 (1): 49–51

(1981b), 'A working paradigm for race relations research', *Ethnic and Racial Studies*, 4 (1): 1–25

(1983), *Race Relations in Sociological Theory*, 2nd edn, London: Routledge and Kegan Paul

Rex, J. and Tomlinson, S. (1979), *Colonial Immigrants in a British City: A Class Analysis*, London: Routledge and Kegan Paul

Rhodes, E. and Braham, P. (1981), 'Black workers in Britain: from full employment to recession', in P. Braham, E. Rhodes and M. Pearn (eds.), *Discrimination and Disadvantage in Employment*, London: Harper and Row

(1987), 'Equal opportunity in the context of high levels of unemployment', in R. Jenkins and J. Solomos (eds.), *Racism and Equal Opportunity Policies in the 1980s*, Cambridge: Cambridge University Press

Rich, P. (1986), *Race and Empire in British Politics*, Cambridge: Cambridge University Press

Richardson, J. and Henning, R. (eds.), (1984), *Unemployment: Policy Responses of Western Democracies*, London: Sage

Richmond, A. (1950), 'Economic insecurity and stereotypes as factors in colour prejudice', *Sociological Review*, 4 (8): 147–70

Roberts, K., Duggan, J. and Noble, M. (1981), *Unregistered Youth Unemployment and Outreach Careers Work: Part One, Non-Registration*, Research Paper no. 31, London: Department of Employment

Roberts, K., Noble, M., and Duggan, J. (1982), *Unregistered Youth Employment and Outreach Careers Work: Part Two, Outreach Careers Work*, Research Paper no. 32, London: Department of Employment

Rose, E. J. B. and associates (1969), *Colour and Citizenship: A Report on British Race Relations*, London: Oxford University Press

Runnymede Trust (1981), *Employment, Unemployment and the Black Population*, London: Runnymede Trust

Ryan, W. (1976), *Blaming the Victim*, New York: Vintage Books

Scarman, Lord (1981), *The Brixton Disorders 10–12 April 1981: Report of an Inquiry by the Rt Hon. The Lord Scarman, OBE*, London: HMSO

Seidel, G. (1986a), 'The concept of culture, "race" and nation in the British and French new right', in R. Levitas (ed.), *The Ideology of the New Right*, Cambridge: Polity

(1986b), *The Holocaust Denial*, Leeds: Beyond the Pale Collective

Select Committee on Race Relations and Immigration (1969), *The Problems of Coloured School Leavers*, London: HMSO

(1972), *Police/Immigrant Relations*, London: HMSO

(1973), *Education*, London: HMSO

(1974), *Employment*, London: HMSO

(1975), *The Organisation of Race Relations Administration*, London: HMSO

(1977), *The West Indian Community*, London: HMSO

Showler, B. (1981), 'Political economy and unemployment', in B. Showler and A. Sinfield, *The Workless State: Studies in Unemployment*, Oxford: Martin Robertson

Showler, B. and Sinfield, A. (eds.), (1981), *The Workless State: Studies in Unemployment*, Oxford: Martin Robertson

Sillitoe, K. and Meltzer, H. (1985), *The West Indian School Leaver*, London: Office of Population and Census Surveys

Silverman, J., Chairman (1986), *Independent Inquiry into the Handsworth Disturbances, September 1985*, Birmingham: Birmingham City Council

Sivanandan, A. (1974), *Race and Resistance: The IRR Story*, London: Race Today Publications

(1982), *A Different Hunger*, London: Pluto Press

Skocpol, T. (1980), 'Political response to capitalist crisis: neo-Marxist theories of the state and the case of the New Deal', *Politics and Society*, 10 (2): 155–201

Skocpol, T. and Ikenberry, J. (1983), 'The political formation of the American welfare state in historical and comparative perspective', *Comparative Social Research*, 6 (12): 87–148

Small, S. (1983a), 'Black youth in England: ethnic identity in a white society', *Policy Studies*, 4 (1): 35–49

(1983b), *Police and People in London, Volume II: A Group of Young Black People*, London: Policy Studies Institute

Smith, D. (1977), *Racial Disadvantage in Britain*, Harmondsworth: Penguin

(1981), *Unemployment and Racial Minorities*, London: Policy Studies Institute

Smithies, B. and Fiddick, P. (1969), *Enoch Powell on Immigration*, London: Sphere Books

Solomos, J. (1983a), 'Black youth, unemployment and equal opportunities policies', in B. Troyna and D. Smith (eds.), *Racism, School and the Labour Market*, Leicester: National Youth Bureau

(1983b), *The Politics of Black Youth Unemployment: A Critical Analysis of Official Ideologies and Policies*, Working Papers on Ethnic Relations, no. 20, Centre for Research in Ethnic Relations, University of Warwick

(1984), 'Black youth and the 1980–81 Riots: official interpretations and political responses', *Politics*, 4 (2): 21–7

(1985), 'Problems, but whose problems? The social construction of black youth unemployment and state policies', *Journal of Social Policy*, 14 (4): 527–54

(1986a), 'Trends in the political analysis of racism', *Political Studies*, XXXIV, (2): 313–24

(1986b), 'Political language and violent protest: ideological and policy responses to the 1981 and 1985 riots', *Youth and Policy*, no. 18: 12–24

(1987), 'The politics of anti-discrimination legislation: planned social reform or symbolic politics', in R. Jenkins and J. Solomos (eds.), *Racism and Equal Opportunity Policies in the 1980s*, Cambridge: Cambridge University Press

(forthcoming), *The Politics of Racism: Theories and Practice in Contemporary Britain*, London: Macmillan

Solomos, J., Findlay, B., Jones, S., and Gilroy, P. (1982), 'The organic crisis of British capitalism and race: the experience of the seventies' in CCCS Race and Politics Group, *The Empire Strikes Back: race and racism in 70s Britain*, London: Hutchinson

Staples, R. (1976), *Introduction to Black Sociology*, New York: McGraw Hill

Stares, R., Imberg, D. and McRobie, J. (1982), *Ethnic Minorities: Their Involvement in MSC Special Programmes*, Research and Development Series, no. 6, Sheffield: Manpower Services Commission

Stevenson, D. and Wallis, P. (1970), 'Second generation West Indians: a study in alienation', *Race Today*, August: 278–80

Stone, M. (1981), *The Education of the Black Child in Britain*, London: Fontana

Tarling, R. (1982), 'Unemployment and crime', *Home Office Research Bulletin*, 14:28–33

Thompson, G. (1986), *The Conservatives' Economic Policy*, London: Croom Helm

Tory Reform Group (1982), *Young, British & Black*, London: Tory Reform Group

Touraine, A. (1981), *The Voice and the Eye: An Analysis of Social Movements*, Cambridge: Cambridge University Press

Troyna, B. (1982), 'The ideological and policy response to black pupils in British schools', in A. Hartnett (ed.), *The Social Sciences in Educational Studies*, London: Heinemann

Troyna, B. and Smith, D. I. (1983), *Racism, School and the Labour Market*, Leicester: National Youth Bureau

Troyna, B. and Williams, J. (1986), *Racism, Education and the State*, London: Croom Helm

Valentine, C. A. (ed.) (1968), *Culture and Poverty: Critique and Counter-Proposals*, New York: Harper and Row

Whitelaw, W. (1980), 'Speech to the Birmingham Community Relations Council', 11 July

Wickenden, J. (1958), *Colour in Britain*, London: Oxford University Press

Wickham, A. (1986), *Women and Training*, Milton Keynes: Open University Press

Williams, J. (1986), 'Education and race: the racialisation of class inequalities?', *British Journal of Sociology of Education*, 7 (2): 135–54

Worsthorne, P. (1978), 'Too much freedom', in M. Cowling (ed.), *Conservative Essays*, London: Cassell

(1985), 'End this silence over race', *The Sunday Telegraph*, 29 September

Young, K. and Connelly, N. (1981), *Policy and Practice in the Multi-Racial City*, London: Policy Studies Institute

Zubaida, S. (1970), 'Introduction', in S. Zubaida (ed.), *Race and Racialism*, London: Tavistock

Index